BLUE
NOTES

BLUE NOTES

JAZZ, LITERATURE, & LONELINESS

SAM V. H. REESE

Louisiana State University Press
Baton Rouge

Published by Louisiana State University Press
Copyright © 2019 by Louisiana State University Press
All rights reserved
Manufactured in the United States of America
First printing

Designer: Michelle A. Neustrom
Typefaces: Sentinel, text; Veneer Clean, display
Printer and binder: LSI

Library of Congress Cataloging-in-Publication Data
Names: Reese, Sam V. H. author.
Title: Blue notes : jazz, literature, and loneliness / Sam V. H. Reese.
Description: Baton Rouge : Louisiana State University Press, [2019] |
  Includes bibliographical references and index.
Identifiers: LCCN 2019006818 | ISBN 978-0-8071-7224-7 (pbk. : alk. paper) |
  ISBN 978-0-8071-7208-7 (pdf) | ISBN 978-0-8071-7202-5 (epub)
Subjects: LCSH: Jazz in literature. | Fiction—20th century—History
  and criticism. | Musical fiction—20th century—History and criticism. |
  Loneliness in literature.
Classification: LCC PN56.J38 R44 2019 | DDC 809.3/04—dc23
LC record available at https://lccn.loc.gov/2019006818

The paper in this book meets the guidelines for permanence
and durability of the Committee on Production Guidelines for
Book Longevity of the Council on Library Resources. ∞

CONTENTS

Acknowledgments / vii

Introduction: *Feeling Blue* / 1

1 In a Minor Key: *The Solo, Improvisation, and the Jazz Short Story* / 30

2 Lonely Women: *Jazz, Gender, and Isolation* / 65

3 Out There: *Jazz and the Out-Narrative* / 96

4 The Real Story: *Jazz Autobiographies, Authority, and Agency* / 128

Epilogue: *So What?* / 162

Notes / 173

Bibliography / 181

Index / 189

ACKNOWLEDGMENTS

This book was born from memories of jazz: Sitting in my grandmother's house, somewhere around six years old, listening to the same Louis Armstrong tunes with my mother that she used to dance to with her dad—a grandfather I never met. I was sitting in his shadow when I felt Satchmo's horn lift something in me. Aged eighteen, on the precipice of truly embracing who I was, sitting in a silent New Zealand theater beside my dad, watching Ornette Coleman shuffle onto stage—seventy-eight and just as mesmerising as ever. The shiver that took hold of me from just the first few notes. The sound of "Lonely Woman" curling up my spine. Walking out into the night, looking at my father, feeling something changed inside.

Usually, the acknowledgments to an academic book riff on the same old lines: "No book is written alone"; "I give my thanks to the community who helped bring this to life." Well—fittingly, for a book on loneliness—that's not quite the case here. This was an introverted, involuted book, written on long train journeys, in solitary hotel rooms, on the far side of the world from most of my family and friends.

I *have* had some truly uplifting voices in support—from my amazing editor at LSU Press, James Long, whose trust and enthusiasm gave me the extra courage to take this project up; and from Alexandra Kingston-Reese, my collaborator, partner, and eternal inspiration, who first entertained my improvised ideas about the harmolodics of prose, who danced with me to Sonny Rollins on our wedding night.

But mostly, my thanks go to my exceptional parents, who brought jazz and joy into my life. You gave me the tools to be alone, to listen to others, to say something myself.

INTRODUCTION

Feeling Blue

"Lonely Woman," the opening track of Ornette Coleman's breakthrough album of 1959, *The Shape of Jazz to Come*, never fails to move and unsettle me. The moaning, dissonant, often wandering conversation between Coleman's alto sax and Don Cherry's pocket cornet evokes isolation and sadness in a beautiful, heartrending way. And as Coleman would recount in later interviews, he composed the piece in an attempt to communicate what he saw as a communal loneliness—a feeling that, he believed, almost paradoxically, joined people in a shared experience of isolation. He explained in one interview that he composed the piece while working in a department store in the early 1950s. Coming across a gallery during his lunch break, he saw "this white lady in a picture with the most shattering expression you could see on her face. In the background there was everything you could imagine that was wealthy—all in her background—but she was so sad. And I said, 'Oh my goodness, I understand this feeling. I have not experienced this wealth, but I understand the feeling.' I went home and wrote 'Lonely Woman.'"[1]

Even if we haven't read the interview, even if we haven't heard the story, or Coleman's music, the narrative he recounts and the desired impact of his music are still more than familiar. Today, they are an almost integral part of the myth of jazz and the jazz musician. As a genre that encompasses an almost impossibly wide variety of possible expressions, jazz can of course evoke more than one affective state. It can be uplifting—joyous even—or loaded with political protest. It can ask you to get up and dance or take to the streets. But more than any other emotion, the feeling Coleman described—a "shattering" sense of loneliness—is consistently associated with jazz.

Indeed, jazz occupies a privileged cultural position (particularly in the United States) as a form of expression that allows its audience to transcend their own sense of being alone through a transformative performance of one individual's deeply felt and keenly expressed solitude and pain. From the start, it is important to recognize this as a story—a narrative about the power of jazz that has wide cultural power, even if it elides so many of the ways that jazz has been performed and experienced. It is an imaginative capital that has been richly mined by writers, whose literary representations of jazz have consistently drawn on both the imagery of the jazz genius and the stylistic qualities of jazz (improvisation, syncopation, a nonlinear structure characterized by riffs, and an ongoing tension between soloist and group) to try and explore the limits of human loneliness; in the world of fiction, jazz can offer pathways for negotiating loneliness, or new perspectives that allow solitude to be seen as a positive, life affirming experience.

I have set out to map this relationship—between jazz, loneliness, and literature—through a perspective that jazz musicians regularly call upon to characterize their own performances: that of the conversation. Even from the first hesitant sketches of this project, I have understood that I wanted to trace the history of literary appropriations of jazz, both as subject matter and as an aesthetic system, in order to show how different kinds of writers have turned to jazz to explore different aspects of loneliness. As such, the following chapters unpack how writers have used the expansive possibilities of nonlinear novels or adapted the minor aesthetics of the short story to fit different conceptualizations of jazz as a *form* for exploring loneliness; at the same time, they look at a range of different subject positions—from African American to Japanese, female to indigenous—with an attention to how the cultural tropes and symbolic potential of the jazz musician are used to parallel the often subjective pains of being cut off from others.

But a one-way conversation is rarely constructive. And in a world replete with artistic cross-pollination, it is clear that musicians have been just as receptive to writing as authors have been to their sounds. Jazz musicians have often turned to literature for inspiration, sometimes obliquely, sometimes at the center of their work. But they have also used the written word as a way to concretely express something to which their music can only allude, or which they must otherwise affectively evoke. In doing so, they mirror the turn by authors toward instrumental music—a form of communication that is abstracted from the language that is their chief resource. In analyzing these exchanges, I try to at once refine and expand the cultural meaning of loneliness; this study is energized by my own belief that, however painful and isolating it may feel, loneliness can also create beauty, empathy, and understanding.

Written literature, as far as it reaches back, imagines our capacity for loneliness as an integral part of what makes us human. The Sumerian epic *Gilgamesh*, which dates back more than four thousand years, even suggests that companionship and loneliness are the two, parallel states that separate humans from other beings. While this study draws on leading research from sociology and psychology, it is not a book on loneliness *per se*. Instead, I look at narratives of loneliness, trying to account for the way this integral aspect of our humanity has been imagined at a particular junction of American (and world) history. In doing so, I consider the ways that these narratives around being lonely have shifted, evolved, and been challenged or reformulated. As Olivia Sagan has recently reminded us, exploring concepts of personal experience through narrative has the doubled benefit of maintaining "the notion of human agency and subjectivity, whilst also attending to the interactional, social and cultural embeddedness of narrative production."[2]

In the same way, this is not, strictly speaking, a study of jazz. I am certainly interested in how writers have imagined themselves appropriating jazz, but unlike several recent studies, this one does not seek to make approximation between the musicology of jazz and literary techniques. Instead, the book investigates the history of *representa-*

tions of jazz, and the cultural narratives that have been associated with it—and have, in turn, shaped readers' judgments and assumptions about the music. In his groundbreaking work of 2017, *Epistrophies,* noted jazz scholar Brent Hayes Edwards concludes by defending his own sometimes unorthodox lines of analysis, pointing out that "a criticism that would be adequate to the interface between music and literature should not proceed like just any criticism."[3] In trying to untangle the complex and deeply rooted narrative that links two distinct, expressive forms (jazz and fiction) with an affective state still not fully understood, I have tried to respond with the same flexibility and investment in narrative that underpins the conversation between jazz and fiction.

Toward this aim, the book at once intersects with and diverges from several related critical discourses. It draws directly on the recent advancements in the social-science field of loneliness studies, where social and emotional isolation has been recognized as a major aspect of negative well-being. But I draw equally on the growing body of humanities research into the relationship between literature and affective states, as part of the larger study of the history of emotions. This book is also indebted to the explosion of jazz studies as an academic discipline over the last twenty to thirty years, which Krin Gabbard describes as the "institutionalization of jazz"—a process that is "consistent with current demystifications of the distinctions between high and low culture" in the academy.[4] The process of demystification has seen a number of critics address the specific relationship between jazz and literature, either in an attempt to theorize their relationship or to explain the history of their interaction. This book does not aspire to anything so universal. Instead, it sets out to trace how a particular psychological condition has driven a series of interactions between jazz and literature, and how these literary representations have in turn shaped the way loneliness is understood and experienced.

WHAT WE TALK ABOUT WHEN WE TALK ABOUT LONELINESS

The first contradiction that faces a study of loneliness is also one of the most persistent. Loneliness is an almost universal human experience. Ami Rokach, a leading figure in the psychological research into loneliness, describes it as a "prevalent, common, and disconcerting social phenomenon"; longitudinal studies consistently shows that an overwhelming majority of people, regardless of cultural or historical background or context, report feeling lonely at some point in their lives.[5] But loneliness is also unavoidably subjective. It can register as anything from a mild discomfort to a physical pain, from a sense of unease in our current situation to a full existential crisis, leaving one crippled, depressed, or suicidal. But depending on one's definition, it can also be a positive, enlightening experience. All of which means that, however unifying and affirmative it might be to assert that humans are brought together by their individual experiences of isolation, what exactly we talk about when we talk about loneliness can make a great deal of difference.

Yet, while precisely what loneliness denotes to each of us depends a lot on our personal and professional backgrounds, there are certain qualities that are fairly consistent. As something that affects both our thoughts and emotions, today loneliness is usually classed as a cognitive and affective condition. Although over the last forty years many theorists have tried to restrict their conceptualization of loneliness to one of these two spheres, as J. Y. Stein and Rivka Tuval-Mashiach point out, because sufferers consistently explain their feelings as an all-encompassing experience, "an adequate conceptualization of loneliness has to rise above the cognitive-affective bifurcation, integrating both cognitive and affective into an experiential conceptualization."[6] An experiential model of loneliness—bridging the emotional and rational split—certainly reflects the way that most literary writers model loneliness in their narratives. Perhaps more importantly, by reading for a broader experiential condition—rather than restricting analysis to either strand—I hope to map out a more complex picture of the role of jazz in stories about being lonely.

There are particularly compelling reasons for attending to what John Cacioppo, James Fowler, and Nicholas Christakis call "the emotional, cognitive, and behavioral consequences of loneliness": the myriad health problems that come with these experiences.[7] Cacioppo and colleagues point out the overwhelming results of nonhuman research, which show that "social species do not fare well when forced to live solitary lives."[8] As one of the most fundamentally social species, humans have health outcomes that (perhaps unsurprisingly) match up to the nonhuman research. With this in mind, psychologists, anthropologists, and humanities scholars can generally agree that loneliness is a product of our evolutionary drive toward socialization and connection. Indeed, Rokach argues convincingly that, "just like physical pain, which, while it is unpleasant, has a protective function and serves as an alarm bell to guard against damage to the organism—loneliness is a social pain that is triggered by disconnection from others, from the group to which the human individual belongs and that can assure us of food, defence, social connection, and support in the struggle to survive (as it did especially for our ancestors)."[9]

The corollary to this psychological defense mechanism is that it can cause loneliness to spread among those most vulnerable to such feelings, who are normally already on the edges of society. Some recent studies even seem to indicate that loneliness can be transmitted; certainly, "loneliness is found in clusters within social networks" and is "disproportionately represented at the periphery of social networks."[10] This has clear implications for narratives that draw on jazz—a music that, despite its initial popularity and (later) high status as "America's classical music," originated on the periphery of mainstream American culture and has a history closely connected to those marginalized by the state or culturally isolated from the majority, both within and beyond the United States.

This attention to loneliness as a social phenomenon—intrinsically related to a larger social context—is only natural, given the basic meaning of loneliness. As Stein and Tuval-Mashiach rightly note, "the concept of isolation may only be understood in a relational context. Isolation is always isolation from something or someone."[11] Philip Morrison and Rebekah Smith explain that "loneliness is caused by the absence of a needed relationship or set of relationships—attachment, social integration, nurturance, reassurance of worth, reliance alliance and guidance."[12] So from this perspective, loneliness can be understood as the feeling that our set of connections with others—our social network—is either too small, or else is unsatisfying: we don't have enough friends, or we aren't close enough to certain ones. In this sense, although loneliness can seem like a highly individualized feeling, almost to the point of solipsism, it is also essentially tied to our connections with others and our unfulfilled social needs. As Jill Stauffer ruefully notes, "selves are formed intersubjectively, in the presence of others, for better and worse and regardless of whether any of us would have willed it to be this way."[13] Despite the pressure in a radically atomized and individualistic society to define oneself as an autonomous being, with our own self-determined identities and experiences, the narratives we use to make sense of who we are—about our tastes, values, and character—do not simply spring into being, but are socially constructed; they "come from what other people say to us, from the values and truths produced by whatever cultures surround us, and from unspoken affective interactions between persons living alongside one another" (10). Feelings of loneliness are no different. Whether we are satisfied with the number and quality of our relationships or not is always tied (whether positively or negatively) to the expectations and standards of those around us.

This only contributes to the larger series of factors that influence how different individuals experience loneliness. Our personality, our history (personal, familial, or perhaps broader still), and the kind of narratives that we associate with being lonely all help determine the extent to which feelings of loneliness are empowering or crippling. Even the stage of our lives plays a crucial role in this experience. Rokach, for instance, not only affirm that "a large proportion of the population feel lonely frequently," but his research has shown that loneliness "is qualitatively a different experience," changing as individuals "move through the life cycle."[14] So although adults in their later stages of life might report loneliness more frequently than young adults, young adults experienced loneliness more keenly on the "emotional distress subscale," which measured "pain, emotional turmoil, sadness, helplessness, hopelessness and feelings of emptiness."[15] By contrast, older participants in the study were more likely to see value in their experiences of loneliness—which is not to suggest, by any means, that it did not also cause them distress, particular given the frequency with which they were likely to experience such feelings.

Indeed, regardless of age, loneliness can have far-ranging consequences, beyond a simple awareness of human isolation. The long-term psychological consequences of loneliness are well documented; depending on its intensity, loneliness can be "linked to depression, anxiety and interpersonal hostility . . . an increased vulnerability to health problems . . . and even to suicide."[16] The visceral pain that is often associated with literary expressions of loneliness, moreover, has scientific approval: studies "have shown that the dorsal anterior cingulate cortex of the brain lights up equally when we are rejected as when we are physically harmed—meaning that the affective component of pain is similar in both situations" (Stauffer 31). Perhaps most intriguing for a study of loneliness in art, however, is the question of creativity. While the ability to spend time easily on one's own has been linked to success in creative or artistic endeavors by a number of studies, as Malka Margalit has also shown, "adolescents who could not tolerate being alone often failed to develop their creative talents."[17] So the way that individuals experience loneliness has urgent and practical consequences for the producers of music and literature.

We can thus say that loneliness depends on a process of internal interpretation. Given the vast differences in how and why different individuals experience loneliness, it is clear that we do not simply trigger an in-built switch when our number or quality of friendships drops below a certain threshold, instigating feelings of isolation. Instead, the conditions for feeling lonely are related to our own perceptions of ourselves, and how we narrate our identities in relation to the outside world. This is particularly the case when it comes to our sense of the *quality* of our relationships; after all, there is no formula for calculating how close we are with others, nor any guarantee that two given people will construct their relationship with each other in the same way. For some researchers and officials, this is seen to be a major impediment to mapping out the occurrence of loneliness across a population: if loneliness is so subjective, how can it be adequately measured? But Cacioppo and coauthors make a compelling case that, rather than a barrier, the subjective nature of loneliness actually helps research. As they rightly note, "humans are an irrepressibly meaning-making species," and ultimately it is our own beliefs about whether we are lonely that most affect our health and well-being; as they demonstrate, "a large literature has developed showing that perceived social isolation (that is, loneliness) in normal samples is a more important predictor of a variety of adverse health outcomes than is objective social isolation."[18] In other words, the stories people tell themselves about their experiences of being alone change the way they feel, to the extent that these stories can demonstrably affect their health.

From this perspective, loneliness is necessarily connected to how we see the world more generally. Clark Moustakas, the pioneering researcher into "existential loneliness" during the 1960s and 1970s, explained that being lonely is "an experience of raw sensitivity" so that, although it creates "a reality of far-reaching social consequence," it is nevertheless "distinctly a private matter."[19] Recent research has shed more light on the complex relationship between loneliness and our ability to make connections with others: alongside the attendant poor health, people who identify themselves as lonelier are "more likely to have poor social skills, have difficulty in forming relationships, and hold negative or hostile opinions of other people."[20] While those who face such difficulties may be more predisposed to feelings of loneliness, it also seems that experiencing loneliness exacerbates such difficulties, leading to loneliness intensifying over time, and becoming harder to escape. As Stauffer notes, loneliness often "starts with everyday losses that are less serious but that may underscore for us—if we take the time to look—our vulnerability, our false ideas about our autonomy, and what matters about the autonomy we do have" (3). In other words, loneliness is not only shaped by our worldview but, as an ongoing experience, it conditions the way we construct our identities and relationships with others.

While loneliness could be imagined justly as an internal narrative, because it also intersects with our relationships with others, it needs to be approached as something more. Indeed, many subjects of recent loneliness studies—especially those who self-identify as "different"—feel their loneliness comes from, or is accentuated by, an inability for their story to be understood. In other words, when it comes to narratives of loneliness, the way we tell our story to others is just as important as how we explain it to ourselves. Jacob Y. Stein and Zahava Solomon describe "this facet of experiential loneliness" as "failed intersubjectivity," using a phrase that "denot[es] the expectation that others will share one's subjective state, but they do not or are incapable of doing so."[21] Immediately, this suggests two social benefits of narratives of loneliness. They demonstrate to lonely readers that their feelings are not unintelligible—that other people can hear and understand their stories. And in the process, they model possible narrative strategies for telling a different story about the experience of being alone.

This is the very question that tends to preoccupy artistic explorations of loneliness: how to transform the experience of being alone into something positive and meaningful. And it points to a major disjunction between scientific and artistic discourse. Within a literary tradition, and into the early philosophical studies of loneliness, the term "loneliness" has not intrinsically implied a negative experience. Moustakas, in the early 1960s, for instance, could describe loneliness as "an experience of being human which enables the individual to sustain, extend, and deepen his humanity" (ix). From the right point of view, loneliness could in fact affirm our sense of self and connection to the world: "Experiencing a solitary state gives the individual the opportunity to draw upon untouched capacities and resources, and to realize himself in an entirely unique manner. It can be a new experience. It may be an experience of exquisite pain, deep fear and terror, an utterly terrible experience, yet it brings into awareness new dimensions of self, new beauty, new power for human compassion, and a reverence for the precious nature of each breathing moment" (7).

Within contemporary scientific discourse, however, loneliness has come to denote a solely negative state. Researchers instead use a term that writers like Moustakas might use interchangeably with loneliness—solitude—to account for the state of being aware of and comfortable with being alone. This is another area where artistic expressions of loneliness can be used to help change the wider narratives around being lonely: for many writers and musicians, there is no firm distinction between solitude and loneliness—and for many, the key to experiencing solitude positively lies in understanding the two states as complementary and continuous, rather than distinct.

However deeply rooted the experience of loneliness might be within our development as a species, commentators in the twenty-first century are quick to point to the seemingly unprecedented intensity of loneliness being experienced today. It can seem almost paradoxical within a culture that appears more connected than ever—and social pundits regularly draw attention to the apparent contradiction of feeling lonely in an age where constant and immediate contact with friends and family on the opposite side of the globe is possible, even describing the phenomenon as a kind of epidemic. Margalit suggests this is a product of "conflicting interpersonal trends" where, "on the one hand, there is an increasing and urgent need for constant connectivity," while "on the other hand, there is a growing recognition for needs of intensified individualism as expressions of the self, encouraging independent mind-set trends, providing increased opportunities for selective meeting of individual choices of living, working, dressing, and leisure activities."[22] But the identification of the current epoch with a sense of loneliness is not, in itself, new—nor is the explanation that Margalit provides. In 1950, David Riesman, along with Nathan Glazer and Reuel Denney, published a groundbreaking sociological study of contemporary American culture, which they titled *The Lonely Crowd*. Although the book was supported by in-depth sociological research, the authors principally saw it as "a book about social character"; the book, often obliquely, set out its authors' vision of how the United States, in an age of technological, economic, and social advancement, could be nonetheless so strongly characterized by conformity and loneliness.[23] Even their formulation of "social character" was based on this connection. Riesman explained that "the link between character and society" was "found in the way in which society ensures some degree of conformity from the individuals who make it up," so that individuals felt increasingly isolated in the face of strong social expectations.[24] Their study drew attention to Americans' increasing sensitivity to the expectations of others, which they argued led to more self-regulation their behavior. Given that, in such a context, "people may be compelled to behave in one way although their character structure presses them to behave in the opposite way," it made sense that individuals felt increasingly dissatisfied with their relationships with others, and perhaps more importantly, alienated from themselves.[25] The work was published, moreover, at precisely the point at which jazz began to be adopted as a subject matter for fiction in new and increasingly frequent ways.

The particular kind of loneliness that Riesman, Glazer, and Denney emphasize is distinct from the two aspects of loneliness that dominate most psychological studies today. A deficit in the size of our network or number of personal connections is referred to as social loneliness; as Morison and Smith explain, this "lack of integration into a social network can be felt even while in a loving relationship," so that "people not only need to be in a stable loving relationship but also need to feel as though they are part of a wider social group." On the other hand, those who experience a (perceived) lack in the quality or intensity of those relationships are said to suffer from emotional loneliness. But the kind of isolation that comes from the sense of self-alienation that *The Lonely Crowd* described—perhaps more familiar to the literary-minded—is termed existential loneliness, and "has been defined as a self-perception of personal isolation, a primary and inevitable condition of existence, related to feelings of personal meaninglessness, helplessness, isolation, aloneness, and loss of freedom."[26]

Moustakas was one of the first to identify this feeling as a specific condition of loneliness, although he attempted to distinguish these different experiences further, by arguing that "the loneliness of modern life may be considered in two ways: the existential loneliness which inevitably is a part of human experience, and the loneliness of self-alienation and self-rejection which is not loneliness at all but a vague and disturbing anxiety" (24). Like the authors of *The Lonely Crowd,* Moustakas drew attention to the origin of these two experiences in the uniformity of postwar culture, where "the individual no longer has an intimate sense of relatedness to the food he eats, the clothing he wears, the shelter which houses him," and "lives in an impersonal urban or suburban community where he meets others not as real persons but according to prescribed rules of conduct" (25). For Moustakas, this characterized the central problem of loneliness: that it arose out of a crisis in identity, but was also a product of the near impossibility of connecting with others. In this sense, he prefigured what is now termed representational loneliness, which "occurs when the awareness of others comes into conflict with the awareness that the self can never be understood by others in its totality because it can never be experienced by anyone else."[27]

Loneliness, then, is not singular; it can be used to describe a range of states of isolation and solitude. It can be used to evoke an individual's need for perhaps just one truly meaningful connection, or their sense that they are cut off from community and friendship at large. It can be used to express our anxiety about other's expectations of us, and our ensuing disconnect from ourselves. In those moments when we become aware of our own singularity, the peculiarity of our experiences, and our inability to communicate them, it can help us describe our dilemma of self-representation. It can even express a pain that our brain translates into the physical spectrum of experience. But equally, if reframed within narratives of solitude, the same awareness of our singularity can represent a peaceful, undisturbed tranquility, an ease with oneself, and an awareness of the pains of others. It can fuel creative expression and facilitate otherwise unimagined connection-making.

Instinctively, I tend to favor a broader use of loneliness: there are clear payoffs from imbuing a generally negatively imagined term with positive implications. And despite its range of possible implications, a broadly construed use of loneliness reflects a persistent social narrative about the solitude and introspection that comes with being on one's own, in whatever sense that manifests. Within the context of postwar American society, however, the experience of loneliness assumed particular cultural status, as a generally negative mode of experience, which was clearly connected to wider social and political changes. So for the purposes of this book, I use the term loneliness in the sense of a lack or absence associated with being alone or cut off from others, and the term solitude to refer to a more affirmative experience of the same conditions.

This usage has the advantage of helping illuminate something of the writers' ambitions (and their texts' effects) when drawing together jazz and loneliness. Given the emergence of loneliness as a concept for defining a national culture, it should not be surprising that writers would seek to explore the limits and possibilities of its affective and cognitive effects with a renewed energy from the 1940s onwards. Nor should it be surprising, given the cultural capital associated with jazz, that they would turn to this uniquely blue form of expression to help them do so.

(SO) BLACK AND BLUE

If we follow the arguments of Riesman and Moustakas, then the new prominence of loneliness in mid-century American fiction can be, in part, explained by the social conditions of late capitalism and early Cold War cultural conformity. Not only were individuals less likely to connect to others, but they were also more likely to feel an inability to communicate their own individuality, or to feel a sense of an essential isolation as a solitary person. It is clear that loneliness is tied to narratives of identity, so it should not be surprising that, in a culture that increasingly saw itself as lonely, authors attempted to tell their own versions of what it meant to be alone. But why would so many writers turn to *jazz* to explore this new, increasingly negative vision of loneliness?

On a relatively superficial (but no less important) level, over the first half of the twentieth century, jazz musicians had accrued stereotypes that associated them with social isolation, nonconformity, and intense, often painful loneliness. As Kathy Ogren notes, as early as the 1920s, listening to jazz connoted interior dissonance and social dissidence, to the extent that it "became the specific symbol of rebellion and of what was new about the decade."[28] As a musical form that developed "from a participatory and distinct black musical culture," jazz attracted those who felt marginalized from, or opposed to, the white mainstream, so that "the music itself and the circumstances under which it was performed embodied social change."[29] There was an early and prevailing assumption, moreover, that jazz was itself inherently sad. Although blues and jazz can express "a wide range of emotions and descriptions of Afro-American life," white Americans (and increasingly, African Americans) came to believe that they "conveyed sad or sorrowful messages exclusively."[30] As such, the realities of the full emotional repertoire of jazz are less important than the way that the music was popularly imagined and discussed. In other words, when considering how writers drew on jazz subjects and structures to consider loneliness, the wide emotional register of African American music is almost beside the point, given how clearly contemporary discourse identified jazz with the mood and emotional cadence of being alone.

The varied (im)precision with which writers themselves have drawn on jazz is not simply a product of broad cultural stereotypes; many writers with comparatively deep historical or practical knowledges of jazz have nonetheless gone on to write quite distinctive, even conflicting, versions of jazz fiction. Instead, this polyphonic representation of jazz in literature can be seen as a consequence of the debate within jazz itself as to its origins and essential elements. As Arthur Knight has appositely noted, jazz "was the first indigenous, (semi) vernacular music in the United States to wrestle explicitly with representing, visually and aurally, its origins and its transactional qualities."[31] In different sounds and stagings, a century of jazz performances has insistently attempted to define or contest the narratives about the music's values and qualities, shaping musical "discourses for debating competing (though often contiguous) visions of the music, for clarifying views of jazz history, and for struggling with the music's value and status." In trying to recover early visions of jazz, moreover, writers have had to negotiate the murky territory between "jazz of the white critic—jazz as mythology and cultural commodity," and "the extensive, elusive, often ignored musics that have been played, usually by African Americans, in various locales throughout the late nineteenth and early twentieth centuries."[32] From this point of view, it is significant that many writers have retreated into what Krin Gabbard calls "jazz myth and jazz culture rather than jazz per se."[33] One essential aspect of this myth, which has contributed to the cultural aura of loneliness around the jazz musician, is that of the solo.

Of course, in a musicological sense, the prominence of the solo is often used to distinguish jazz from other forms of music. It is not so much mythical as intrinsic. But for many practitioners, critics, and listeners alike, the jazz solo is considered such a defining feature of the genre that the image of "the jazzman" has become synonymous with the spotlighted soloist. Frederick Garber has pointed to this tendency to idealize the moment of the solo, noting that it tends to be regarded as the "essence of jazz in terms of a singular immediacy."[34] The implication of this narrowed focus is that representations of jazz often treat the music as the ephemeral production of an inspired individual, where ideal performances "take their origin and end from the moment in which they are made and the lonely figure who makes them."[35] This sense of loneliness can actually be exacerbated by the presence of other band members; by stepping out of the group and asserting an individual voice, the soloist seems to reject (or at least stand outside of) the group dynamic of sociability. This dynamic is not accidental, nor a product of, say, a public taste for displays of virtuosity. Instead, it derives from the specifically African American musical tradition from which jazz developed—what Ogren calls "the participatory qualities of its origins," including the "rich exchange between performers" on the one hand, and between the group "and their audiences" on the other.[36] As many writers suggest (or explicitly point out), jazz owes its origins to the history and conditions of slavery and racial oppression in the United States.

One of the central debates in jazz discourse, since at least the Harlem Renaissance, has circulated around this racial dimension of jazz. This includes the extent to which it should be considered a peculiarly, or even solely black form of expression, and the part that it ought to play in helping bridge racial tensions in America. Edwards makes a convincing case that, more generally, we need to attend to "the infinitely fertile interface between music and literature in African diasporic culture."[37] Certainly, there has been more at stake for black musicians and writers alike when it comes to jazz and literature. For many, the appropriation of jazz by white critics and authors is particularly contentious, given that "formerly enslaved Africans and their descendants locate themselves in a social-political history of exclusion," against which their aesthetic tradition, including spirituals, blues, and jazz, is a form of resistance.[38] As A. Yemisi Jimoh argues, "for many African Americans artists . . . a history of aesthetic ideas has been situated within the contexts of a struggle for freedom from chattel slavery and from its reformulations"; from this perspective the role of the solo, as a form of individualistic expression, can be considered an "articulation of experiences of alienation and fragmentation."[39] Like many critics, moreover, Jimoh argues that this personal sense of fragmentation acts as the point of cohesion in a jazz performance so that, whatever particular model of jazz one subscribes to, the genre is almost always defined by "a style of improvisation" that "allows each musician to comment simultaneously on the musical fragment that serves as the jumping-off point."[40] So, from the point of view of a writer, both the group dynamic and the nature of the solo connote estrangement from others, personal isolation, or in Garber's terms, the "lonely figure."

In addressing the relationship between jazz and racial politics, critical and popular discussions alike frequently turn to the question of the relationship between jazz and blues. This is clearly vexing terrain. Both forms of music are tied to an African American tradition, and in some definitions are simply imagined as variations of the same meta-genre—to the point where the terms are even used interchangeably. While this kind of blurring is more likely in popular discourse, it is readily apparent in what musicians themselves say about their music—or even in the titles of their albums and pieces, from *Blues and Roots* to *Blue Train* to *Kind of Blue*. At first listen, the jazz solo might seem like the most distinctive element of jazz—but in comparison to the blues, it is actually the group dynamic that is most important.

Even Jimoh, who places so much pressure on the solo, accepts that, although both forms emphasize "multiple, unique personal expressions—innovative personal style," in "contrast to Blues, Jazz moves away from singular expression firmly situated within and largely informed by group experiences."[41] Vic Hobson's recent detailed study of the relationship between the blues and early New Orleans jazz helps explain both the underlying common ground between these forms and their critical divergence. As he notes, it is clear that, by the early 1920s, a "recognizable New Orleans style of jazz had developed. This was a largely improvised, polyphonic music, rooted in the tonality of the blues."[42] As his detailed documentary and musicological detective work reveals, both forms ultimately derived from the vocal practices of black barbershop quartets; these shaped "the tonality of the blues" and, in turn, "the polyphony of New Orleans jazz." Like Jimoh, Hobson emphasizes that, although jazz as a distinctive form was characterized by "harmonic features" that were "associated with the tonality of the blues," it also departed from its tonal brother in its movement toward a different group dynamic. This distinction is more than academic—the question of how a single voice related to a group is central to narratives of loneliness and jazz alike.

The association of the solo with loneliness, particularly in written engagements with jazz, means that although there is, as Ryan Jerving has impressively documented, a substantial body of early jazz literature, many of these first writers were more interested in a big-band style of jazz (strongly associated with white musicians) where the role of the solo was diminished or completely cut. So although white writers of the 1920s might "explore Afro-American themes," "they rarely used the music as a source of innovative language."[43] Indeed, as Ogren points out, even F. Scott Fitzgerald—whose *Tales of the Jazz Age* contributed so much to a popular association between the early twentieth century and jazz—was more successful in trying "to capture the affection of young white college students for jazz than in his accuracy about musical performance."[44] On the other hand, as the culture of jazz performance shifted toward a heightened emphasis on both the solo and improvisation, writers began to increasingly co-opt jazz as a symbol for loneliness.

The cultural pressures of loneliness and the increased emphasis on the individual in jazz collided in the early 1940s, with the emergence of bebop as the most discursively powerful genre of jazz. Again, this is not to make claims about the number of performers working within different genres of jazz, or even their artistic value, but to recognize the cultural capital attached to bebop, which is very clearly reflected in the number of stories that focus on beboppers (as opposed to, say, swing bands or older New Orleans jazz groups). Eric Lott has argued that the technical virtuosity privileged by bebop offered black musicians a way to "reclaim . . . jazz from its brief co-optation by white 'swing' bandleaders," and the implication behind his claim— that bebop was, overwhelmingly, defined in racial terms—is repeated insistently by jazz critics.[45] Knight, for one, echoes Lott's claim by arguing that "the shift from swing to bop marked a change in jazz from a mainstream popular music to an explicit art music, which was (at least initially) assertively black and (at least nascently) cultural-nationalist."[46] Bebop, in other words, was marked as an outsider form through its rejection of commercialized tastes, and its assertion of ethno-nationalist aesthetics. Its confrontationally virtuosic performances "allowed black musicians to seize their discourse from the white-dominated culture industry and to create something less likely to be appropriated. The various social codes stressed by bop are a part of this creation of a counterdiscourse."[47]

Many of the cultural tropes about the jazz musician that continue to circulate in films like 2015's *Miles Ahead* and *Born to Be Blue*, therefore, date not to the earlier eras of Dixieland or swing, but to the attitudes and appearance, at least as caricatured by the opponents—and many fans—of the bebopper. These artists were characterized by "excessive musical acrobatics" on the one hand, and "elitism, hostility, and avant-garde posturings" on the other, all packaged in "unconventional dress and morally suspicious life-styles."[48] When the virtuosic bebop pianist Sonny sends his brother a letter from jail early in James Baldwin's story "Sonny's Blues," he tries to explain his isolating, destructive behavior by protesting that it doesn't have "anything to do with me being a musician. It's more than that. Or maybe less than that."[49] His very protest, however, reflects the cultural assumptions about the jazzman that musicians like Dizzy Gillespie and Charlie Parker seemed to cultivate: the idea that their free, unfettered music was intimately connected to an unconventional, even irresponsible life. Certainly, from a musical point of view, bebop could be easily identified as individualistic: it was, as Lott notes, "a soloist's music, despite the democratic ethos of jazz (in which soloists assume a momentary universality in a highly musical context), and particularly of bop (its dependence on unison riffs, the extreme sympathy required between players to negotiate the rhythms)."[50]

In her landmark study of improvisation and interaction, Ingrid Monson observes that, since "the extended solo became one of the most prominent characteristics" of jazz, "those fascinated by the beauty, power, and complexity of the jazz tradition have focused primarily upon the activities and achievements of individual soloists."[51] So it is only natural that, from the 1940s onwards, as writers turned their attentions increasingly toward the "lonely crowd" dynamic of American society, they would co-opt the jazz musician as an emblem for individual isolation. But equally, as writers and critics built a cultural mythology around the idea of being a jazzman, musicians themselves turned to writing as a way to regain control over the construction of their own identity. As Christopher Harlos explains, "For jazz musicians, the turn to autobiography is regarded as a genuine opportunity to seize narrative authority," and it is interesting that "dissatisfaction with jazz writing is a theme that immediately surfaces in a number of autobiographical works."[52] Even as their music was being idealized and their identities mythologized, jazz musicians used writing as a way to express something personal—individual, even exceptional—about their own experiences, in contrast to the universalizing tendencies so common in contemporary fiction and criticism.

This reflects what I see as the central place of narrative in jazz. Jazz musicians themselves have long conceptualized group improvisation as a form of conversation—a communal storytelling—but as a musical genre jazz is defined by the way it can recreate experiences and bring them freshly into being for the audience. If this sounds a little abstract, a simpler description might simply term this concept "immanence"—something that has long been seen as a defining feature of jazz. As Edwards nicely puts it, to say "that jazz is defined by musical immanence means not only that it is a self-reflexive medium but also that—without being programmatic or somehow simply mimetic," this genre creates performances where "sound itself can capture and retain and even revisit ... a precise historical transcript of the most complex affective experience."[53] In other words, jazz has the ability to recreate experiences for the audience as they listen, through an act of improvisation that mirrors the affective turn of spoken narrative.

BEYOND LONELY: LONELINESS AND INVISIBILITY

While many authors have written thoughtfully, emotionally, or wittily about classical music or the modern world of pop, few writers of fiction have turned to other musical forms for stylistic, structural, and thematic cues to the same extent that so many twentieth-century writers have turned to jazz. The ever-growing body of new research on jazz and literature bears this out. I would guess that the inherent narrative impulse underlying immanent jazz has something to do with this wider phenomenon—for it is certainly the foundation for writers drawing on jazz to engage with loneliness.

Whatever else they think of loneliness, the writers on whom I focus are keenly attuned to its subjectivity. Many were decades ahead of psychological research in their recognition that loneliness is rooted in the stories that we tell. Like Edwards's conceptualization of jazz immanence, these stories are a form of self-expression that is in the present tense, in the process of coming into being—and it is by drawing together literature, jazz, and loneliness within this framework that I hope is to broaden the understanding of not just literary texts, but the conditions of loneliness itself. This is at the heart of not only fiction writers' work, but the work of musicians like Duke Ellington and Charles Mingus in their various writings, which recast isolation as an empowering assertion of individuality.

In an intriguing chapter that closes the 2008 *Companion to Emily Dickinson,* noted poet and scholar Joshua Weiner covertly advances a similar claim. Weiner begins with the bold claim that "when I listen to Thelonious Monk I hear Emily Dickinson; and when I listen to Emily Dickinson I hear Thelonious Monk"; admitting the ahistoricity of his comparative reading of these two radical figures' work, he nonetheless maintains that it is the way that their work "brings empty space—a musical pause or rest that signifies a greater silence—into the very structural principle of their respective art that announces their relation as artistic cousins."[54] Here Weiner implicitly draws a distinction between the different forms of the isolated and the invisible that Dickinson regularly employed as subject matter (which were often tied to the restrictions of her place and conditions—what we might call her loneliness, or at least solitude) and the aesthetic *strategies* that she and Monk both employ to coordinate their work, arguing that these can be understood in commensurate aesthetic terms. It is in these same terms that the unnamed narrator of Ralph Ellison's *Invisible Man* introduces his state of invisibility. Although initially he appears to attribute his condition to other people—"the invisibility to which I refer occurs because of a peculiar disposition of the eyes of those with whom I come in contact"—as the novel continues, it becomes clear that his invisibility is also a choice, a deliberate strategy on the part of the narrator.[55] So, too, is the loneliness that characterizes even his most intimate exchanges with other people; in many ways, Ellison's novel (the most frequently scrutinized exemplar of "jazz fiction") undertakes the same project as this book—to refigure loneliness as an active, generative state.

The prologue that opens *Invisible Man* both explicitly announces the novel's preoccupation with invisibility and defines it in terms closely linked to the syncopated, improvisational world of jazz. In a striking image, the narrator explains that he likes the music of Louis

Armstrong "because he's made poetry out of being invisible" (8), and in doing so, establishes one of the novel's key aesthetic registers. Ellison himself is almost as well known for his jazz criticism as he is for *Invisible Man*, to the extent that his essays on jazz have come to be considered as the intellectual successor to his debut novel; David Yaffe has argued that to "be a jazz scholar at the beginning of the twenty-first century is to write in the shadow of Ralph Ellison."[56] A trumpeter from the age of eight, the young Ellison had even anticipated a career as a professional musician, and as Horace A. Porter aptly notes, the "study of music taught him something about the art of fiction as he began his transformation from aspiring classical composer to novelist."[57] This is witnessed in the configuration that the narrator sets out in the prologue, which suggests that invisibility can be understood as a poetic fusing of language and music. From this perspective, the narrator's adaptation of jazz poetics into a code of character identity—emblematized by Armstrong—also informs his style of first-person narration, as well as the aesthetics of the novel at large.

This is not, in itself, a new observation. As Timothy Spaulding notes, "many critics have characterized the novel as a 'jazz novel' and have explored, in general terms, the elements of a jazz aesthetic in the novel."[58] But underneath this consensus lies a fundamental contradiction between jazz, on the one hand, as a racialized form of expression and, on the other, as universal mode, so that when critics like Brennan Maier use Ellison's jazz criticism as a lens through which to read his anxieties "about the ability of Negro nationalism to reproduce itself as a social formation," they also reinforce *Invisible Man*'s status as a protest novel, where the narrator's race determines his visibility.[59] Simultaneously, however, Ellison's reflections on jazz stand out as "some of the first to provide a thorough cultural analysis of the origins and aesthetics of jazz," and reflect his broader interrogation of history and culture in terms that bypass race and speak instead to America as a whole.[60] For Ellison, discussions of influence "impose [. . .] racial considerations which don't belong to discussions of culture"; although jazz was "Afro-American in origin," it was also "more American than some folks want to admit."[61] When the narrator identifies his acts of social resistance as the political equivalent of Armstrong's music, therefore, he both identifies with an African American tradition and broadens the implications of his experiences of solitude beyond race.

This tension between individual and group identity is inevitable, given Ellison's attitudes to jazz aesthetics (predominantly that of bebop) and their specific application in the novel.[62] In his criticism, Ellison decried the solipsistic element of the new wave of bebop musicians, increasingly focused on the individual performance; in his seminal essay "The Golden Age, Times Past," he argued that they "were intensely concerned that their identity as Negroes placed no restrictions upon the music they played or the manner in which they used their talent," suggesting that their emphasis on honing individual talent as *artists* isolated them from their culture.[63] Although they "resented" earlier musicians like Armstrong, Ellison implied that their interest in the improvised virtuosic did little to advance the cause of African Americans, where swing music had valorized black culture. This logic underpins "Ellison's antipathy to bebop" and indicates why it is the poetry of Armstrong's music that the narrator most closely identifies with: unlike the self-conscious bebopper, "he's unaware that he *is* invisible" (*Invisible Man* 8).[64] But this reflects an internal contradiction in the narrator's ideal of invisibility; although his own actions lead him to a highly reflexive position of social isolation and resistance, he distances himself from any external group (whether racial, political, or otherwise) by adopting this role.

On the other hand, as Addison Gayle argued, "Ellison's protagonist" seems to choose "the path of the individual instead of racial unity."[65] From this perspective, the performed nature of jazz inflects its aesthetics of invisibility—particularly given that, as he or she is in the spotlight, the jazz musician also participates in the domain of the visible. It is here the narrator's distinction is useful; Armstrong is an artist of invisibility because his music lacks a recognizable language of visibility. As Yaffe puts it, it "was the conflict between the mediated forms of representation and the liberating content that interested Ellison."[66] Indeed, the narrator translates Armstrong's aesthetic mastery into language through a coming from invisibility to visibility—from silence to words.

Although for the majority of the novel the narrator's strategies of invisibility work in his favor, at the end he is confronted by the limitations of isolation—the point at which psychologists would argue it becomes an experience of loneliness. This transgression occurs against the backdrop of the haunting possibilities of violence and rape. In the spirit of *Invisible Man*'s subversive attitude to racial and gender identity, however, rather than a physical rape, the narrator violates the cultural and political attitudes that the woman in question embodies.

Disenchanted with the pseudo-communist Brotherhood for whom he is working, the narrator decides to seduce one of their wives to leverage them. His target, Sybil, quickly proves to have no interest in her husband's politics, and is only concerned with "casting" the narrator "in fantasies in which I was Brother Taboo-with-whom-all-things-are-possible" (391). Recognizing that this scenario would reinforce her objectification of his black body—embodying Sybil's dehumanizing image of "a brute, huge, with white teeth, what they call a 'buck'" (392)—the narrator refuses to conform to the prescriptive and demeaning paradigm of a "domesticated rapist" (394). While he had imagined the violation of a powerful, white woman as an act of liberation and resistance, as Sybil increasingly urges him to "join her in a very revolting ritual" (391), the narrator starts to question "who's taking revenge on whom" (393). His solution is to take an action that reasserts his agency, without forcing him into a politically and psychologically compromised position: he convinces her that he has already raped her, writing in lipstick on her stomach: "SYBIL, YOU WERE RAPED / BY / SANTA CLAUS / SURPRISE" (395). Inscribing his subversive refusal to play an imaginary role (as a kind of sexual Santa) onto her body leaves her "lit up like a luminescent sign" and reinforces the ethos of subversion that underpins his use of invisibility. As he maintains in the novel's opening monologue, "irresponsibility is part of my invisibility; any way you face it, it is a denial" (11).

On its own, this disarming message reflects the narrator's appropriation of invisibility as a strategy for insurrection. But the neon violence of his action—while presumably less repugnant than play-acting rape—proves to be a catalyst for a crisis of conscience within the narrator. Having just admired his handiwork, he changes his mind, "rubbing out the evidence of my crime" (395). Here, Ellison deftly invites the reader to question the narrator's logic: What crime does he believe he has committed, and why does he withdraw his statement of rebellion? Clearly, the crime is not an act of rape. There is no opportunity within the narrative for this to happen and, in any case, Sybil openly invites him into consensual sex, calling to him, "come on, beat me, daddy—you—you big black bruiser" (394). A more likely interpretation might be that he feels remorse for pretending to have violated her, compromising his own integrity and invisibility.

The narrator's actions speak against this, too. As Sybil wakes up, he continues to convince her that he has fulfilled his fantasy, to which she is "delighted" (396). When she drunkenly asserts, "You were such a strong big brute you made me give in. I didn't want to, did I now, boo'ful?" he responds that she "brought out the beast in me," maintaining the same illusions that his message created. One reading of this passage argues that the crime is in fact the narrator's impotence, and that it is here that "Ellison begins to undo the herero- and phallocentric logic of agency that has so far subtended the novel."[67] While I would not go so far as to identify the narrator's "crime" as impotence per se, Douglas Steward does highlight an important aspect of the narrator's dialogue with Sybil: rather than inflicting something upon her, he shares responsibility with her in cocreating an alternative narrative. The crime that he erases is his use of Sybil's body as a weapon or, as he refers to it, "a lecture on an aspect of the woman question" (395), and he does so out of recognition of their shared invisibility.

Earlier in the evening, Sybil remarks to the narrator that they are "kind of alike" (393). This straightforward observation underpins the narrator's increased feelings of remorse after his political act of violence, and is magnified when, as they co-narrate their virtual rape/ sex, she takes him aback by stating, "I've never seen anyone like you" (397). As someone who has cultivated their anonymity through invisibility, the narrator is understandably confronted by the idea of being seen, in spite of his acknowledgment that "it's good to be seen." What Ellison prompts us to ask, however, is what exactly Sybil believes she has seen. Is it the racialized, hyper-masculinized stereotype he is now laying claim to—someone who "rapes real good" (394) when they're drunk—or is it the man he really is, subversive and fraudulent? Looking "at her out of a deep emptiness," the narrator asks himself, "what had I done to her, allowed her to do? Had all of it filtered down to me?"

(397). On the one hand, his emptiness suggests that he understands that she has seen through his performance, that she has recognized he has not risen to the task. On the other, his sense of contamination implies that he feels that, by perpetuating the illusion of having raped her, he has been compromised by her ideal of him as a "domesticated rapist."

But, a third possibility exists: in spite of the lurid context, a genuine moment of recognition has occurred to pierce his invisibility. This reading is supported by the narrator's difficulty in articulating his feelings about "My action [. . .] my—the painful word formed as disconnectedly as her wobbly smile—my responsibility?" Despite trying to maintain, almost as a protest, that "I'm invisible," this emphasis on responsibility recalls his early equation of irresponsibility with invisibility. Asking, in the opening chapter, "to whom can I be responsible, and why should I be, when you refuse to see me?" the narrator explains that "responsibility rests upon recognition, and recognition is a form of agreement" (11). Here the narrator's agreement with Sybil to maintain the pretense of rape allows for a moment of recognition; it is this recognition that undermines his sense of integrity in invisibility, instilling him with feelings of emptiness. In the sequence that follows, the question of recognition seems more physically at stake, as the opposing factions contesting the city at large make claims on him through false recognition. But where these oppositional moments of identification only serve to validate the narrator's invisibility, the small instance of shared responsibility represents a genuine threat to his identity by revealing his ability to be seen.

This moment of recognition creates a rupture in the narrator's perception of himself, which helps to account for what many critics have seen as an unsatisfying conclusion to the novel. The narrator's final act, proleptically signaled by the novel's opening, is to withdraw into subterranean isolation, in a "retreat" that Jaffe notes many critics would "dub a cop out" (64); from one perspective the rupture in his self-image becomes a hole into which the narrator disappears. But as his final question indicates—"Who knows but that, on the lower frequencies, I speak for you?" (455)—the narrator is also seeking a connection with the reader, hoping to be seen. Here, isolation is not a permanent strategy; as his interactions with Sybil clarify, he is seeking to transform the reader and achieve a mutual visibility, his final question daring us to acknowledge him, and in doing so, break his loneliness. This process of recognition, moreover, is created not just in terms of sight, but through shared storytelling. It is the alternative narrative that he and Sybil shape, regardless of its problematic subtexts, that reminds the invisible man of the possibility of shared experience.

THE SHAPE OF THINGS TO COME

It is telling that Ellison's narrator turns to a jazz *musician,* rather than an abstract discussion of the music, to explain his isolation. Implicitly, his novel responds to earlier literary engagements with jazz that privilege and mythologize the soloist—most prominently a set of short stories that replicate such similar tropes and structures that they constitute an (unrecognized) genre: the jazz story. Such pieces focus on a prodigiously talented jazz musician (usually black), whose musical genius correlates to unconventional behavior, dissident attitudes to society, and an often overwhelming sense of loneliness. While these stories might trace an entire career, they almost always magnify a particular incident, in which the musician's loneliness, expressed through a virtuosic performance, opens up new paths for conciliation and conversation. The first chapter of this book traces the history of this genre, in both its pulp and high-literary manifestations, considering how social context, literary aesthetics, and the cultural connotations of jazz have been brought together to figure loneliness as a transformative experience. It pays particular attention to stories by figures as disparate as Eudora Welty, Langston Hughes, Julio Cortázar, James Baldwin, and Geoff Dyer, to show how ideas of improvisation and conversation have allowed writers to explore the solitary, isolating form of the short story.

In his account of the "new aesthetic discourses" that developed around jazz between 1942 and 1946, Bernard Gendron points out that the contesting definitions of the form "were laced with the idioms of commerce, politics, gender, and race."[68] Chapters 2 and 3 take up these contested questions of gender and race by looking at how writers have used the subject and aesthetics of jazz as a way to explore the isolation that comes from being marginalized by society—in the process, often questioning the racial and sexual politics of the music and its representation. In particular, the history of jazz has tended to occlude and exclude female practitioners—with the notable exception of a handful of vocalists—even as musicians like Coleman attempt to articulate, musically, the exclusion that women faced in the twentieth century. Chapter 2, then, looks at how female writers, including Zadie Smith, Gayl Jones, Toni Morrison, and Candace Allen, have negotiated this double bind, celebrating jazz as an empowering aesthetic model, even as they interrogate the narratives of masculinity that surrounds the genre. In turn, chapter 3 explores the importance of jazz as a way for writers to respond to racial othering, particularly outside the context of the United States. For even as African American musicians staked out an independent identity through a nonconformist, aesthetically complex form of expression, writers from Asia and the Pacific saw the potential for this music to express their own sense of marginalization and resistance. Reading the global circulation of jazz through its literary application, this chapter considers the work of Michael Ondaatje and Haruki Murakami, alongside a comparison of the use of jazz by indigenous writers in New Zealand and the United States.

While loneliness might suggest a feeling of smallness—social isolation, emotional numbness, physical paralysis, mental fog—this book concludes on a note of expansion and openness. Moving from fiction to autobiography, I focus on two canonical figures in twentieth-century jazz, Charles Mingus and Duke Ellington, and the concerted way that their writing contests their own exclusion from the defining narratives of jazz. Critics often draw attention to the difficulty of describing music in prose; as Leland Chambers argues, "the description of music most usually becomes impressionistic (focusing on how the listener reacts while listening or else what the player feels while playing), or it is technically precise but lifeless (at least for the purposes of fiction), or else it leans on metaphors from other areas of human experience."[69] Mingus's and Ellington's writing does not simply respond to the loneliness that comes through social marginalization; their written work uses the medium of language as a way to express something about isolation that their music cannot, pointing to the corresponding difficulty that musicians face in expressing concrete ideas in an abstracted form. I conclude by drawing together the disparate ways that writers have responded to this alternative, expansive side of solitude, by looking at how jazz writing offers readers a remedy for loneliness—helping them to reimagine their solitude through narratives of connected isolation.

IN A MINOR KEY

The Solo, Improvisation, and the Jazz Short Story

The short story has enjoyed a (comparatively) long and intimate relationship with jazz; from the literary critic's perspective, jazz almost begins with the short story, in the guise of F. Scott Fitzgerald's 1922 epoch-naming volume, *Tales of the Jazz Age*. Not only did this book represent, even cement, the status of jazz as the defining aesthetic of the American 1920s and 1930s, it also authorized a particular association between short stories and jazz (as subject, tone, and stylistic influence). The ongoing importance and commercial success of this relationship is best exemplified by the number of volumes—including Chris Parker's 1986 collection *B Flat, Bebop, Scat: Jazz Short Stories and Poems*, Richard N. Albert's 1990 volume *From Blues to Bop: A Collection of Jazz Fiction*, Marcela Breton's *Hot and Cool: Jazz Short Stories* (of the same year), and Sascha Feinstein and David Rife's 2009 *Jazz Fiction Anthology*—that anthologize and valorize the jazz short story as its own identifiable genre. But although these collections almost all include stories that range from Fitzgerald's jazz age to their present moment, by looking at the way this genre has evolved since the 1920s, one rapidly sees that particular tropes and narrative patterns started to recur in jazz fiction around the middle of the twentieth century, distinct from those initial appropriations of jazz.

As anyone who has been disappointed by Fitzgerald's volume will know, earlier short-story writers tended to overlook the musicians who created jazz, and focus on the music itself as a ready-made form of cultural capital. Indeed, as Ryan Jerving argues, jazz was "most often sounded" in 1920s literature in order to express "an affirmative relation to its time and place."[1] This tendency in turn reflected the commercial nature of the short story at the start of the twentieth century, where a writer like Fitzgerald saw himself as "whoring his talents" writing short stories for "the popular magazines" whose financial support "sustained him throughout his writing career."[2] Starting in 1934 with an early (perhaps originating) version by Langston Hughes, however, and with prominent examples by writers as disparate as Eudora Welty, James Baldwin, Ralph Ellison, and Richard Yates, a distinctive genre of "jazz story" developed over the 1940s and 1950s that instead focused squarely on the jazz *musician*: in particular, a virtuosic performer who struggles with isolation and loneliness.

That this period should see writers increasingly turn to jazz as a way of grappling with the parameters and possibilities of loneliness should not be surprising. The period that Riesman characterized as the age of "the lonely crowd" was bookended by works like Carson McCullers's 1940 novel *The Heart is a Lonely Hunter* and Yates's 1962 collection *Eleven Kinds of Loneliness*; the subject was clearly at the forefront of the American literary psyche. Indeed, as Mary Caputi argues convincingly in *A Kinder, Gentler America: Melancholia and the Mythical 1950s*, the pressures of conformity and homogeneity led to an endemic experience of "loneliness and despair."[3] In turn, the performance of jazz was itself increasingly staged as an act of independence and nonconformist rebellion; Steven Elworth has shown that, by the 1940s, jazz was "no longer an important element in the dominant pop music of the day," and instead was promoted as "an art music created primarily by young urban African Americans, part of a subculture with its own somewhat scandalous cultural codes and the use of various illegal drugs."[4] The jazz musician was consequently associated with individuality, nonconformity, and social isolation. At the same time, the popularity of the short story as a literary form, particularly among established writers, grew significantly over the course of the 1940s. Indeed, reflecting on the previous year in an article from 1951, the prominent critic Leslie Fiedler noted in wonder that there had "never been so favourable a moment for the short story," echoing similar summative reviews by Irving Howe, Nolan Miller, and Edith Mirrielees.[5] But this popularity was not commensurate with an authoritative status—instead, the short story continued to be associated with a narrow focus and limited social relevance. Within the context of American publishing and criticism, it remained a minor form compared to the dominant mode of the novel.

Indeed, it was the minor aesthetics of the short story—in terms of its limited focus, constrained size, and oppositional relationship to the novel—that led writers as early as Hughes to turn to the short story as a structure for exploring the concept of loneliness through jazz. As Mary Louise Pratt has shown, critics' frequent recourse to the qualities of the novel when trying to define the short story is not in itself a sign of laziness, but instead a direct consequence of a tendency in "highly institutionalized forms of discourse, like verbal art," toward "pairs of short and long genres."[6] Although specialists in the short story like to maintain the idea that it is "an autonomous genre," Pratt makes the useful observation that (in English, at least) the form of the short story is essentially defined by its brevity; given that "the conceptual aspect is that shortness cannot be an intrinsic property of anything, but occurs only relative to something else," whenever writers come to define the short story, they almost inevitably do so in contradistinction to the "long story," or novel.[7] This is because the qualities that critics have routinely ascribed to the genre since the essays of Edgar Allan Poe—self-containedness, compression, focus on an individual rather than a group or community, unity of effect—all rely on an implicit contrast with a longer form that emphasizes the alternative. From this perspective, the form of the short story is not just minor for being short, but minor in that it embraces the qualities neglected by the major form of the novel.

In one light, this is a positive quality of the form; Poe certainly valorized the unifying effect of a narrow, constrained aesthetic model. Many critics, particularly in the mid-twentieth-century United States, however, equated the minor aesthetics of the short story with fragmentation and isolation. In a 1945 essay on "The Structure of the Modern Short Story," for instance, A. L. Balder observed that "the modern short story is plotless, static, fragmentary, amorphous—frequently a mere character sketch or vignette, or a mere reporting of a transient moment, or the capturing of a mood or nuance."[8] His charge that in such stories "nothing happens" in fact conflated two frequent attacks on the short story: sometimes it implies "that nothing significant happens," while sometimes it means more generally that "the modern short story is charged with a lack of narrative structure." These critiques had a particular urgency at a time when American critics were concerned with promoting the more democratic form of the novel; equally, they echo comments that continue to be raised against the short story. They point to the "lurking associations" behind the juxtaposition of short fiction and novels: "if the short story is not a 'full-length' narrative it cannot narrate a full-length life; it can narrate a fragment or excerpt of a life. And if from that fragment one can deduce things about the whole life, then the more novel-like, the more complete, the story is."[9] It makes sense, then, that the short story should be associated with isolation and loneliness, for its minor aesthetics—as Deleuze and Guattari argued of Kafka—offer a way for writers to retreat from the sociability and totality associated with the novel. As Hughes's story "The Blues I'm Playing" demonstrates, moreover, the short story also offers the writer aware of the rhetoric around the two genres a way to question the prevailing assumptions about loneliness *and* the short story, by emphasizing the expansive possibilities of both.

PLAYING THE BLUES: LONELINESS, THE SOLO, AND IMPROVISATION

Hughes's early jazz story "The Blues I'm Playing" (from his 1934 volume, *The Ways of White Folks*) had a profound effect on the way other writers would construct stories around jazz soloists. Focused on a prodigious black female pianist, "The Blues I'm Playing" deliberately points to the long-established tropes around isolated artistic brilliance. Rather than simply eliding the virtuosic jazz musician with the larger mythology of the isolated and tormented romantic genius, however, Hughes instead emphasized that brilliance as a musician came from a connection with a wider community, in the process moving the music's register from the blues to jazz.

At least on the surface, however, the formal elements of the story would seem to contradict this thematic movement toward connection. As theorists like Pratt are quick to emphasize, because it is defined by its limited size, any short story must inherently narrate events limited in scope, detail, or both. Nobody writing in the 1930s exemplified this trend more than Hughes's contemporary Ernest Hemingway, whose "famous prose style—plain words, simple but artfully structured syntax, the direct presentation of the object"— was coupled with a subject matter that focused insistently on "the fragmentary nature of modern life, with its small local victories and defeats, its focus on the present moment and its prevailing mood of disillusion."[10] In the American short story of the 1930s through the 1950s, then, this intrinsic quality of "limitation" was elevated to the defining stylistic feature—and "The Blues I'm Playing," with its close focus on a pair of characters and their relationship, and a narrative organized around a final turning point or moment of epiphany, foregrounds precisely such stylistic compression. The title, moreover, immediately suggests a connection between loneliness and jazz, riffing on the popular connotations of "the blues," so that, on the surface, the formal limitations of the story appear to reinforce the protagonist's isolation, and the pain that is associated with her music. Hughes's story was to prove so influential, however, because of the way it subverted the expectations established by both the title and the oppressive loneliness within the story, to offer a redemptive, expansive vision of being an individual, and being alone.

The story charts the relationship between an elderly white widow, Mrs. Ellsworth, and her "protégée" (78), the talented young (and crucially, black) pianist, Oceola. A patron to a number of artists, Mrs. Ellsworth expects Oceola to dedicate her life to perfecting her music, living the "beautiful life" of one of "the few beautiful people who live for their art—and nothing else" (83). Idealizing a romantic narrative of sacrifice, wherein the artist rejects earthly pleasures in dedication to art, she encourages Oceola to give up her teaching and performances at churches, believing that "she must learn to sublimate her soul" (78). Crucially, this means rejecting love and emotional fulfillment; Mrs. Ellsworth tries to talk Oceola out of marrying a black medical student, Pete, and after they are engaged, blames "Pete's influence on her protégée" for a less-than-perfect performance: "All that time you were playing on that stage, he was here, the monster! Taking you out of yourself, taking you away from the piano" (81). The kind of "beautiful" art that Mrs. Ellsworth wants her to create, moreover, is restricted to traditional genres: despite Oceola's love of jazz, Mrs. Ellsworth expects her to only play classical pieces, believing still "in art of the old school, portraits that really and truly looked like people, poems about nature, music that had soul in it, not syncopation" (78). Hughes takes great pains not only to expose the coldness that lies beneath traditional expectations of genius—that "art is bigger than love" (83)—but also to show the incompatibility of such isolation with jazz.

Ultimately, Oceola rejects her patron's expectations of her lifestyle as an artist, and the kind of music she can produce. In the final action of the story, she breaks free from her patron's stifling expectations, performing an earth-moving jazz improvisation at Mrs. Ellsworth's house. By the time Hughes depicts this climactic, syncopated performance, however, he has already shown Oceola regularly questioning the validity of her patron's idealized artistic life, wondering why "white folks think you could live on nothing but art?" (83). For a period, Mrs. Ellsworth pays for Oceola to live and study in France, where for the first time she mixes with a group of "serious" (rather than syncopated) artists. She cannot, however, understand how they can "argue so much about life or art," juxtaposing their pained and intellectualized engagement with art against her own organic, holistic experience of music: she "merely lived—and loved it" (79). In defiance of her patron's sacrificial expectations, moreover, Oceola maintains that she doesn't need to be isolated from other to create beautiful music. She forcefully demonstrates this not only through her relationship with Pete, but her insistence on continuing to perform in her community: "she still loved to play for Harlem house parties," where she no longer performed for money, but instead "out of the sheer love of jazz" (78).

Indeed, her joy and success as an artist are directly connected to her relationships with others. It is telling that, despite the reference to "blues" in the title, within the story Hughes describes Oceola's performances as "jazz." Like recent theorists, Hughes himself defined jazz in terms of its group dynamic—so that, in his well-known speech on "Jazz as Communication," he argues that the blues is a form of jazz when it moves toward communication. Within "The Blues I'm Playing," certainly, Hughes characterizes Oceola's jazz performance as a form of musical expression that gains strength from a sense of community. It is what allows her to break down the loneliness that she otherwise feels in Paris: performing jazz at a black club, her music transcends the question of technical skill and instead takes on a communicative function. In a moment of transcendent signification, she makes "the bass notes throb like tom-toms, the trebles cry like little flutes, so deep in the earth and so high in the sky that they understood everything" (79). This sense of shared understanding, bringing together the members of the audience and the performer, is reinforced by their unity of movement, and the pure pleasure Oceola feels when "the night club would get up and dance to her blues." Far from living *for* her art, Hughes asks us to see Oceola as living *through* her art.

Beyond the harmony created in the club, however, the story probes a broader question of community, to which Hughes would return a number of times in his career: whether art, particularly music, can overcome the racial divide in America. Oceola, on the one hand, seems to reject the idea that music could facilitate cross-racial unity, simply declaring "Bunk!" to the "cultured Negroes who were always saying art would break down color lines, art could save the race and prevent lynchings" (79). And her stance seems justified, in light of Mrs. Ellsworth's disdain for jazz, and horror at her performance in the final stages of the book. But equally, Oceola herself comes to define jazz as a form of artistic expression that brings together black and white, characterizing it through a bivalent aesthetic that encompasses dual emotions—"Listen! . . . How sad and gay it is. Blue and happy—laughing and crying"—a dual-gender identity—"How much like a man. . . . And how like a woman"—and, crucially, a racial harmony: "How white like you and black like me" (84). Hughes affirms and valorizes Oceola's definition through the final action of the story. In a moment of call-and-response, Mrs. Ellsworth allows herself to be moved by the music, and as Oceola sings "I'd go up on de mountain . . . and call my baby back," Mrs. Ellsworth "rising from her chair" responds that she "would stand looking at the stars." Like the audience at the club, Mrs. Ellsworth rises up to symbolically join the performer, imaginatively placing herself on the mountain top together, healing their relationship through the music and creating the first moment of equality in what has been, until that point, a highly unequal system.

This moment is so emotionally loaded in part because of the loneliness that both characters experience—not the heroic isolation of Mrs. Ellsworth's romantic ideal, but the quotidian loneliness that comes from finding yourself disconnected from the people around you. In this sense, jazz is figured by Hughes as a form that is antithetical to loneliness; Oceola performs jazz (until the conclusion) for groups with whom she believes she has a connection, where that sense of connectedness feeds into, and is affirmed by, the power of her music. But as the title of the story also indicates, jazz for Hughes is also a highly personalized, even private form of expression. In her final performance, Oceola fervently affirms, "this is mine" (84), making it clear that her music is a way for her to assert her identity against the attempts by her patron—and white society at large—to dictate what kind of art she can produce, and how she is allowed to live her life. At the same time, unlike the sublimated art that Mrs. Ellsworth values, this personal expression is a way of valorizing the individual's voice and experiences, but not at the expense of one's own identity and desires. This individualizing impulse sits against the allegorical register of story, framed within a collection with the fablesque title *The Ways of White Folks,* and in which the artist's patron wildly generalizes about "the Negro girl" (72), her "black friend" (76), emphasizing the importance of maintaining a distinctive, individual voice. So as a bivalent form that combines happiness and sadness, connectedness and individuality, jazz offers a way of transforming individual experience into something shared, and affirmative, just as the limitations of the short story ultimately affirm the value of being alone as the common ground that can bring individuals together.

This affirmation relies on a particular quality of Oceola's music, which firmly associates it with jazz: it is improvised, thus evoking an individuality that classical music, however emotionally felt, is denied in an American discourse. Monson has described the act of improvising jazz as a "magical projection of soul and individuality by musical means," and by joining Oceola and Mrs. Ellsworth through such an act of self-projection, Hughes's final scene ultimately privileges jazz over other forms of musical expression, as a form uniquely capable of communicating individuality and shared isolation.[11] Their dialogue, moreover, reinforces the emotional exchange that this display of individuality has opened up, echoing what Monson has called the recurring "verbal aesthetic image" of "saying something" within both popular and professional conceptualizations of jazz.[12] For Monson, however, the importance of saying something in jazz also insistently "underscores the collaborative and communicative quality of improvisation," and it is worth noting that, by contrast, Hughes is only able to make such strong connections between the narrow focus of the short story and the collective individualism of Oceola's improvised music because she is a soloist; more than that, the style of jazz that she plays requires only tacit collaboration from the audience, not musical accompaniment. Even when a musician is associated with group performance—as is Armstrong in *Invisible Man*—the thematic need to construct the soloist as a virtuosic individual means that writers often blur their backing band into an indistinct musical smudge, to create this spotlighted effect.

From a musical perspective, however, the act of improvisation developed through a long history of group dynamics, so that "saying something [in jazz] requires soloists who can play" and equally "accompanists who can respond."[13] The development of bebop over the mid-1940s shifted this dynamic further. Although bop developed, as Eric Lott explains, as "a soloist's music, despite the democratic ethos of jazz," the kind of improvisation that bebop cultivated depended on a close, almost intuitive connection between soloists and accompanists, due to its "dependence on unison riffs" and "the extreme sympathy required between players to negotiate the rhythms."[14] These structural changes "redefined the tradition," and in turn, changed the way that writers sensitive to jazz responded to, and appropriated, the aesthetics of improvisation.[15]

Indeed, in literary terms, Timothy Spaulding has argued that the "bebop aesthetic" can be understood as one where individual expression is only ever achieved through listening to, taking inspiration from, and reciprocating the thoughts and expressions of other.[16] He suggests that in *Invisible Man*, for instance, "Ellison constructs the unnamed narrator as a literary bebop improviser who draws on the voices and reflections of other characters, redefines and comments on their statements, in order to emerge with his own improvisational voice by the end of the text." In some ways, Oceola's epiphanic improvisations do reflect the experiences of those she had met—Hughes certainly suggests the "reciprocal and multi-layered relationships among sound, social settings, and cultural politics that affect the meaning of jazz improvisation"—but because she performs alone, her ability to "say something" is crucially compromised.[17] For although it is easy to read Mrs. Ellsworth's final words as responding affirmatively to Oceola's expression of isolated selfhood, they can equally be understood as a rejection of her call to collective singularity. By turning away from her former protégée, and staring instead at the stars, she could be seen to refuse the call for recognition in Oceola's music, returning instead to her own idea of collective, cosmic beauty. Through this ambiguity, Hughes suggests the limitations of Oceola's music to offer consolation in the face of loneliness. However well she plays them, they are only ever *her* blues; the loneliness of Oceola is unique and, as a consequence, perhaps ultimately unconsoling.

Like Ellison, James Baldwin wrote in the wake of the bebop "revolution," and his use of jazz aesthetics in his much-anthologized "Sonny's Blues" marks a development in the genre of the jazz story: loneliness in this work always sits in relief to communication with others, just as jazz within the story is characterized by means of an individual who can only communicate something personal within the context of a group performance—in conversation with others. Like Hughes, Baldwin deliberately plays with the boundary between jazz and the blues, but here the focus is much more squarely on the role that the two musical traditions can play in the process of forming new stories for imagining the self in relation to others. As Tracey Sherard has argued, Baldwin "deals not only thematically with the crossroads between the blues and jazz, but addresses the need for a new form of cultural narrative as a repository for the experiences of

African Americans."[18] Constructing these new, historically rooted, narratives is a communal act for Baldwin—one that counters loneliness and fragmentation through building social ties.

Indeed, from the very beginning of the story, Baldwin establishes the status of loneliness as a specifically social affliction, initially through the narrator's observations of his students. A high-school teacher, he wonders about his students' attraction to "the darkness of the movies," imaging the cinema as a place in which "they now, vindictively, dreamed, at once more together than they were at any other time, and more alone (104). This emphasis on a contrasting physical proximity and emotional disconnection, underlined by their sinister, "vindictive" dreams, is unconsciously mirrored in the narrator's own interactions with his brother, Sonny.

Although he is a keen, almost poetic observer of his brother, paying close attention to his physical appearance—he remarks that "when he was about as old as the boys in my class his face had been bright and open, there was a lot of copper in it; and he'd had wonderfully direct brown eyes, and great gentleness and privacy" (103)—the narrator struggles to connect with Sonny's interior being, or what he refers to as "the life that Sonny lived inside" (110). Indeed, part of the story's pathos comes from the narrator's growing awareness of this gap between their sudden physical proximity, once Sonny is released from prison and moves in with the narrator, and their growing emotional distance. This "difference," in the narrator's mind, "lay between [them] like a chasm," so that moments of recognition, such as when "the baby brother I'd never known looked out from the depths of his private life, like an animal waiting to be coaxed into life," ultimately only reinforce the isolation that both men feel in the face of one another. Here Baldwin stages a process of affective reflection that recent research so clearly affirms: the loneliness of others tends to amplify our own sense of being alone.

Both men recognize that this gap is further exacerbated, if not caused, by their mutual inability to communicate. And the initial image of the narrator's students at the movies, physically close but psychically isolated, suggests the same thing: staring at the screen, their dreams remain private and uncommunicated, perhaps incommunicable. Between Sonny and the narrator, however, there is at least a willingness to *try*. In their interactions, what Baldwin emphasizes instead is the limitation of words alone to express one's inner life. Sonny, in particular, tries to use his body to communicate something that he does not have the vocabulary to express: at one point in the story "he paused, looking hard at me, as though his eyes would help me to understand, then gestured helplessly, as though perhaps his hand would help" (120); later, he again uses his eyes to try to translate his thoughts to his brother, looking at him "with great, troubled eyes, as though, in fact, he hoped his eyes would tell me things he could never otherwise say" (131). Through these observations, the narrator seems to shift responsibility to Sonny, as if their distance is the fault of his expressive failures. But Sonny inverts this equation, reminding his brother, and the reader, that connection and communication require active listening as well; when the narrator tries to encourage Sonny to stay in school and put off his dreams of being a musician, Sonny pulls away, explaining, "I hear you. But you never hear anything *I* say" (124). Steve Tracy points to "a half dozen explicit instances" of Baldwin describing the act of listening, reflecting the story's preoccupation with failures in conversation.[19]

For Baldwin, this two-way problem in communication is not a minor issue: as the story progresses, psychic dissonance is increasingly registered as a physical pain, to the extent that loneliness becomes the characteristic feature of human suffering. The pain that the narrator feels in his isolation from his brother—for example, when he recognizes what "both were seeking . . . was the part of ourselves which had been left behind"—is equated with the visceral ache of a phantom limb; as he explains, "it's always at the hour of trouble and confrontation that the missing member aches" (112). In an equally telling moment, when the narrator describes the loss of his daughter, what causes him the most grief is when his wife, Isabel, cries in the night, dreaming of her death: it is this isolation that hurts him most, so that "where Isabel is weeping against me seems a mortal wound" (127). Where the narrator is unable to move beyond describing his pain, Sonny is able to analyze it: "'It's terrible sometimes, inside,' he said, 'that's what's the trouble. You walk these streets, black and funky and cold, and there's not really a living ass to talk to, and there's nothing shaking, and there's no way of getting it out—that storm inside.

You can't talk it and you can't make live with it, and when you finally try to get with it and play it, you realize *nobody's* listening. So *you've* got to listen. You got to find a way to listen'" (133). This marks one of several moments where Baldwin suggests that, as a jazz musician, Sonny has a particularly privileged understanding of loneliness. He is better able to recognize it, but also better equipped to actively transform his own experiences, through the agency of listening.

Of course, it might be more accurate to say that the qualities that make Sonny sensitive to loneliness and pain are also those that give him virtuosic powers as a musician. In part, Baldwin suggests that this association is a product of the cultural connotations of jazz, where the apparently loose, improvised nature of the music seems to carry over to every aspects of the musician's life. The narrator "didn't like the way [Sonny] carried himself loose and dreamlike all the time" because it betrayed a kind of moral decay associated with jazz; he even suspects that "his music seemed to be merely an excuse for the life he led. It sounded just that weird and disordered" (126). The narrator's wife and his family find Sonny similarly difficult to understand: for them, living with Sonny "wasn't like living with a person at all, it was like living with sound" (124), to the point that they felt "as though Sonny were some sort of god, or monster. He moved in an atmosphere which wasn't like theirs at all" (125). But Sonny himself suggests an alternative reason for the close relationship between jazz and loneliness: the jazz musician needs to feel a heightened pain in order to produce something beautiful. Listening to a woman singing at a barbecue across the street, he explains how "it struck me all of a sudden how much suffering she must have had to go through—to sing like that. It's *repulsive* to think you have to suffer that much" (132). Yet Sonny also recognizes how generative such isolation can be, where it "was actually when I was most *out* of the world, I felt that I was in it, that I was *with* it, really, and I could play or I didn't really have to *play,* it just came out of me, it was there" (134). It is in this translation of inner isolation to external expression that, for Baldwin, the value of jazz seems to lie: it offers the potential to transform the fundamentally painful experience of being alone into one of communion and harmony.

One sign of Sonny's success at listening is his ability to draw inspiration from any kind of music—not just an instrumental form of jazz. On the whole, critics have tended to focus on the connections that Baldwin establishes with bebop throughout the story; Sherard notes that, while the story is titled "Sonny's Blues," the description of Sonny's playing "strongly supports a reading that it is jazz, and more specifically "Bebop," that Sonny plays in the culminating scene."[20] But Tracy has recently pointed out that, although the "blues that Sonny is playing" is "in a jazz style influenced by Charlie Parker and his generation of boppers," the story draws together jazz, blues, and spirituals in a way that is "strongly reminiscent of the quintessentially musically oriented African-American writer, Langston Hughes."[21] Convincingly, Tracy connects this conversation between musical genres to the story's thematic focus on communication, suggesting that, as synthesized by Sonny, these three genres "transcend the philosophical, spiritual, and artistic differences that characterize them. Like a jam session, they engage each other, not to destroy, but to produce a wholeness that comes from listening and hearing different points of view."[22] Like Hughes, then, Baldwin stages a pivotal performance that parallels a conversation between musical forms and one between isolated individuals.

In the final moments of "Sonny's Blues," the narrator goes to see his brother play for the first time, and it is through this beautifully evoked performance that Baldwin unpacks the power of jazz to communicate and relieve pain. Listening to his brother's quartet, the narrator draws together two elements of loneliness that Sonny has remarked on earlier: the importance of listening to things that people normally ignore, and the need to make people listen. As the band begins to play, the narrator reflects that, on the one hand "not many people ever really hear" music, and that when they do, and "something opens within, and the music enters," what they "mainly hear, or hear corroborated, are personal, private, vanishing evocations" (137). By contrast, the jazz musician is able to hear things that the ordinary person can't. He or she is able to hear "something else, is dealing with the roar rising from the void and imposing order on it as it hits the air. What is evoked in him, then, is of another order, more terrible because it has no words, and triumphant, too, for that same reason." Listening to his brother and his group play what is unmistakably bebop, he recognizes that these musicians are able to hear not just their own internal loneliness and isolation, but something greater, almost communal—the roar rising from the void—and translate it into a redemptive experience, for as he concludes, "his triumph, when he triumphs, is ours."

Why does Baldwin privilege jazz over other musical forms here? Sonny has clearly drawn from other African American musical genres throughout the narrative, but in this transformative moment we can recognize something of Charlie Parker (to whom the story alludes) in the driving, polyphonic, instrumental narrative. Baldwin's insistent focus on conversation suggests one explanation: it is because the group dynamic of jazz is itself a kind of conversation, communicating not through singular voices, but through a staged interaction: "Creole let out the reins. The dry, low, black man said something awful on the drums, Creole answered, and the drums talked back. Then the horn insisted, sweet and high, slightly detached perhaps, and Creole listened commenting now and then, dry, and driving, beautiful and calm and old. Then they all came together again, and Sonny was part of the family again" (139).

But equally, what stands out about jazz expression here is that, although it makes the audience feel they are experiencing something new—as he improvises, Sonny seems "to have found, right there beneath his fingers, a damn brand-new piano"—the music also communicates something fundamental to human nature, something that lies at the core of the blues and spirituals alike. It is only when the bandleader, Creole, steps in again, and "hit something in all of them" (which also "hit something" in the narrator) that the music "tightened and deepened, apprehension began to beat the air," and the narrator understands "what the blues were all about. They were not about anything very new" (139). Instead, the band are "keeping it new, at the risk of ruin, destruction, madness, and death, in order to find new ways to make us listen" to the story of human suffering; confronted by their music, the narrator finally recognizes that "the tale of how we suffer, and how we are delighted, and how we may triumph is never new, it always must be heard. There isn't any other tale to tell" (139). In this way, Sonny's blues (both the music within the story and the story itself) are recast as the archetypal narrative, a metonym for storytelling itself. Not only does the relationship between improviser and group create a bridge between loneliness and community, but the staged storytelling speaks to an underlying shared experience between musicians and audience.

In many ways, Baldwin's treatment of improvisation as a communal affirmation of individuality owes as much to a literary precedent as a musical one. Eudora Welty's 1941 story "Powerhouse," which Sascha Feinstein and David Rife describe as "the second most famous jazz story" after Baldwin's, follows a much more authoritative jazz virtuoso, the eponymous bandleader, as he breaks up his group's improvised performance by responding to a telegram announcing his wife's death.[23] Based on Welty's own experience hearing a performance by the proto-bebop pianist Fats Waller, the story signals its interest in a different kind of jazz to Hughes's story through the structure and effect of the music: a series of highly complex solos, the performance is so technical that the audience cannot dance along. Not only does this distance between audience and band indicate the difference in genres of jazz—it also reflects the lack of shared community between the white southern crowd and the black bandleader.

Indeed, the audience stands at once entranced and intimidated by the musicians, especially the bandleader, who is initially presented as a kind of inspired romantic poet: following the euphoric announcement "Powerhouse is playing!" (201), he is described as being "in a trance; he's a person of joy, a fanatic" (202). But rather than a spontaneous expression of individuality, his music is a communicative response to those around him, where the audience "watch[es] them carefully, hear[s] the least word, especially what they say to one another, in another language" (202), listening to the way their music summons and responds to one another's voices. The effect of this harmonious individuality is that, in spite of their isolated solos, the band members sound unified, coming "down the first note like a waterfall" (203). As Leland Chambers has noted, moreover, the collective individuality of improvisation is represented not only through the music, but through "the stories Powerhouse tells about the death of his wife"; because "the descriptive language of narrative cannot adequately report the sounds of music and consequently the activity of improvisation," Chambers argues, Welty instead tries to capture the effect of improvisation through storytelling, where "the nature of jazz improvisation becomes exemplified and clarified" through analogies with narrative.[24]

Both Baldwin and Welty draw explicit analogies, then, between telling stories about loneliness and playing jazz. In "Sonny's Blues," the narrator hears in his brother's music a story both of general human suffering and of Sonny's particular experiences of aching isolation; Powerhouse's improvisation echoes his attempts to come to terms with the loss of his deepest personal connection. Even in "The Blues I'm Playing," Oceola's music is accompanied by words—a song about the loneliness of loss, of calling back her baby. In each case, this process frames the writer as a kind of jazz musician, asking the reader to view the processes of storytelling and playing jazz as complementary, and to make a connection between the effect of the music within the story (unifying the audience, resolving the crisis of individual pain through a recognition of shared humanity) and the effect of the story they are reading. The implication of this jazz-story logic is that, although the piece may focus on one individual case of loneliness, it will resonate with readers and provide them with a new way of understanding their own solitude.

Of course, within "Powerhouse" and "Sonny's Blues," the solo performance is also part of a conversation, a dialectical exchange. Like Baldwin, Welty stresses the collaborative atmosphere that generates improvised genius, both in the band's individual solos and in the role of other musicians in encouraging Powerhouse's storytelling, as they riff together on the same narrative themes. Improvisation, which Hughes portrayed as a solitary act of expression, is treated by Baldwin and Welty as an act of shared creation. As Chambers argues, storytelling is "a collective enterprise, in which the chief improviser/storyteller, Powerhouse, is pushed on by his fellow musicians throughout several choruses . . . just as it is with jazz."[25] Indeed, across both stories the process of jazz performance is characterized by such a process of encouragement and response. Powerhouse, for example, "has to keep encouraging" his "bass fiddler from Vicksburg," and the narrator asks, almost in wonder, "when you heard him like that on records, did you know he was really pleading?" (204). Looking at the stories metatextually, these internal conversations map out another exchange, between the reader and the story, where the text, like a bandleader, elicits a response from readers—asks them to perform their own solo, map out their own blues, express their own solitude in an affirmative way.

As with both "The Blues I'm Playing" and "Sonny's Blues," however, the question of the genre of music in "Powerhouse" has been contested—and as in Hughes's and Baldwin's texts, there is more at stake than just a label. As Kenneth Bearden notes, while "critics have been able to arrive at a fairly congruous reading of the text ... which highlights both Welty's incorporation of a jazz style and the protagonist's attempt to end his feelings of alienation by connecting with his audience," they may have failed to listen closely to the music in "Powerhouse," which he argues draws on a hybrid "blues-jazz aesthetic."[26] Why should we care about this kind of hybridity? Because, as in "The Blues I'm Playing," there is a crucial distinction between jazz as a form of communication, and the blues as a singular or unilateral performance. Bearden supports his reading by pointing to a crucial mismatch between audience and musician, noting the "continual indications" that "the narrator and fellow audience members fail to even understand what it is they hear."[27] From this perspective, the communication between musician and audience that is so central to the meaning of "Sonny's Blues" is missing. Sarah Gilbreath Ford's extremely sensitive reading supports this, pointing out the narrator's racism and hostility toward Powerhouse, even when the narrator is trying to convey admiration. Here, she argues, "Welty's fiction only thinly veils the realities of racism, exploitation, hatred and violence."[28] Both Bearden and Gilbreath point to the confluence of the white audience's commodification of Powerhouse and his band, and the narrative of exploitation so central to the story that Powerhouse tells them; together, both stage a failed communication.

This is not to diminish the power of Powerhouse as a musician or a storyteller. Indeed, by co-opting a blues sensibility here, Bearden argues, Powerhouse takes on the role of manipulative trickster who parodies his audience's expectations: his "unique position—on the border between white and black worlds—permits Powerhouse to manipulate the very words the white audience loves to hear, thus creating multiple meanings which are only visible when one adopts a different perspective."[29] In particular, Powerhouse works stereotypically racist assumptions about sex and violence—consider the connotations of the name "Uranus Knockwood"—to at once satisfy and undermine his audience. Ford quite rightly points out that "the violence" in Powerhouse's story "both entertains the audience and allows Powerhouse to gain the power indicated in his name"—but she also ties this to the "blues strategy of making the evil thing present... to diminish its power."[30] Where Hughes implied a possible failure to communicate, then, Welty deliberately stages an ironic performance, which blends both the polyphonic, communicative qualities of jazz with the singular, even solipsistic elements of the blues.

This deliberate distancing on the part of Powerhouse is clearer in the original ending of the story. While the final song certainly confronts the audience, and thus the reader, with their own distance from Powerhouse, encouraging a closer connection, as Bearden has shown, in the first draft of the story (rejected by her editor), Powerhouse played the popular piece "Hold Tight": a song whose lyrics "were in fact deemed sexually suggestive."[31] Even without the salacious references to seafood, it is hard to avoid reading "the pleasure the audience expresses is a kind of sexual release," where their titillation is ultimately at their own expense.[32] I think that Bearden's argument needs to be taken a step further, however, as it is not just Powerhouse who is manipulating an audience, but Welty herself, by means of a deliberately alienating narrator and persistent second-person address. Welty forces the reader to engage on a different level with the marginalized, isolated Powerhouse "by constructing the reader as a white racist sympathetic to the disturbing racial politics that lead to violence." Either we identify with the narrator and are thus implicated in his racism and objectification, or we must reject the narrator's viewpoint and actively "read . . . against the grain," so that "the reader's response of denying the racism becomes the point of the story."[33] In effect, Welty is drawing attention to our own isolation—ideally, reminding us of our difference from the crowd, and our shared ground with Powerhouse.

From this perspective, the traditional associations of the short story with fragmentation and incompletion contribute directly to these stories' attempts to reframe and reimagine loneliness. While Pratt helpfully points out that "the short story is always printed as part of a larger whole, either a collection of short stories or a magazine, which is a collection of various kinds of texts," she concludes that, "except in schools, perhaps, individual short stories are usually read as part of a larger reading experience."[34] This is to say that the short story asks to be completed by being brought into conversation with other stories. But as Welty and Baldwin show, the other stories necessary to complete the jazz-story-as-solo are not necessarily those in the same volume (particularly given that both stories were originally published in magazines), or even ones that are written down. Instead, they are those the reader supplies, the responses that the stories plead for, just as Creole or Powerhouse plead with their players to tell the stories that matter.

THE CRITIC'S JAZZ: TROPES AND OWNERSHIP

On the surface, Julio Cortázar's story "The Pursuer" seems to rehearse the same themes and structures as "Sonny's Blues" and "The Blues I'm Playing" as a kind of exemplary jazz story.[35] First published in Cortázar's 1959 volume *Las Armas Secretas,* the story is dedicated to the memory of "Ch. P.," and as a consequence, the story's protagonist, an isolated and drug-ravaged saxophonist named Johnny, has tended to be read as a thinly veiled portrait of Charlie Parker.[36] Superficially, Cortázar's story does draw parallels between the isolation and physical collapse of Johnny, the music he plays, and the confined form of the short story. From early in the text, the narrator, a critic named Bruno, emphasizes Johnny's exceptional talent—he played the saxophone "like I imagine only a god can play an alto sax" (185)—which seems conditional on his own isolation from the people around him, including his own band members, who would not even "risk lending Johnny an instrument" (184). So when Johnny exclaims that "everybody knows the dates except me," he is reinforcing his status as a privileged figure, who is so talented that he circumvents the usual strictures of space and time—but who also suffers as a consequence. Indeed, this "preoccupation" with time is characterized as a "mania" of Johnny's—which Bruno confesses he still "explains and develops" in conversation "with a charm hard to resist"—and is at once the source of his brilliance as a musician, and of his isolation. In one episode that Bruno recalls early in the story, Johnny suddenly disrupts a near-perfect rehearsal with Miles Davis, shouting "I already played this tomorrow, it's horrible, Miles"; from that point onward, "everything was lousy" (186). But equally, it is this temporal dissonance with others that makes him great, giving him an "astonishing step forward... over any other musician" (189). Throughout the story, Johnny insistently stresses his physical and psychological isolation from others, culminating in his anguished cry, "I'm as alone as that cat, much more alone because I know it and he doesn't" (239).

But even as the attentive reader recognizes the conventions of a typical 'jazz story,' tracing the fall of a lonely, brilliant individual whose music contains something that transforms human experience, she will also inevitably recognize that Cortázar has dramatized the *construction* of this narrative. Through Bruno's narratorial asides, and consistent references to another text—his successful biography of Johnny—Cortázar draws our attention to the ways in which Bruno is trying to fit Johnny into a particular set of tropes, so that his "story" can be unpacked into a certain kind of allegory. In part, Bruno attempts to reduce Johnny to a force within a historical trajectory that he himself has theorized, noting that "anyone who's interested can read my book on Johnny and the new postwar style" (199), but at the same time, it is also clear that, within the narrative we are reading, Bruno is attempting to construct a different kind of narrative around the ideal of Johnny; as he explains, "this is not the place to be a jazz critic." Naturally, such a comment might make the reader wonder what kind of place *this* (the story) is, and question the status of the text presented to us as a pseudo-confession. Cumulatively, Bruno's asides suggest that we are to understand the story as a parallel text to his biography; when Bruno describes trying "to drag him [Johnny] back to reality," for instance, he follows with a parenthetical comment: "(To reality: I barely get that written down and it disgusts me)" (217), reinforcing the reader's impression of reading a document, not listening to a story.

Graciela Garcia has argued that "the text of 'The Pursuer' is constructed as a kind of intimate diary, that is, a personal notebook containing the unofficial 'dossier' privately kept by Bruno," and the advantage of looking at the text as a kind of reflective confession is that it encourages an attention to Bruno's motivations.[37] In a moment of reflexive honesty, Bruno admits the extent to which he is attempting to interpret Johnny: "I know very well that, for me, Johnny has ceased being a jazzman and that his musical genius is a façade, something that everyone can manage to understand eventually and admire, but which conceals something else, and that other thing is the only one I ought to care for" (207). Bruno thus compromises his own narrative by revealing his own attempts to mythologize his subject and transform him into an ideal. By exposing the author of the text we are reading as someone less interested in his subject as a human than as a concept, Cortázar not only critiques the genre in which he is ostensibly working—the jazz story—but forces the reader to engage in their own process of "critiquing" Johnny.

The honesty of Bruno's self-examination grows over the course of the story, to the point where it becomes clear that, despite their apparent friendship, Bruno actually looks down on—even despises—the musician around whom he has built his career. Cortázar gestures to this at the start of the story, when a detailed account of Johnny's idiosyncratic philosophy is contrasted with a disdainful commentary; Bruno even admits that "I never pay too much attention to the things Johnny says" (184). Such casual disregard is further colored by racism—he describes Johnny as an "uncivilized monkey" (233)—and a final confirmation that Bruno only cares about Johnny as an idea: in the face of the jazzman's failing health, he asks, rhetorically, "what does his life matter to me?" (237). This might suggest that, as a writer, his subject is more important to him as a concept than as a living being, but Bruno then admits that, even as an idea, Johnny stands in the way of the aesthetic concepts the writer wants to apply to his life: "he's waiting for me, maybe, to deny all the aesthetic bases on which I've built the ultimate structure of his music, the great theory of contemporary jazz which has resulted in such acclaim." This revelation reinforces Cortázar's dominant theme: that Bruno is ultimately interested in his subject as a concept around which he can hang his own "structures"—structures that, it is clear, have more to do with Bruno's own white, middle-class life than Johnny's marginal black life. Earlier in the text, Bruno realizes that, "if I go on like that, I'm going to end up writing more about myself than about Johnny" (223), unconsciously registering the extent to which the story he is building around Johnny is really a way of defining himself. This leaves the reader with one solution: to discard the analysis that Bruno provides and construct an alternative reading of the central character.

Indeed, Cortázar encourages the reader to draw her own conclusion about Johnny by exposing Bruno's motivations, and emphasizing the gap between Johnny's actions and statements on the one hand, and Bruno's commentary and analysis on the other. Lanin Gyurko has even argued that "The Pursuer" should be considered as "three texts—Bruno's first-person account, the text-within-a-text or the book about Johnny that the critic has written, and, finally, the text that the reader himself must write in order to explain the phenomenon that is Johnny."[38] Johnny himself generates some of this pressure on the reader through his critique of Bruno's book. Although he at first claims that "it's very good your book," Johnny then qualifies his verdict, explaining that reading it is like looking "in a mirror," when he had hoped that "to read something that'd been written about you would be more or less like looking at yourself and not into a mirror" (223). Puzzled by Johnny's observation, Bruno declares that "mirrors give faithful reflections"; however, Johnny maintains that "there's things missing, Bruno." It is this missing information—both in the fictional biography and the text of "The Pursuer" itself—that Cortázar tacitly directs the reader toward constructing. In doing so, he grants Johnny's philosophizing the status that a musical solo has in a typical jazz story: his views on time and space, interpreted by the reader, take on that "collaborative and communicative quality of improvisation" that Monson argues is characteristic of jazz.[39] In other words, the fragments of Johnny that Cortázar presents demand a communication between reader and subject that breaks through the isolation that Johnny is otherwise subjected to.

Rather than asking the reader to respond with her own solo, then, Cortázar instead calls for an act of interpretation. He engages with the question of loneliness less from the perspective of identity than from that of interaction and representation, by questioning how we deal with the individuality of others, and mapping out, through the gaps of Bruno's narrative, an alternative, subject-driven counternarrative. In doing so, Cortázar actively interrogates the tropes that cluster around jazz fiction, asking us to listen sensitively, rather than blindly (often callously) mythologizing others; Johnny's loneliness in the story comes from nothing intrinsic to his skills as a musician, Cortázar implies, but from the cultural capital attached to them. Yaffe has noted that "getting jazz wrong in literary writing has often been a case of underestimating the complexity of jazz musicians—even in intended admiration," and in this sense, "The Pursuer" presciently identifies a major problem in the literary mediation of jazz: by privileging the jazzman as a symbol, writers inevitably simplify, even dehumanize, their subject.[40] Christopher Harlos has demonstrated the extent to which musicians themselves have voiced such complaints, noting that "dissatisfaction with jazz writing is a theme that immediately surfaces in a number of autobiographical works."[41] And it was this process of commodification that bebop's technical virtuosity sought to circumvent; as Elworth argues, "bop also allowed black musicians to seize their discourse from the white-dominated culture industry and to create something less likely to be appropriated."[42] Through his reimagined Charlie Parker—preeminent bebopper that he was— Cortázar reinvests the musician with the authority to tell his own story, one that can bypass the easy structures that critics use to circumscribe the meaning of his life and music.

A LONELY GUY: *BUT BEAUTIFUL* AND THE SOLO IN CONVERSATION

In many ways, Cortázar's work marks the genre of the jazz story coming into maturity; his story at once follows the conventions of the genre and raises questions about the guiding tropes and structures that define the form. His critical—and unsympathetic—portrayal of Bruno points to a central problem with writing about jazz musicians: the tendency to obscure their individual character and identity by remolding their narratives to fit preexisting tropes and structures. Even in nuanced and sympathetic portraits like those by Hughes, Welty, and Baldwin, the hero-musicians are deliberately shaped to fit a part, where their unconventional life and social isolation are part of a necessary sacrifice for their art; while Hughes, for instance, might try to contrast the conventional Romantic expectations of Mrs. Ellsworth with Oceola's more socially integrated model of artisthood, the narrative arc of the story, moving from alienation to unity through a transcendent, even sublime, performance (evoking mountains and stars) ultimately reinforces the Romantic ideal of the artist. Indeed, it is the primitive, instinctive, and "natural" (both in the sense of relating to the natural world and of relating to one's intrinsic character) qualities of jazz that make it so attractive to short-story writers as a thematic structure for writing about loneliness; more widely, as Michael Titlestad notes, "the history of literary jazz is dominated by tropes embedded in Romantic nostalgia and atavism."[43] And in spite of the critical distance he tries to establish, it is hard not to see an analogy between Cortázar as writer and Bruno as writer. Both inevitably resort to the same idealizing approach, pursuing their subject in differing but complementary ways. Geoff Dyer's 1991 work *But Beautiful,* subtitled *A Book About Jazz,* at once probes the limits of the conventions of the jazz story and offers potential solutions to the problem of being bound in conventions when trying to write about individuality.

Dyer's text is constructed around a series of eight portraits of jazz musicians, threaded through with observations of Duke Ellington and Harry Carney as they drive across the (usually dark and uninhabited) landscape of the United States. In his brief preface and critical essay affixed to the end, Dyer emphasizes two qualities that, in his eyes, mark his own project out as peculiarly tied to its subject: like jazz, his book is both improvisational and personal. Although he admits the work began as "conventional criticism," what he eventually composed is recognizably fiction—a series of "scenes" that "were still intended as a commentary either on a piece of music or on the particular qualities of a musician."[44] Although, from my perspective, the text looks like a sequence of jazz stories, Dyer notes that, as he composed, he "was unsure of the form it should take," which "was a great advantage since it meant I had to improvise and so, from the start, the writing was animated by the defining characteristic of its subject" (vii). Immediately, then, Dyer signals an explicit connection between the form of jazz and the form of the story within his conceptualization of the work; he has taken an internal analogy, comparing the writer of the story to the musician within the story, and made it a conscious component of his construction of the text. He argues, moreover, that his blending of history, popular anecdotes, and fiction is the writerly equivalent of a musical solo, drawing on "a common repertory of anecdote and information—'standards,' in other words"—around which he improvises, "departing from them completely in some cases," so that, although "this may mean being less faithful to the truth," he nonetheless "keeps faith with the improvisational prerogatives of the form" (viii). "Jazz musicians," he argues, "frequently quote from each other in their solos . . . the same thing applies here" (viii).

The cover of my 2012 Canongate edition of Dyer's hybrid text is plugged with three words from jazz pianist Keith Jarrett: "a little gem." And as a text now into its twentieth year and umpteenth edition, the Somerset Maugham Prize–winning book is easy to categorize as a well-established literary treasure. Certainly the positive reviews that greeted the text (and grace its back cover) attest to the book's broad appeal; equally, they mask the intense criticism that the book has faced, and it is telling that there have been no sustained critical engagements with the work. The text's hybrid status, somewhere between fact and fiction, has certainly contributed to this critique; David Widgery, writing for *New Statesman,* argued that, although "*But Beautiful*'s promise, the application of a European literary sensibility to American genius, is exciting," the end result is "more modest."[45] A review in *Kirkus* took a stronger line, noting that, although "Dyer has a neat turn of phrase and can aptly sum up a musician's style in prose," because "the reader has no idea where fact ends and fiction begins, these essays are more frustrating than illuminating. And because much of the material Dyer draws on is easily available in the jazz literature, one would be better served by referring to the original material rather than relying on his high flights of fancy." Echoing Widgery's ambivalent judgment, the *Kirkus* reviewer concludes that the book strikes "a false note in the history of jazz criticism." Both reviews point to a central problem with the stories: by focusing on the musicians' characters, Dyer neglects the music—or, as Widgery argues, "the narrative form Dyer uses ducks difficult aesthetic judgments" by "deflect[ing] attention from what the musicians actually play" (44).

Indeed, these critiques draw attention to problems not simply with Dyer's text, but with the tropes of the jazz story more generally.

Widgery sums up the collection as providing "an oddly conventional storyline: sex and drugs and bebop all ending in incomprehending dialogue in psychiatrists' offices"; these charges could just as easily be leveled against any number of jazz stories, or jazz autobiographies like Mingus's *Beneath the Underdog,* and Widgery's critique seems to be aimed less at Dyer than at the prescriptive narrative structures that still seem to dictate writing about jazz musicians more than fifty years after Hughes's prototype. Richard Bernstein, in an otherwise glowing review for the *New York Times,* also pointed to the repeated structures and imagery that recur across each story: "Common to all of the dramatis personae is a struggle with the dark forces, with violence, despair, self-destruction, racial hatred, heroin addiction, alcohol and the unbearable pressure to keep the touch of genius in an art form whose very essence is spontaneity and improvisation. Mr. Dyer looks in on most of his musicians just at the moment when the touch is disappearing, or when they stare Early Death in its pallid face."[46]

In trying to account for this conventional structure, Bernstein turns to Dyer's own explanation, in his critical conclusion, that there is something dangerous about jazz. But Dyer's insistent application of such romantic tropes of the doomed jazz musician, Bernstein argues, actually suggests the opposite emphasis—that there is "something dangerous in the men who adopt jazz as their medium of expression." From this perspective, then, *But Beautiful* seems to play out the final stages of the jazz story, endlessly recycling the same archetypes, revealing a cultural failure to represent jazz outside the conventions of cathartic pain, and self-destructive, socially beneficial isolation. This kind of reading views Dyer as relatively uncritical, trapped in the commodification of jazz-as-destruction-and-redemption.

Dyer himself, however, acknowledges the conventional structures toward which his work is drawn. As Bernstein notes, in his final critical commentary Dyer does in fact argue that "a sense of danger—of risk—surrounds the history of jazz" (196), where the "collapse" of Chet Baker's "once handsome face" serves as a "convenient expression of the symbiotic relation of jazz and drug addiction" (197). There is an ironic bivalence to Dyer's use of "convenient" here, which we might easily read as "too convenient"—particularly in light of his opening notes, where he identifies the structures of his stories as guided by popular narratives around jazz musicians, which he describes as the literary equivalent of standards. Not only is Dyer aware of the conventions of the jazz story, then, but he is also aware that he cannot avoid them, just as even the most talented jazz musicians produced their most inspired work by quoting from the tunes of others, by responding to the existing musical discourse. Returning to his concept of creating the text through a process of improvisation, it seems that the characters also emerge in Dyer's text through improvisation *within a pre-existing structure*. Like Cortázar, Dyer recognizes that writing about jazz musicians is often tied to a process of idealization, but where Cortázar undermines the myths surrounding Johnny even as he himself inscribes them, Dyer makes a lateral equation between the very genres of the short story and the jazz improvisation, showing that, in both, individuality is always marked by deviations with a limited form. Titlestad suggests a similar relationship, arguing that "Dyer's evocative, if rather mythomanic, collection of fictional jazz portraits . . . immediately suggest possibilities in terms of the relation of desire and the symbolic to emergent identities."[47] Individuals need recourse to symbolic structures to define their individuality, Titlestad argues; by repeating the same conventional narratives, Dyer emphasizes that musical and personal identity emerge through the presence, not the removal, of conventional expectations.

Dyer's critical positioning of the work, moreover, encourages the reader to draw parallels between the musicians as composers, and Dyer himself as an equivalent musical improviser. This equivalency, established by his rhetoric of innovation, is reinforced by his claim that, in the book, his "purpose was to present the musicians not as they were but as they appear to me" (viii). In other words, his relationship to his subject is almost the inverse of that in "The Pursuer," where Cortázar urges the reader to look through or beyond the narrative mediation of Charlie Parker, as the fictionalized Johnny, in order to access the musician as he truly was. Dyer seems to suggest that the only way to legitimately engage with jazz is from a subjective position, adopting the conversational model that he ascribes to jazz production—particularly given that, as Dyer himself suggests, his book is less about the artists as individuals, and more as the creators of music. His very subject is the act of creation, where he sees himself as "not describing musicians at work so much as projecting back onto the moment of the music's inception the act of my hearing it thirty years later" (viii). In the "Note on Photographs" that follows the preface, Dyer emphasizes his interest in the idea of capturing a (subjectively experienced) moment of artistic creation by drawing a comparison between the aesthetics of the short story and those of the photograph. He pays particular attention to analyzing an image that is included as a frontispiece to most editions: a snapshot taken by Milt Hinton of Ben Webster, Red Allen, and Pee Wee Russell. Dyer emphasizes that, like a good short story, the photograph contains a small moment that suggests a much larger pattern: "although it depicts only a split second the *felt duration* of the picture extends several seconds either side of that frozen moment to include—or so it seems—what has just happened or is about to happen" (ix).

Each portrait can be read in these terms of immanence, then, both in Titlestad's sense of identity formation—the artist coming into being—and in Dyer's photographic sense, of capturing a moment before it unfolds. The brief narrative interludes that separate each of the individual portraits, following Duke Ellington and Harry Carney as they travel through an empty American landscape, amplify the formal limitation of each story, often providing literal blank space, as well as images of emptiness. But given the book's preoccupation with creation, it should not be surprising that these empty sites quickly become spaces for new production; the first page of the "fiction" begins with a "blackness ... so uniform that the driver found himself thinking that no road existed until the headlights scythed a path through the wheat writhing stiffly in the shock of light" (1), while later, Duke muses on how "virtually everything he encountered found its way into his music," which he imagines as a "personal geography of the earth" (60).

This might immediately suggest a particular parallel between Dyer as author and Duke as composer, with the musician an internal proxy for the writer, and Dyer underlines this relationship through the conceit of Duke imagining a new artistic project that sounds strikingly like the book the reader is holding. In Duke's words, it "was going to be something specifically about jazz. Not a chronicle and not even history really, something else," but instead "what he had in mind now was a series of portraits" (30). So within the text, Dyer argues that the only way to truly represent jazz as music and history was through portraiture and individual stories; moreover, through Duke, he seems to suggest that such a portrait of a musical form can only emerge through conversation between smaller individual parts. Even a more conventional composer like Ellington, Dyer argues, "worked from small pieces, things that came to him quickly. His big works were patchworks of smaller ones" (30). Not only does Dyer reinforce the idea that jazz is fundamentally a conversational form; he also justifies his use of small, repetitive stories rather than a larger, synthetic narrative: it is the closest literary equivalent to jazz composition and performance.

The collection's opening portrait is of Lester Young, the pork-pie-topped tenor saxophonist known as "Pres." As Dyer warns the reader, there is no moment of actual artistic creation within the story; even the brief descriptions of Young's playing are sparse and incidental. Instead, the narrative accesses jazz at an angle, through the musician himself. This does not mean that the story avoids the idea of creation; like the repeated choruses of Duke's trip, the story places great emphasis on immanence and coming into being. Indeed, the opening image foregrounds the importance of Young's self-creation, by describing him "touching [his] hazy reflection like it was a painting," and tracing "wet lines around his eyes, mouth, and head until he saw it turning into a drippy skull-shaped thing that he wiped clear with the heel of his hand" (5). Later in the story, when Young is brought before a military tribunal, he compares giving testimony to the self-definition of performing jazz: "taking the stand to give evidence—it was like taking the stand to play a solo. Call and response" (22). In both images, the artist asserts his authority in self-definition. But Young also recognizes the limitations of what he can improvise. He notes ruefully that, "just like a solo, you had to tell a story, sing them a song they wanted to hear" (23), and in doing so prefigures the critique leveled against the book: his self-representation, he seems to say, is constrained by the demands of his audience.

This sense of constraint is keenly developed as the story progresses—the affirmative act of creation juxtaposed against a diminishment and melting away. Young is described as feeling as though he is "shrinking, fading to nothing" (5), and as the story progresses, he continues "to thin himself down even more" (6), to the point where he is "fired from a gig in Harlem because he hadn't had the strength to stand." Dyer suggests something dehumanizing about this process of self-dissolution, characterizing Young as "swilled out and fading away" (7), and in doing so, emphasizes that this personal collapse is tied to his peculiar style of playing. When he is criticized for his "wispy skating-on-air tone," and is "bullied" to play more like Coleman Hawkins, Young resists: "he just tapped his head and said, — There's things going on up here, man" (6). On their own, these images of physical collapse also suggest emotional emptiness, but Dyer takes this equation a step further, by showing that Young suffers an intense loneliness specifically tied to his career as a jazz musician. He illustrates this most effectively through the platonic intimacy of Young and Billie Holiday, where in a striking moment of free-indirect discourse, the narrative takes on the collective voice of the pair, who meditate that "it wasn't that jazz musicians died young, they just got older quicker," so that Holiday could feel "she'd lived a thousand years in the songs she had sung, songs of bruised women and the men they loved" (19). Young's loneliness, however, originates not necessarily in the music he plays, so much as in the conflict between his belief in jazz as a music of individuality, and his painful awareness of the broader social expectations of conformity. He believes firmly that "jazz was about making your own sound, finding a way to be different from everybody else" (8), but also recognizes that society expects certain narratives (the stories he knows he needs to tell in his solos), exemplified by his treatment as a soldier, where he sees that "the army wanted everyone to be the same" (9).

It is not the social isolation that wears Young down in Dyer's portrait, then, but a more personal experience of loneliness, originating in his fractured connection with his own identity. The story's insistence on the schizophrenic dynamic of jazz builds as the story progresses, so that Pres is increasingly caught between others' expectations and the desire to make his own sound. The pressure progressively modifies his performance, so that his "sax tilted off to one side" as though "the horn was getting lighter and lighter" (7), reflecting his increasingly tenuous hold on his identity. After one particularly ethereal performance, another saxophonist harangues him, declaring "you're not you, I'm you"; this appropriation of his identity crystallizes into an awareness of an intense self-alienation: he realizes that he "was being thrown out of his own life for not sounding enough like himself" (7). Later, he reflects on a moment when the photographer "Herman Leonard had come to photograph him," and had "ended up leaving him out of the picture altogether, preferring a still life of the hat, his sax case, and cigarette smoke ascending to heaven"; he recognizes that "the photo was like a premonition" (10) of his own disappearance from his own narrative. It is here that the implications of Dyer's paralleled, almost stereotypical narrative arcs—so criticized by some of his initial readers—become clearer. His portraits dramatize the problems of having an individual identity within a discourse that carries as much cultural weight as jazz. Young loses his connection to himself precisely because his audiences have such a strong idea of who he ought to be. This is why he appears so insubstantial: in the face of his own reputation, "he was disappearing, fading into the tradition before he was even dead ... he limped along after himself" (7).

But Beautiful continues to rehearse the theme of improvisation as spontaneous creation in one of the most nuanced of Dyer's portraits, that of Thelonious Monk. Early on, the narrator asserts that "part of jazz is the illusion of spontaneity and Monk played the piano as though he'd never seen one before. Came at it from all angles" (39); later, the voice of Monk emerges, to reflect that such improvisation is the only way for many individuals to say something meaningful. He wonders whether in other art forms "they'd've had their idiosyncrasies ironed out," before noting that "spelling and straight-line stuff don't matter necessarily in jazz, so there's a whole bunch of guys whose stories and thoughts are not like anyone else's who wouldn't've had a chance to express all the ideas and shit they had inside them without jazz" (42). Monk himself exemplifies this trend, as Dyer shows him consistently falling between the gaps of social expectation, just as his music sits in between the notes an audience expected him to play. In conversation, he "swallowed as he spoke, forming words reluctantly as if language were a foreign language" (37), while when he composed, "a logic was operating, a logic unique to Monk: if you always played the least expected note a form would emerge, a negative imprint of what was initially anticipated" (40). Through this portrait of Monk, Dyer not only suggests that improvisation is a form of self-expression that bypasses conventional narratives, but also reminds the reader of the extent to which the musician's identity is bound to their style of performance. Observing that Monk "didn't play around the tune, he played around himself," the narrator implies that the off-kilter, angular playing that made Monk's music so idiosyncratic was directly tied to something peculiar in the musician himself—that "he was at the heart of it, he was in it" (38).

Repeating the narrative arc of Young's story, Monk's tale moves inexorably toward loneliness and isolation. Instead of an internal conflict, however, Monk is driven by the very introspection of his style that the narrator valorizes toward an increasingly destructive introversion. Initially, Monk's internal focus seems positive (if somewhat solipsistic); others observe that "even if he was composing it made no difference what kind of bedlam was going on around him" (34). The narrator, moreover, juxtaposes Monk's composure against the next subject in the sequence of solos, Bud Powell, by suggesting that, although "Monk was weird, coming and going out of himself like he did ... Bud was a wreck" (36). But this introspection develops into a complete dissociation from the world, as in those times "when he felt the world encroaching," and "he became very still, retreated right down into himself" (44). This act of self-protection—developed because "whatever it was inside him was very delicate, he had to keep it very still, slow himself right down so that nothing affected it" (45)—becomes more acute over time, so that eventually Monk retreats entirely into himself. Rather than being cut off from his own identity, as Young was, Monk protects his inner self at the expense of his connection to others; the narrator notes that "silence settled on him like dust. He went deep inside himself and never came out" (55). An unnamed interlocutor notes that, although "it wasn't despair," Monk's overwhelming emotion *was* one of loneliness, and that "there was a lot of sadness in him" (56). Dyer again reinforces the thematic connection between jazz and sadness, and as with Young, traces it to the disjunction between the individual and the narratives that others build around them.

In both portraits, loneliness comes from the musicians' difficulties connecting to others; these difficulties arise because of a clash between their individualistic form of expression—so intimately tied to self-definition—and the popularity of their music, which is increasingly co-opted and reimagined by critics, fans, and other musicians. Dyer takes the tendency that Cortázar identified in "The Pursuer" and repeats it across a series of reiterated performances. Like the series of solos that Dyer compares these portraits to, however, the individual causes and kinds of loneliness that each musician communicates are individual and idiosyncratic. Their peculiarity only emerges in relief to the other portraits, through repetition and variation, through the call-and-response that occurs across a coordinated whole.

The implications of Dyer's reiterative structure and patterns of loneliness are expanded at the end of this portrait. Taking on Monk's voice, the narrator extrapolates his peculiar existential isolation out to a larger pattern of loneliness, where all the city's longings acquire the clarity and certainty of sudden understanding. The day comes to an end, and people are unable to evade any longer the nagging sense of futility that has been growing stronger through the day, knowing that they will feel better when they wake up and it is daylight again but knowing also that each day leads to this sense of quiet isolation—and knowing also that these thoughts do not represent any kind of revelation because by now they have themselves become part of the same routine of bearable despair (57–58).

Although the lives of the book's readers may not be like those of Monk or Young, Mingus or Duke—they might not find themselves falling into the cracks and gaps of everyday life in the same way—this unifying image of separation reinforces the key theme of Dyer's portraits: we all lose something of ourselves in the patterns of life, and in doing so, lose our connection to others. Isolation is inevitable. Earlier writers suggested that the performance of jazz could overcome human isolation, transfiguring pain into something empowering and progressive. Perhaps one reason for the tendency to critique Dyer is that, although his characters are sacrificed, broken down, and hollowed out, this process lacks the emotional payoff that readers of jazz have come to expect. It is here that Dyer's title is so instructive. Readers might well wonder just what Dyer is qualifying as beautiful here, and if the title is read as a reference to the jazz ballad of the same name, then the answer would be love. But Dyer places the phrase in a character's mouth late in the book, when Art Pepper is trying to explain jazz. In keeping with the book's imagery, he decides that, although "the blues is a lot of things, a feeling," it really is "a guy alone." Having heard the pain of this lonely guy, Pepper's interlocutor begins to understand: "All that hurt and pain, she said at last. But . . . but . . . —But what? —But . . . beautiful?" (167). For Dyer, jazz is not a way to redeem loneliness, to make it universal. His patterned narrative is crafted to stress the opposite—that, even though we all suffer from it, everybody's loneliness is unique. But loneliness, his portraits of jazz show, is also beautiful.

LONELY WOMEN

Jazz, Gender, and Isolation

Despite her close attention to her subject's lavish style—her famous mink coat, alligator handbag, twinset, and pearls—beauty is not at the forefront of Zadie Smith's masterful story "Crazy They Call Me." Like Dyer's story-portraits, "Crazy" sees Smith reimagine Billie Holiday through a subjective and highly focalized narrative. But Smith's eye is less romantic than Dyer's; instead, she dramatizes the tension between Holiday's passion, fire—even anger—and her cool self-control. From the start, Smith reminds us that Holiday is carefully curating not just her appearance but her whole personality ("can't let anybody mistake you for that broken, misused little girl: Eleanora Fagan," she thinks in the story's second sentence), and by the end of the first paragraph, it is clear that the question of individuality is central to the story.

While Holiday herself likes to focus on her singularity—after all, for her, "there is no more Eleanora, there isn't any Billie, either. There is only Lady Day"—Smith plays a careful game setting the two sides of Holiday's individualism against one another. Certainly, Smith emphasizes the fierce pride that Holiday takes not only in her individuality, but in her solitude—perhaps best exemplified in her desire to turn to a reporter and say "*Motherfucker I AM* music" (emphasis in original). But Smith also addresses the intense loneliness and isolation that come with needing to maintain her role. In fact, her brilliant retort is undercut by her recognition that she cannot say what she really wants: "a lady does not speak like that," the story closes, "and so you did not." This reflects her general isolation from the people around her, whether the women she can't get on with or the audiences who "don't want to hear about dogs and babies and feeling your way into a phrase, or eating your heart out"—in other words, all the things she'd like to share. And as signaled by that phrase, "a lady does not," Smith directly takes on the gendered expectations that exacerbate Lady Day's loneliness.

Even those who miss the allusion in the title of Smith's story are sure to recognize Billie Holiday's name as one of the leading jazz vocalists of the twentieth century. Despite what critics might make of her limited register, Holiday's status as a great jazz singer is undisputed: the improvisational quality of her performances driven by her oft-reported ambition to make her voice sound like an instrument. Her collaboration with some of the leading soloists of the bebop era—particularly her close friendship with Lester Young—added to her stature in the musical world. But strangely, for a story so shadowed by music, Smith seems at first to distance her writing from the world of song. Structurally there is nothing experimental to the work—a conventional monologue, it has more internal consistency and narrative flow than many of, say, Dyer's stories. And in an interview for the *New Yorker* where she discussed writing the story, Smith admitted she "never listen[s] to any kind of music when writing," especially not here.[1] Instead, as those first physical details suggest, Smith developed the story through visual prompts. In fact, like Dyer's stories, "Crazy" was originally written in response to photographs— in this case, as a critico-fictional introduction to a new collection of shots of Holiday, *Jerry Dantzic: Billie Holiday at Sugar Hill*. Smith describes evocatively the way that "critical writing should meet its subject in sympathy. If you write about Borges, get a little Borgesian. If you write about Bergman, write Bergmanly," before explaining that "Billie's voice is so distinct I couldn't find a way to write about it from any distance at all. In the end I just looked at the pictures and felt my way in." Certainly, from the beginning of the story, Smith captures a double image of Lady Day—we seem to, at once, see through her eyes and stand outside her, seeing her as she thinks others do.

This play between interiority and exteriority reflects Smith's interest in a different kind of double-consciousness: she imagines Holiday's ability to balance loneliness and solitude as part of "that tension between delight and pain that she had." And while she may not have been listening to it as she wrote, Smith admits that as she crafted the story she "was certainly thinking of 'Crazy He Calls Me,'" which she describes as a "a beautiful, masochistic song" where you can "hear all the suffering laid out right next to the declaration of love." What interests me most is that the source of the pain and loneliness that Smith identifies in Holiday is not of the same order as in, say "Sonny's Blues" or "The Blues I'm Playing." There, the musicians struggle with an interpersonal loneliness—but for Holiday, at least as Smith imagines her, it is not a lack of specific connections that is painful. Indeed, her intense confidence seems to counteract any worry she might have about her social circle. Instead, what stands out for me is the underlying sense of injustice in "Crazy They Call Me." Smith insistently implies Holiday's persecution by society; she is cut off from support, marginalized and victimized. While Holiday might try and make this a strength—she takes pride in the way that she doesn't "ask anything at all from them ... that's your secret"—she is also aware that, if she lets her guard down, "everybody in the place would think they had permission to leap right down your throat and eat your heart out."[2] Clearly this is not the same kind of loneliness taken up by the stories in chapter 1; even Welty's "Powerhouse" only addressed obliquely the danger that the musician faced of being consumed by his or her audience.

Instead, Smith targets a broader affective dissonance here, suggesting that Holiday is missing a larger connection with society—that when she steps on stage "it's like there's nobody out there in the dark at all." This kind of loneliness is reminiscent of the existential isolation with which earlier writers like Moustakas were concerned—a pain that emerges from the inability of others to understand you. Smith even works in a quotation from one of Holiday's radio interviews, where she explains, "I only do it for people who might understand and appreciate it." The implication here—that these people are few and far between—is made explicit by Smith, who has Holiday follow up with the observation that "people are idiots." Given the ongoing sexism in the West, particularly within performance industries, it is probably not a shock that recent research has shown gender impacts on this broader kind of loneliness, specifically that "loneliness spreads more easily among women than among men."[3] With this in mind, one can see why so many narratives around female experiences of jazz turn to this existential loneliness: after all, as Smith's story implies, jazz might be a genre that can communicate "three hundred years of heartache," but its long history is still characterized by gendered restrictions and limitations.[4]

Indeed, as contemporary musicians are quick to affirm, these longstanding cultural narratives associated with jazz continue to have power over individuals and their sense of identity. In a 2016 interview for *Pitchfork*, for instance, the leading contemporary jazz bassist and vocalist Esperanza Spalding emphasized the extent to which these stories continue to have cultural currency, so that "to be called a jazz musician—it's a big responsibility."[5] Throughout this interview, Spalding draws attention to her own attempts to resist what she sees as the gendered limitations of these narratives. When the interviewer notes that "Jazz can feel generally very male . . . ," Spalding agrees; in another interview, she has suggested that "jazz is kind of like a boys' playground."[6] Yet she describes herself as "insubordinate by nature" and draws special attention to her attempts to create a new space for women in jazz.[7] She also points out that this underlying sexist bias is not limited to jazz. In the *Pitchfork* interview, she even expands the problem to a larger question of a male gaze, where, in art, "everything is male, man. Everything is male."

In order to explain the gendered constraints she experiences as a jazz musician, and articulate her own insubordination of this patriarchal framework, Spalding draws a comparison between herself and Joni Mitchell, explaining that "It's weird being a pretty woman doing something real now, but for her 50 years ago . . . I've seen videos of her performing where you can tell the guys are so uncomfortable. They can't even smile right because they don't know what to do because she's singing, writing, and producing them under the table. And it's not just about her voice. It's the whole thing."[8]

Here Spalding valorizes unashamed individual talent as a radical response to male expectations; elsewhere she has described herself as aspiring toward Mitchell's "individuality" and skill at "really exploring what she hears, not worrying about what category it falls into." It is precisely this conflict between individualism and social categorization, however, that has proven central to the history of jazz, animating artists in their attempts to "break ... out of the stereotyped place that American society had for black music."[9] In other words, jazz represents a paradox: a music that valorizes individualism, but where women are still forced into limited categories because of what trumpeter (and Quincy Jones Professor of African American Music) Ingrid Monson identifies as "the gendered assumptions in our society about what instruments are appropriate for women to play"—assumptions that further shape the roles they can occupy within a larger imaginative discourse.[10] Is it surprising, then, that for women like Spalding or Zadie Smith's interpretation of Billie Holiday the imaginative power and cultural discourse of jazz are a source of, as much as a solution to, loneliness?

While Smith's and Spalding's intercessions might seem a product of contemporary reexaminations of the way gender and social connectivity intersect, it is also true that women have been writing about jazz since at least the 1920s. Many, like Zora Neale Hurston, have done so without questioning the way the music enforces certain gender roles, instead valorizing jazz as an affirmation of a shared African American identity. Hurston, who researched and wrote widely on traditional African American music and spirituals alongside the blues and jazz, used jazz most evocatively in her 1928 essay "How It Feels to Be Colored Me," where she contrasts her own emotional involvement in the music with the disengaged intellectualism of a white male companion. Although she is often untroubled by her own racial identity, she notes that "when I sit in the drafty basement that is The New World Cabaret with a white person, my color comes."

She attributes this awareness to the affective power of the music, to which she cannot help but physically respond: "it constricts the thorax and splits the heart with its tempo and narcotic harmonies"; "I dance wildly inside myself; I yell within, I whoop; I shake my assegai above my head, I hurl it true to the mark yeeeeooww! I am in the jungle and living in the jungle way." By contrast, her white, male companion responds impassively, remarking "good music they have here," as he "drum[s] the table with his fingertips." Hurston differentiates these experiences not only through their qualities—"he has only heard what I felt"—but through what this contrast implies: explaining that "he is so pale with his whiteness then and I am so colored." Hurston emphasizes that their responses to the music are based on their (lack of) identification with larger cultural, and racial narratives associated with jazz. For her, the unifying, affirmative aspects of jazz, which align her with the (presumably male) musicians and *against* the white, male interlocutor, are more important than any disparity within the culture of jazz. The experience of jazz isolates the white man, but provides a space of unity and connection for her. But for several of Hurston's contemporaries it was less easy to write positively about a discourse from which they felt themselves to be excluded.

As Spalding and Monson make clear, moreover, this is not simply a historic problem; an aggressively masculine discourse continues to govern jazz, excluding women even as it promotes the music as a symbol for democracy. Indeed, scholar-saxophonist Tracy McMullen points to precisely this contradiction in her analysis of Wynton Marsalis's highly successful (and sometimes controversial) Jazz at Lincoln Center, where she emphasizes that, "somewhat in contradiction to the image of 'jazz as democracy,' Marsalis's face of jazz has coalesced around the visage of the sophisticated, upper-class black man."[11] On the one hand, this recurrent imagery can be attributed to Marsalis's traditionalist/revivalist attitude toward jazz, evoking the canonical performers whose music his program champions. But on the other, as McMullen points out, Marsalis is not merely tied to old ways of thinking about gender and jazz, but is actively exploiting them in order to meet "the needs of a white capitalist culture that understands the selling power of black male mystique." Indeed, by continuing to emphasize a "black masculine mystique associated with the classic era of jazz," Marsalis's program entrenches this inequality "through the use of the exemplary archetype that men play, write, and are the foundation of jazz."[12] By contrast, in taking up the challenge to write about jazz against the gendered grain in ways that trouble such archetypes, authors are able to expose this commercialized inequality, and in the process contest jazz as a larger cultural space.

Such critiques have often focused on one particularly intransigent narrative around the jazz musician: that of romantic hero, sacrificing himself to his art. This trope faced early challenges from writers like Hughes, but nonetheless continues to enjoy significant cultural capital, directing stories about jazz toward allegories of self-sacrifice and sublimation for the benefit of all. Nor are these tropes limited to fiction; if anything, they exercise more power in the world of cultural history, influencing the narratives of figures like "Bud Powell and Charlie Parker," whose lives are made to "epitomize the tragic and romantic mythologies" of self-sacrifice that fuel public fascination with jazz and its practitioners.[13] As Titlestad argues, the "life and early death" of an artist like John Coltrane "almost perfectly exemplify the Romantic and religious tropes that have characterized jazz discourse": "After purging himself of his drug and alcohol habits and undergoing a spiritual reawakening in 1957, Coltrane was able to combine the roles of dedicated artist, committed professional, humble religious devotee, and race hero. He was thus fully vested with both the musical authority and personal authenticity that jazz lovers have venerated."[14]

As much as it elevates the status of jazz musicians, however, such mythologizing also divests the artist of authority and individuality; he becomes a vessel for the spiritual awakening of his audience. In other words, these pervasive narratives "comprise discursive journeys into jazz which subjectify both its practitioners and audiences." Their ability to create connections with others—in a way that, as Hurston's essay affirms, had the power to overcome individual loneliness—necessarily came at the expense of their own well-being. This process, moreover, obviates specificity and authority: the musician no longer has control of his or her own narrative, to the extent that their individual character can be smoothed away. So by encouraging a sense of universality, these acts of romanticization disempower men and women—but, given their already marginal status within jazz discourse, these tend to have an exaggerated effect on female performers and audiences. As such, this process marks an important site for women to assert alternative narratives, grounded in individuality and ownership—the kind of narrative that Spalding advances for herself and her imagined precursors like Mitchell; the kind that Smith envisages in her treatment of Holiday.

But as Spalding's comments show, this kind of alternative narrative also relies on writers and musicians acknowledging that this universalizing tendency is part of a cycle of exploitation. Nick Stevenson notes that, although "jazz is understood as representing a shared global culture of freedom," what this "progressive view of jazz" neglects "is how it has been converted into a commodity by the culture industry."[15] Like Marsalis's program at Lincoln Center, globalizing, universalizing narratives ultimately encourage a commodified image of jazz, emptied out of its historical capacity for individualism and resistance.

Taking a longer historical view, it is clear that jazz only enjoys its special cultural status because of this revolutionary capacity. A form of expression born out of cultural marginalization, jazz originally offered African American musicians a way of reasserting control of their own narratives and expressing their individuality in a nuanced, personalized way; the development of individual solos, marking out distinct voices within a group dynamic, was the natural culmination of a profoundly idiosyncratic music. So the tendency to romanticize jazz musicians sits uncomfortably against the history of jazz, not least because it threatens to smooth over and obscure the revolutionary by repackaging the music's intrinsic individualism as a consumable ideal.

In questioning the gender politics of jazz, writers might be upsetting traditional expectations around the instruments women can play, or their authority within the music's larger discourse, but they are also reaffirming this original revolutionary aspect of jazz—resisting their own marginalization through virtuosic individual performances. By doing so, however, they also trouble larger narratives, whereby jazz is commodified into a ready solution for loneliness: listen to this heartfelt expression of pain, and feel catharsis. If jazz can be a symbol of individuality, then the loneliness that writers express needs to do more than provide a moment of relief for the audience: it needs to make them stop and recognize the performer as someone singular, accentuating, not alleviating, loneliness. On a broad level, writers have questioned the discourse around jazz—the way that it is represented, and the expectations that these rules lay out for performances of gender—showing the ways that the often affirmative evocations of jazz often work to isolate and alienate women. More specifically, writers have explored the conditions of being a female jazz artist, using historical and fictional musicians to show the challenges and isolation of their search for fulfilling self-expression—and opening up possible new spaces for empowered female expressions of individuality.

TONI MORRISON: JAZZ AND GENDERED OPPRESSION

In her 1992 novel *Jazz*, Toni Morrison treats what she terms "race music" as more than just a subject; she foregrounds jazz as a stylistic influence, a compositional strategy, a way of looking at the world, and ultimately as a model for historically located ways of being. Given this dazzling, dexterous handling, and Morrison's status as one of the foremost American novelists of the twentieth (and twenty-first) century, it should not be surprising that *Jazz* has been the subject of more jazz criticism than any literary text since Ellison's *Invisible Man*—and even then, looks to have outpaced its prototype. Although it is now more than twenty-five years old, and firmly located in a historical period that transitions from the 1870s to the 1920s, the model this novel develops for radical, black, urban identities is still striking and unique. In spite of critics' assiduous attention to the text's syncopated stylistics, however, few have acknowledged that (even with the novel's passion and urgency) Morrison also shows the limits of this jazz mode of being, in ways that draw attention to the twinned questions of gender and of loneliness. By focusing on what her characters have lost in their migration to the city—alongside their obvious gains—Morrison questions the consequences of adopting an identity that the novel associates with jazz, even as it valorizes such a way of being.

Perhaps because of the contradictions implicit in the "why," critics have overwhelmingly turned toward the "how" of *Jazz*, proposing varying, sometimes contradictory explanations of the ways that the novel is structured according to certain principles of jazz. Taking the broadest possible view, Rachel Blumenthal proposes that "*Theme, Bridge, Solos, Theme* is the form of most jazz music and the schema for Morrison's novel *Jazz*"; Chad Jewett has narrowed this structural argument to suggest "the compositional strategies and blues-based interpolations she attempts are far more akin to this narrative-resistant strain of free modal jazz than any other jazz genre, including the highly constructed bebop or the song-based music of the Roaring Twenties in which *Jazz* is set."[16] Both arguments offer a way of approaching the novel through the formal patterns of jazz, and in doing so, as Jurgen Grandt notes, make larger claims about the novel's status: "because the text's structure and style contain certain elements derived from jazz music—improvisation, the riff, call-and-response, et cetera—Morrison's novel thus becomes jazz literature."[17] But as Grandt also points out, the novel is perhaps more overtly influenced by jazz in its finer use of language and voice. Suggesting that "perhaps the most jazz-like aspect of the novel's technique of storytelling is its narrative voice," Grandt argues that the seemingly spontaneous, circular language that Morrison cultivates in the voice of the narrator—coupled with several obvious moments of self-correction—give the novel the impression of being composed almost at the moment of reading, to the extent that "the narrator's storytelling is truly improvisational."[18]

Whichever specific structure(s) of jazz that critics apply to the form of the novel, they almost always reach the same conclusion: Morrison's work not only experiments with ways of telling, but in turn forces the reader to adopt new ways of seeing and/or listening. If, as Robin Small-McCarthy argues, meaning in the novel "is not to be found in time-ordered or causal sequencing" because, like jazz, "the structure is episodic, with happenings woven together through the commonality of theme," then it makes sense to conclude that the reader is "asked to relinquish conventional thought patterns, to participate in the creation of the text by pulling together the seemingly disconnected or random threads of the story, and to go with the flow that may eventually lead to catharsis."[19] In other words, Morrison's use of a jazz-like structure is important in so far as it forces the reader to engage with the text in a participatory, perhaps even antiphonal way, much as I have argued the structure of the jazz story often solicits a direct response from the reader. As several critics have noted, however, the complexity of Morrison's novel lies (in part) in the way that this structure is both musical *and* historical, reflecting the peripatetic movement of rural black communities to the urban centers of the north—most obviously to Harlem. Grandt, for one, maintains that "the novel's aesthetic gesture connects with jazz history," while Andrew Scheiber even comes close to acknowledging the problems of this structure, when he notes that the novel's model of "journey and transformation—of the music as well as the people—is fraught with paradox," suggesting that, although "*Jazz* is a love letter to the City as a field of black possibility," it also "takes the measure of urban life's capacity to empty vernacular forms of their power to counter the confusions and seductions of modern life."[20] In engaging with the musicality of the text, these critics argue, we invariably engage with the larger questions of black history, for Morrison has intertwined the two.

In spite of Scheiber's reservation, critics have tended to read this transformative strategy, and Morrison's eliciting gestures, affirmatively. The call for response is also a call to action. As Caroline Rody stresses, the "suggestive ending" of the novel in particular invites the reader to respond to the text, where "the speaker addresses us as 'you' and alerts us to our role in this performance, urging us to do something."[21] This antiphonic address establishes a conversation between the narrator and the audience; in the terms of the jazz discourse, critics have variously figured Morrison's text as eliciting responsive solos from the reader or as staging a form of cutting contest, calling on the reader to trade licks with the text. From either perspective, the jazz aesthetics of the novel draw the reader into the textual performance, inviting a form of engagement that casts the act of reading not as passive, but as an active, ethical form of engagement. Small-McCarthy goes so far as to argue that this structure reinforces the novel's patterns of community, in that "Morrison's use of the jazz aesthetic requires her readers to be more than passive recipients of text, for jazz is a communal art form."[22] This is a particularly attractive reading, insofar as it treats musical aesthetics as empowering, and aligns the work with many of Morrison's other novels, where "the central character operates in relation to others so that the narrative gives rise to a spirit of community."[23] Such a reading is problematic, however, for precisely the same reason: by emphasizing community, it neglects the loneliness and isolation that is at the heart of *Jazz*.

It makes sense that critics have read the text so enthusiastically, given the passion that energizes both Morrison's prose and her reflections on it. In an interview for *Paris Review,* she admits that the "playful aspect of *Jazz* may well cause a great deal of dissatisfaction in readers who just want the melody"—which she defines as "what happened, who did it and why"—but advocates forcefully for her own approach, stressing that "the jazzlike structure wasn't a secondary thing for me—it was the raison d'être of the book."[24] For Morrison, moreover, jazz seems to have played a greater role in shaping the construction of the text—in terms of both its finished structure and its composition—than it did in determining the subject of the book. She contends that "the process of trial and error by which the narrator revealed the plot was as important and exciting to me as telling the story," and in the foreword to the novel, she further foregrounds this improvisational quality by describing the text as a "project."[25] In this sense, Morrison valorizes jazz not only as a cultural signifier in its own right, but as a model for a new way of composing texts. Adopting an improvisational approach, she implies, challenges the conventional relationship between reader and narrative, demanding a different form of engagement, predicated on contingency and response.

This kind of engaged readership necessitates a reinvestment in a historical moment; for Morrison, the aesthetics of jazz acted not simply as a compositional guideline, but an access point into the broader culture of black life in the 1920s. In approaching this period, Morrison notes that she required "a specific lens—one that would reflect the content and characteristics of its music (romance, freedom of choice, doom, seduction, anger) and the manner of its expression" (ix). Her narrator's improvisational voice, therefore, was crafted in such a way as to equate (perhaps even collapse) jazz with a competing range of impulses and emotions, suggesting that, in her eyes, music and history can be communicated through a singular, coherent style. This places enormous cultural weight on jazz, privileging it as a unique, historically specific sensibility that can nonetheless speak outside its own moment to affective states that transcend its contemporaneous conditions. Indeed, Morrison does, to some extent, romanticize jazz by figuring it as a source of (or even metonym for) freedom. Part of Morrison's expressed interest in writing about jazz-age Harlem was her desire to explore how "relationships were altered" by "a certain level of liberty," particularly in the wake of her focus on the trauma of slavery in *Beloved* and the way that *those* conditions had, themselves, altered relationships. Indeed, Morrison proposes that jazz acts as a kind of weathervane, making the connection between freedom and new forms of love "abundantly clear" (x). As a marker of broader African American culture and life, jazz created a "moment when an African American art form defined, influenced, reflected a nation's culture in so many ways: the bourgeoning of sexual license, a burst of political, economic, and artistic power" (xii)—in other words, jazz was responsible for a new cultural freedom and authority.

Perhaps the novel's most striking connection between jazz and freedom comes in the form of an early image, provided by the ambiguous narrator. The reader is presented with a disarming sight that, for the narrator, seems unremarkable: "a coloured man floats down out of the sky blowing a saxophone" (8). This image, showing an African American empowered and literally released from all bonds, hovering over the heads of everyone in the city, has sometimes been read as an allusion to the iconic saxophonist Charlie "Bird" Parker. Even without this (anachronistic) reading, however, the symbolism of flying (or in this case, floating) is clear, and resonates with another image of freedom that Morrison returns to repeatedly in the text: the protagonist, Violet, releasing her caged birds out into the street. This recurring motif establishes and cements the novel's insistent association between jazz and flight, providing the work with its dominant theme: jazz as liberation.

This is not simply a historical liberation—although, as Morrison herself stresses, it is tied fundamentally to a particular time and space—but a physical one, deeply associated with control of one's body. For Dorcas, mistress to Violet's husband, Joe, this music is particularly associated with a sexual freedom—the "life-below-the-sash" of jazz was "all the life there was"—that is also an affirmation of individual freedom; listening to jazz represents her "resisting her aunt's protection and restraining hands" (60). Such liberating individualism, from a different perspective, can look a lot like solipsism, and Dorcas's aunt criticizes jazz for precisely those reasons her niece embraces it. She thinks of jazz not as music but "a kind of careless hunger for a fight or a red ruby stickpin for a tie," an "appetite" or purely personal desire that "did not make her feel generous" (59). So even as Morrison celebrates jazz, she also draws attention to the way that such freedom breaks down traditional forms of community and togetherness. Scheiber suggests that she "is concerned with the way in which newness and freedom threaten to break the bonds of community—both across time, in terms of historical memory, and in the present moment, in terms of love" (482), and it is worth remembering the words that Violet loses when she releases her birds: the voice of her parrot calling "I love you." Freedom and individuality come at the expense of loneliness and loss.

 The difficulty for characters like Alice, Dorcas's aunt, is that the whole of the "City" (reverentially capitalized by the narrator) is imbued with jazz. This is not simply a rich symbolic association, but an aural one; the characters cannot help but hear the echoes of jazz in the noises of the cityscape whenever they interact with it. It is, for instance, "impossible to keep the Fifth Avenue drums separate from the belt-buckle tunes vibrating from pianos and spinning on every Victrola" (59), so that the very city itself seems to be performing jazz. Of course, the strength of this association lies in the reciprocity of the relationship: the sounds of jazz in turn evoke the noises of the city, so that one song's "greedy, reckless words" might sound "loose and infuriating," but the music nonetheless remains "hard to dismiss because underneath, holding up the looseness like a palm, are the drums that put Fifth Avenue into focus" (60). Through this antiphonal exchange between city and music, Morrison draws together the historical end of slavery and subsequent mass-migration of African Americans to the city—embodied in the characters of Joe and Violet—with the development of jazz into an urban, rather than rural, aesthetic. As she explained in her interview with *Paris Review,* although "when the ex-slaves were moving into the city" in the late nineteenth century, they were "in a very limiting environment"; if "you listen to their music—the beginnings of jazz" then you can hear them "talking about something else . . . the music reinforced the idea of love as a space where one could negotiate freedom." In this sense, music for Morrison is intrinsically spatial, mapping out an imaginary equivalent to the social freedom that the city represented for ex-slaves. So when the narrator describes it as "a City seeping music that begged and challenged each and every day. 'Come,' it said. 'Come and do wrong'" (67), she is simply reinforcing an intrinsic relationship between the conceptual freedom of jazz and the literal freedom of their new environment.

As a writer, however, Morrison consistently refuses to smooth over uncomfortable aspects of race and gender relations; for all of its positive energy within the novel, jazz is depicted as a problematic, politicized field. In one of the novel's first direct descriptions of the music or its practitioners—a telling aside about a fictional band— Morrison signals the gendered dimensions of jazz, in a way that at once celebrates and contests its sexual politics. As Violet tries to discover more about the life of her husband's teenage mistress, Dorcas (now deceased), she learns that the girl's "favourite band" was "Slim Bates' Ebony Keys" (5). Even if we put aside the novel's title and its insistent evocation of jazz aesthetics, given the setting in 1926 Harlem and the connotations tied to the band's name, it would still be safe to assume the Ebony Keys are a jazz group. But as elsewhere in the novel, even as Morrison foregrounds the musicians' race, she *refuses* to name the style of music they play; as many critics have noted, Morrison does not use the word "jazz" within the work, outside of the title. In an interview with Angels Carabi, she explained that, although the "etymology [of jazz] has been contested," she sided with "most people" who "agree that it is French 'jism,' meaning an ejaculation, semen"; from this perspective, "the word comes out of a vulgar, sexual term, which is why many black musicians abhor the word jazz."[26] By valorizing the music, without giving it its name, Morrison can evoke all of its "implications of sex, violence, and chaos," while pointing to the problems within a broader discourse. By juxtaposing the word's prominence in the title with its absence in the many descriptions and discussion of the music within the book, Morrison invites the reader to question not only what is in a name, but whether there is something exploitative or exoticizing in its usage.

For surely these sexual implications are not neutral. They implicate a profoundly masculine sense of sexual dominance and mastery, from which the female is excluded. Indeed, the discovery of Dorcas's penchant for the Ebony Keys does not pass without comment: instead, the text stresses that the band choice "is pretty good except for his vocalist who must be his woman since why else would he let her insult his band?" (5). Here, Morrison underscores the sexual imagery that surrounds jazz (the singer must be in a relationship with the bandleader), and the hypermasculine identity that it connotes—the singer is *his* woman (emphasizing ownership), not able to occupy a jazz identity in her own right. Nor, as this aside implies, are women competent enough to keep up with the men—and throughout the novel, Morrison reinforces this early observation with a recurrent absence. Women may listen to jazz, they may dance to jazz, but they do not play it; the performance of jazz is a male space, associated with male ownership and sexual aggression. Caroline Brown notes that, within Morrison's novel, jazz is both a "carefree indulgence of the now" and "a marginalized population's assertion of selfhood, of cultural vitality and artistic pride."[27] But, in the way that she draws attention to the gendered limitations around jazz, Morrison also suggests that in certain respects it confirms and enforces restrictive gender roles, marginalizing women as actors and crafters of their own identities.

On the one hand, this marginalization is a symptom of the radical, individualistic model of freedom that is associated with jazz and urban identities in the novel. Almost every character in the book expresses a sense of isolation and loneliness, from "Joe Trace, driven by loneliness from his wife's side" (12), to the narrator herself, who confesses she had "lived a long time, maybe too much, in my own mind. People saw I should come out more. Mix" (9). The novel encourages us to understand this loneliness as a product of the solipsistic lifestyle encourage by the City (and its sensual, aural counterpart, jazz), which, almost paradoxically, give "you a taste for a single room occupied by you alone as well as a craving to share it with someone you passed in the street" (118). Indeed, loneliness in Morrison's text is not just a sense of isolation from others, but a much deeper kind of self-alienation, or mode of double-consciousness. Richard Hardack has argued that jazz, for Morrison, "represents the reified and personified hunger of double-consciousness, of a self which can never be complete in itself"; this process is perhaps best exemplified by Violet, who experiences (as the novel progresses) a dramatic break in her internal coherence.[28] Finding herself "wondering who on earth that other Violet was that walked about the City in her skin, peeped out through her eyes and saw other things" (89), Violet begins to imagine herself as two distinct characters, one of whom she is completely cut off from. Of course, on one hand this break is caused by her husband's affair, and her own increased obsession with Dorcas. But it is also a product of the extreme internalization she experiences on moving to the City—a voicelessness exacerbated by the masculine tempo of this new life.

So on the other hand, the case of Violet implies that women are more affected by loneliness in the novel than men—and Morrison certainly emphasizes that they are excluded from the discourse and dynamics of the City (and by extension, of jazz). The atomization of urban life spells an end to the kinds of supportive communities that characterize the characters' memories of their own rural past, and the new opportunities open to women tend only to exacerbate their isolation. The novel places particular emphasis on the fragmentation of Violet's interactions with women in their own homes (where she finds work as an unlicensed beautician), suggesting that her new lifestyle has contributed to her internal schism. When Joe tries to voice his unhappiness with his wife, it is her inability to communicate on which he focuses: "the quiet. I can't take the quiet. She don't hardly talk anymore, and I ain't allowed near her" (49). Brown describes this as Violet's descent into an "aggressive and eccentric egoism," suggesting that she begins to take on the fragmented quality of jazz herself.[29] But from a different point of view, given her lack of a stable community, it makes sense that Violet loses the capacity to communicate— particularly when the City itself excludes her. Throughout the novel, she remains on the outside of the urban landscape, her interactions characterized by an invisibility that recalls Ellison's narrator: an absent presence, the traces of her are wiped out almost as soon as they are made, as when "the snow she ran through was so windswept she left no footprints in it" (4). This invisibility provides one of many links between Violet and the unnamed, unseen narrator, whose commentary on the action of the story only underlines her total absence from the text. If, as many critics have done, we read the narrator as a female voice, then she can be seen as the necessary consequence of the alienation felt by women like Violet: so completely withdrawn from a community that she literally disappears.

Just as, for Zadie Smith, the music of Billie Holiday holds pain and love in constant tense, for Morrison jazz is more than just a musical form: it is a way of being that brings together freedom, strength, and joy with loneliness and alienation. It is clear that jazz, as a lifestyle in tune with the city, provides the urban characters of Morrison's novel with a model of living that allows them to experience a new kind of freedom and individuality. But at the same time, it also encourages an isolating atomization—not only by breaking down communal ties, but by encouraging a discourse that alienates women and seems to entrench (if not exacerbate) their social marginalization.

Thus the narrator is at once attracted to jazz—to the point where, if we agree with certain critics, she embodies its aesthetics—but also distanced from it, even to the point where she can recognize her own alienation. She explains to the reader that "it was loving the City that distracted me and gave me ideas. Made me think I could speak its loud voice and make that sound sound human. I missed the people altogether" (220). Here, the narrator at once collapses any distinction between the city and jazz (the two become synonymous), and acknowledges that their combined spatial and sonic discourse tends to obscure the individual, rendering them invisible (much like the narrator herself). But while the narrator is unable to interact with the characters, she does directly address the reader, and as Rody notes, when "the speaker addresses us as 'you,'" she "alerts us to our role in this performance, urging us to do something with the hands we hold around her, as it were. We hold the book, so we can offer or withhold the response—that 'kick' of an answer—for which this speaker longs."[30]

Not only is the narrator conscious of her isolation, but she actively seeks to bridge it. She is attracted to jazz, moreover, because in spite of its alienating potential, it also offers a model for connection (through antiphonal response) and the affirmation that this recognition provides. Michael Nowlin argues that the "alien discourse" of jazz "continues to hold" power over the narrator, in spite of its tendency toward atomization, because "it seems to promise a language that might reconnect her to the community she has left behind, a language on the other side, so to speak, of the representational discourse of a white patriarchal order."[31] As a model for authentic expression and direct engagement, jazz has the potential to bypass gender divisions, rather than simply enforcing them. In this sense, the ready connection critics make between Morrison and Ellison is not without basis. Both novels close with a gesture of apostrophe, turning out toward the reader, searching for community. Both draw on jazz to do so; clearly, for Morrison, the music is so powerful because it is at once a cause of loneliness, and the source for a new, connected individualism.

GAYL JONES: BLUES AND JAZZ—ONE VOICE, MANY

One reason that Morrison is able to establish such broad, thematic connections between jazz, loneliness, and gender is that she never ties her novel's evocation of jazz to one specific style or musician. Her characters are not performers, or even fans of one particular artist—instead, they engage with jazz solely as an abstract, animating spirit or discourse. This can be seen as a strength of her work—in that she acknowledges at once the range of meanings jazz has had over time (this is why her anachronistic reference to Charlie Parker seems important to me) and critiques a discourse that creates power imbalances within the music and its culture. But it can also be seen as a weakness of the text in that, by the end of the novel, the concept of jazz seems so broad that it is hard to tell if it means anything at all.

Like Smith, then, many writers have chosen an alternative path, focusing on women who are musicians themselves. Not only does this give a specificity to the way such texts imagine jazz, it also changes the relationship between music, identity, and loneliness within these works. After all, what happens when women are not merely part of a diffuse jazz culture, but are practicing musicians themselves? Given the gendered restrictions of the jazz world, not to mention the sexualized connotations of *performing* jazz, it is hard to imagine that characters who identified as musicians would find their loneliness *lessened* by these isolating conditions.

Despite their closer attention to the specifics of different genres of jazz, however, writers who have focused on such characters tend not to limit the scope of their critique to just the kind of patriarchal discourse that Monson and Spalding describe within jazz communities. Instead, their explorations of the gendered constraints of jazz act as a kind of metonym for the pervasive isolation and loneliness that women (especially those of color) experience in the face of a profoundly sexist culture. Focusing on a vocalist and trumpeter (fictional and historical, respectively), Gayl Jones and Candace Allen have both crafted novels where their protagonists' experiences pursuing careers in jazz help explain a broader social and existential loneliness, intimately tied to gender and cultural standards of femininity.

Jones's 1975 novel *Corregidora* centers on Ursa Corregidora, a blues singer whose oppressive relationships are juxtaposed against a multigenerational family history of sexual violence at the hands of a Brazilian slave owner, Simon Corregidora. In a sometimes confronting display of narrative virtuosity, Ursa's crumbling relationship with her first husband, Mutt (who attempts to stop her from singing), and the barman Tadpole (in whose club she sings) are interwoven with dreamlike imagined discourses between Ursa and her female ancestors. This formal experimentation has led critics to discuss the novel largely in terms of blues traditions and aesthetics—most prominently Donia Allen, who argues that "Jones adapts formal devices, among them repetition, call and response and the blues break to reveal crucial aspects of her character's lives and struggles, as well as important themes."[32] On one level, this reading seems natural; Ursa describes the genre of her own singing several times as "the blues." But, when asked about the formal aesthetics of her writing, Jones herself associated her style with jazz, rather than the blues, suggesting that the "nonchronological, flexible, jazz-time" of her fiction is a product of her "interest ... in getting the greatest flexibility in the rendering of time/place/space in fiction"—a balance she compares to the "coherence and flexibility of jazz improvisation."[33] This discrepancy is not just a generic quibble—it is central to understanding the relationship between loneliness, performance, and history at the heart of *Corregidora*.

Although the exact criteria for and consequences of defining the difference between jazz and blues are contentious, there is at least one obvious difference on which most critics agree. While both forms share common historical roots, are both associated with improvisation and idiosyncratic expression—what A. Yemisi Jimoh calls "multiple, unique personal expressions—innovative personal style"—and both share musicological characteristics (a blues tonality), the two are differentiated by the number of voices. Blues focuses on a single voice; jazz is polyphonic. As Jimoh argues, "in contrast to Blues, Jazz moves away from singular expression firmly situated within and largely informed by group experiences" toward a democratic, multivocal expression, where "*many* singular voices are brought together to comment musically on a particular idea."[34] In "Sonny's Blues," Baldwin worked to synthesize these two distinct modes of expression, offering a way of mediating multiple cultural traditions into a single conversation.

But in *Corregidora*, the two forms are not reconciled. Instead, it is around this tension between singular and multiple voices that Jones structures the novel, where the prose alternates between a single voice, striving to distinguish itself in relation to the history of a family, and a polyphonic exchange, where the singular voice is reduced to one of many. So loneliness for Ursa occurs at multiple levels: in her personal life, where romantic relationships are quickly reduced to abusive, asymmetrical exchanges; in her musical life, where the subject of her music and her mode of delivery emphasize her isolation; and existentially, where she struggles with a sense of dissonance and disconnection with her foremothers, whose moments of jazz-like polyphony underline her otherwise isolated, singular voice. As Elizabeth Yukins appositely notes, "Ursa is both a part of and apart from the matrilineal history that drives her story, and it is this consciousness of proximity without legitimacy—her bastard consciousness—that shapes her testimonial narrative."[35] Jazz, then, offers Jones a framework for exploring an individual's dissonance with her own history, and a culture's larger disconnection from a traumatic past of gendered violence.

In fact, with its jarring, uncompromising images of violence and coercion, the novel opens in a way that forcefully draws together these elements of gender identity, loneliness, and competing jazz and blues modes of expression. Ursa's initial narration locates the reader in a fixed point in time—1947—and a particular set of circumstances: her husband foreclosing her career as a singer, cutting her off from others, and from possible new identities. Explaining that Mutt "didn't like for me to sing after we were married because he said that's why he married me so he could support me," Ursa draws the reader's attention to Mutt's rationale—financial support—and in the process encourages the reader to recognize that his personal and professional expectations of her are framed by the cultural conditions of gender. It is not appropriate for her to sing, because it would imply he is not an adequate husband, or that he is failing as a man.[36]

He sees the act of public performance, moreover, as one of sexual display, reliant upon the objectification of women. Explaining that "I don't like those mens messing with you" (although they don't physically molest her, he claims that they "mess with they eyes"), Mutt not only projects feelings of control and ownership over his wife, but also denies her subjecthood: her performance cannot be understand in *her* terms of agency, only from the perspective of the men for whom (Mutt imagines) she performs. More than any physical act of control over her, it is this failure to understand that most affects Ursa. Although she tries to explain to him that singing is central to her identity—"I said I didn't just sing to be supported. I said I sang because it was something I had to do"—he refuses to listen, with Jones emphasizing Ursa's incipient loneliness and isolation through her declarative epiphany: "he would never understand that." From its first exchange, then, *Corregidora* foregrounds the loss that women suffer within the gendered discourse of jazz-blues performance, implying that Ursa has lost something more than her connection with her husband: she has been denied her purpose for being, that "something" she had to do.

Throughout the novel, Jones plays out the consequences of scenarios when women are denied creative expression, where Ursa's loneliness is connected as much to an inability to express herself as it is to the inability of others to listen. This is reflected in physical terms through the loss of her womb—a climactic, visceral denial of reproductive creativity that Jones again foregrounds through dramatic staging. Ursa's loss is depicted at the very start of the book. Following their emotional break, Mutt pushes his wife down the stairs, and in the following operation, she undergoes a hysterectomy—tellingly, without her consent. Ursa is, herself, aware that this physical loss is linked to a larger loss of creative power, "feeling as if something more than the womb had been taken out" (6), and emphasizes her own lack of agency; here, women's creative power is controlled by men. Indeed, Ursa imagines inverting the situation in terms that reflect the novel's strong association of physical and imaginative potency, by asking "What if I'd thrown Mutt Thomas down those stairs instead, and done away with the source of his sex, or inspiration, or whatever the hell it is for a man, what would he feel now?" (40–41). What fuels this desire to see her former husband in the same situation as herself? It is, again, Ursa's frustration at the inability of others to understand her situation, their failure of empathetic connection. On one level, then, Jones presents jazz as a way for Ursa to express herself that others will understand—a creative solution to loneliness that takes on an added weight with the loss of her bodily source of creation.

Ursa is so acutely—even somatically—conscious of the misogyny that conditions her loneliness precisely because of her awareness of her family's history of rape and objectification by men. Indeed, she can only imagine her (great)grandfather in terms of commercialization and exploitation: to her, he was "old man Corregidora, the Portuguese slave breeder and whoremonger" who "fucked his own whores and fathered his own breed. They did the fucking and had to bring him the money they made" (8–9). Even the names of her foremothers bear traces of this objectification; her great-grandmother was called "Dorita. Little gold piece" (10). These women's act of creative resistance has been to have daughters to whom they can pass on their story, acting as future witnesses. From Ursa's removed perspective, this act of testifying is also a bulwark against loneliness—these daughters provide a bridge of understanding and continuity that contrasts with their abject status as objects. But it also places intense psychological pressure on Ursa, who cannot carry on the line, and is thus caught without anyone to share in this witnessing. The familial refrain, "Ursa, you got to make generations" (10), only emphasizes Ursa's isolation, cut off from her dead ancestors and cancelled descendants.

Given this internal fracture, it makes sense that singing the blues takes on greater importance to Ursa as the narrative progresses—especially given that her internal alienation from this matrilineal narrative is coupled with an increased emotional distance from those around her, especially her new lover, Tad. In conversation with others, Ursa makes it explicit that her need to sing is connected to this loneliness—"Are you lonely?" "Yes." "'Do you still fight the night?" "Yes." "Lonely blues" (97)—but crucially, it is in the wake of her hysterectomy and separation from Mutt that her expression takes on a different quality. One of her admirers notices that something has changed; although he admits, "if I hadn't heard you before, I wouldn't notice anything. I'd still be moved," he declares that "it sounds like you been through something" (44). This suggests a kind of bivalent relationship, where Ursa relies on the blues because of her need to connect to others, but finds the only way to connect is through increased pain and isolation. Although before this point her singing "was beautiful too," now her audience acknowledges that "you sound like you been through more" (44). The blues offer a way for Ursa to draw together her pain, isolation, and psychological burden into something she can express to the people outside of her—but also internally, to the dissonant voices of her mother and grandmother. Speaking inwards, she affirms the value of music to a ghostly presence she imagines as her mother: "*Yes, if you understood me, Mama, you'd see I was trying to explain it, in blues, without words, the explanation somewhere behind the words. To explain what will always be there. Soot crying out of my eyes*" (66, emphasis in original).

Yet even as she voices her pain, Ursa also acknowledges that it will not leave her, and in doing so, implies that the blues are not a permanent solution. They give her a way to put her experiences into words, but they do not relieve her. As she affirms elsewhere, however, it is precisely because of their temporality that the blues offer her a reprieve, locating her in the present through connection with others. She sings, at one stage, "*Trouble in mind, I'm blue, but I won't be won't be blue always*" (44, emphasis in original).

Nonetheless, in contrast with the apparent strength of her singing, as Yukins has convincingly argued, Ursa struggles with feelings of inauthenticity, repeatedly "expressing a consciousness of illegitimacy."[37] While Yukins connects this to a genealogical sense of (il)legitimacy, focusing on the family history of rape and incest, I would contend that it applies equally to Ursa's feelings toward her singing—particularly in her growing awareness of the need to express not only her own identity and story, but that of her family. Indeed, the burden of this inherited narrative obscures her own story, leaving her less room to articulate a sense of self. She even figures this in spatial terms, recognizing her mind is filled with *"their memories, but never my own. They slept in the bedroom and I slept on a trundle bed in the front room"* (100, emphasis in original). This self-alienation helps to explain why the blues are, on their own, not enough to overcome the loneliness that Ursa feels—as a solipsistic mode of expression, they do not allow her to reconcile her own story with the other voices that crowd hers out.

Despite the clamor of these other voices, however, Ursa's singing is ultimately affirmative, offering her a mode of expression that reconciles her communal dreams (which fracture both her consciousness and the stability of the text) with her independence and autonomy. When asked why she "go[es] making dreams," Ursa certainly emphasizes this ideal of independent agency, explaining that she will keep singing "till I feel satisfied that I could have loved, that I could have loved you, till I feel satisfied, alone" (103). She imagines a possibility where being solitary is empowering, at once contrasting being alone with the state of being lonely and also suggesting a sense of inner coherence and unity. Many critics, including Yukins and Stephanie Li, have argued that Ursa's success in reconciling her internal historical voices with her own comes through an act of public performance. Yukins posits that it is through "assertions, denials, queries, and refusals" that "Ursa's first-person, blueslike narrative moves into a public realm not pursued by her mother or grandmothers and articulates her demands for patrilineal accountability in a self-reflexive rather than a repetitive manner," attributing her success to her own self-conscious performance of self; Li places a similar emphasis on "performing the blues," which helps Ursa to "shift her narrative position from passive recipient to active storyteller."[38]

While the act of performance *is* significant in Ursa's internal reconciliation, however, these summaries ignore the changes in her performance over time. Both fail to explain why it is not until the end of the novel that she is able to achieve the autonomy she desires. This shift can only be explained if we see Ursa as moving from a blues mode of expression—solely individualistic—to a polyphonic jazz mode of expression and identity, where her own experiences can sit equally beside those of her mother, grandmother, and great-grandmother. Ursa tells the reader as much herself, explaining that she "wanted a song that would touch me, touch my life *and* theirs" (59). This bivalent mode of singing echoes the kind of expressive power that Zadie Smith suggests Lady Day possesses: a form of communication that goes beyond narrating a singular state, to hold loneliness and connection together.

AN EXPANSIVE LONELINESS: CANDACE ALLEN AND THE LIMITS OF JAZZ SOCIABILITY

Candace Allen's 2004 novel *Valaida* differs dramatically from both *Jazz* and *Corregidora*. Following the career of the trumpeter Valaida Snow from her childhood in southern poverty during the early 1900s to her death backstage from a brain hemorrhage in 1956, the long novel reimagines not only a historical figure, but an accomplished professional musician who rejects any expectations that she limit herself to the traditionally female roles of singer or dancer. This focus alone is unusual; as Gwen Ansell noted for *Jazz Times,* Allen "treats Snow first and foremost as a musician."[39] Even in a story like "Crazy They Call Me," writers tend to be more interested in the psychology of female musicians than in their practice. Snow's story is, moreover, intriguing in itself—in part because her career bridged the transition from swing to bebop, and the movement of jazz from a local, domestic form of music to an international one, but also in part because of her own independence from the trends around her. Not only did Snow maintain a successful (if ultimately flagging) career as a trumpeter, but she also remained aloof from the "girl bands" that formed during World War II—even as she acted as a model for their growth. Allen's is not the only fictional treatment of Snow. She makes a moving appearance in John Edgar Wideman's 1989 short-story collection *Fever,* and as recently as 2012, the French writer/artist team of Maël Rannou and Emmanuel Reuzé produced a short stand-alone comic about her life, accompanied by a two-CD collection of her music. But *Valaida* does stand out as a sustained, critical piece that interrogates the relationship between gender and loneliness through the framework of jazz with every bit as much coherence and complexity as Smith, Morrison, or Jones.

While it might share their ambiguous stance toward gender roles and jazz, Allen's novel also differs from its predecessors in a number of ways. Unlike the female protagonists of Morrison's and Jones's novels, Valaida is not presented by Allen as overtly marginalized for her gender. Despite the decline of interest in her music, moreover, she continues to attract admiration and support until her death. This means that, to an extent, the novel's critique of the gendered limitations of jazz is more muted than in the earlier works—and an inattentive reader might in fact overlook the intense loneliness that persists throughout *Valaida*'s narrative. The text is also less formally experimental than *Jazz* or *Corregidora,* so that, in conjunction with Allen's own relatively low profile as an author (*Valaida* remains her only novel), the work has so far received almost no critical treatment. It did garner broader attention from popular periodicals, but these responses were characterized by frequent comparisons between the author and the subject, often tinged with thinly veiled objectification. Writing for the *Telegraph,* for instance, Michael White explicitly equated Allen with her subject, arguing that, "although the semi-fictional Valaida and her author come from different social backgrounds—one a poor girl from the American South, the other raised among East Coast professional intelligentsia—they have much in common."[40] Sue Fox echoed this appraisal in the *Independent,* by beginning somewhat unnervingly with the observation that "there are some women who would look a million dollars dressed in a bin-liner. The writer Candace Allen, understated but head-turning, is one of them. Another is the subject of her first novel, *Valaida.*"[41] Despite its thoughtful treatment of a uniquely successful female musician, then, the novel has been denied the status of serious literary work—surely exacerbated by the lower status that the academy has traditionally accorded historical fiction.

All the same, there are several stylistic features that seem to align *Valaida* with other works of "jazz fiction," aside from its subject matter. The descriptive language is rich, emphasizes contrasts, and is often syntactically compressed, further highlighting the juxtapositions Allen has crafted. One of the first vivid images in the novel is of Valaida's "cotton sateen dress, its ivory lustre pleasing contrast to the yellow-brown of her leg, the figure of its print playing subtle background riff to the deep chestnut of her hair."[42] This syncopated imagery evokes the fragmented, visually stark aesthetics of jazz poetry, as do later descriptions which "riff" through repetition of phases: "Cool blue. Cooler styles, cooler thoughts, cooler notes, cooler times. Softer, mellower. Cool. But hot too, staccato heat. Focused, intense, like a blowtorch flame" (7). Although such formal disruptions do not disturb the otherwise realist narrative to the same extent as Jones's or Morrison's verbal flourishes, they *are* similarly reinforced by temporal dissonance, which is again used to create the effect of multiple voices and syncopation.

Richard Williams has noted that "the device of chronological interleaving makes demands on the reader, but the layers gradually build into a satisfying richness,"[43] while Anna Dvinge, in the only critical work on the novel to date, spends her article developing this observation, arguing that the use of time is part of the novel's stylistic use of jazz. In terms that echo Jones's account of *Corregidora,* she contends that "music has the power to transcend or change not only circumstances, but also space and time. Its very tangible qualities can be used as a ride or stepladder to another plane or space, with the physical place around it changing character as well."[44] Like Jones, Dvinge equates temporal jumps and transitions with the aesthetics of musical progression—and in this case, with the disjunctive time signatures of jazz. Although several critics have taken issue with the simplistic equation of literary structures with musical ones, it does not really matter whether this is, in itself, a valid equation—clearly, Allen is breaking from the conventions of realist prose in order to signify a jazz aesthetic to her readers.

These stylistic markers of jazz are frequently tied to Valaida's experiences of loneliness, often underscored by the inclusion of fragments of jazz lyrics. For instance, late in the novel when Valaida confronts her isolation directly—even embraces it—Allen deploys lyrics from J. C. Johnson's 1920 piece "Trav'lin' All Alone": "she was craving a bit of comfort. More than comfort, oblivion. What she wouldn't have given for a bit of sweet oblivion. *Trav'lin,' Trav'lin,' all alone . . .*" (469, emphasis in original). This might seem to be a relatively straightforward association. Allen, however, does not reduce Valaida's experience down to a simple conflation of jazz, gender, and marginalization. Instead, the novel develops a complex pattern of contrasts: between performance in open spaces, and containment at home, traveling, or backstage; between the externalizing acts of projection, sharing, and collaboration, and the introversion of privacy and solitude. Indeed, the two impulses often intersect, as when Valaida reflects on the physical containment inherent in performance. Although she "hates a girdle, instrument of the devil sent to reduce the most steadfast woman to a whimpering, low-count slave," she also recognizes the social pressure to embody this containment on stage, conceding that "you can't be playing without your underclothes" (3). Valaida's uncomfortable suspension between the two states is introduced and foregrounded through the novel's framing episode: Valaida's preparation backstage before her final performance in 1956, with which the book opens and closes. Catching the trumpeter in between privacy and performance, it holds her in a liminal state throughout the novel—one that is accentuated by the book's final image of her death. Allen described Valaida literally suspended in the air as she "blows her way towards the light," her spirit intertwined with the noise of her trumpet, hovering over the Palace Theatre.

Given that Allen dwells on Valaida's imprisonment in occupied Denmark between 1941 and 1942, it is perhaps surprising that the novel's focus on isolation and containment does not reach its climax within the walls of the Danish prison, but only after her release. Yet it is in the scenes of apparent freedom of ship-life (open skies, an open ocean, open movement) that Allen concentrates her attention to enclosure. Valaida is still haunted by both "the leaden oppression of her European winters and falls" (437) and "the frigid darkness of its winters and the reserve of its inhabitants" (438), where the very openness of the sea only reinforces her feeling of limitation. She feels that she is enduring "weeks of confinement," which she equates with the "many other months of diminutive enclosures, the clubs, her rooms, narrow stairways and winding side streets" (438); the expansiveness of freedom is as oppressive as enclosure to her. Again, Allen forcefully aligns this oppression with loneliness: on board the ship, she feels an intense isolation, both as "the only Negro," and as one of a handful of passengers onboard a ship built for "a couple of thousand," which seems "barren of white people" (438) as a consequence. But if Valaida's loneliness derives from an intersection of freedom and containment, then so do her feelings of happiness. Standing at the prow of the ship, Valaida discovers a freedom in an expanded isolation, with the narrator observing that "the sky goes on for ever, and Valaida finds beauty in this fact alone" (437). Around other people, where she inhabits the role of performer, Valaida feels oppressed, but on her own, she discovers an aesthetic of isolation that troubles her earlier experiences as an extroverted musician.

This shift—toward loneliness within, rather than outside of, music—is reinforced by the changes in musical culture and style that have occurred in the United States during her absence. Unlike Ursa, whose experiences of performing are curtailed by her gender, Valaida finds that there are more female musicians than ever when she returns; Allen seems determined to show that it is not Valaida's gender that leads to her marginalization, but the dissonance between her style of jazz and that which is current. In fact her playing style is shown to be old-fashioned and out of favor—Valaida herself is blown away by the pace and technical virtuosity of the early bebop that she encounters, which Allen describes in synesthetic imagery that suggests Valaida is blinded by this new style: "what she's hearing now is light, white-hot, like the sun full on you, right up there against your nose" (456). Unable to identify with this jarring aesthetic, Valaida begins to feel increasingly isolated from the music she performs, wondering where she "would . . . find herself in a music blazing this bright?" Intriguingly, the novel seems to argue that this alienation comes, in part, from changes in the tone of jazz. Where once it had been resilient, uplifting, now it was dominated by an uninflected sadness.

Listening to her contemporaries on her return, Valaida feels that they "seemed to be inviting you to step inside of her pain, like you had her bleeding heart in your hand. This had not been the way for Valaida and the folks she had come up with. They had gone out and entertained. Their business had been good times, even with the blues. Some blues were sad, but they were always strong. If your heart was quivering and bloody, that was nobody's concern but your own" (470). Again,

Allen juxtaposes privacy and performance. Valaida feels alienated from a style of jazz predicated on public expressions of loneliness, which she experiences as oppressive, given that, for her, solitude is to be experienced privately, where it can be expansive and empowering.

Whatever differences there might be between the settings, structures, and stylistics of *Valaida, Jazz,* and *Corregidora,* the three novels are unified in the way they expand jazz beyond a form of music. In each text, jazz is presented as more than music, more even than a mode of expression: it is a model for different ways of being. As a discourse associated with otherness and alterneity, it gives female characters across all three novels a way of imagining their own identities that valorizes their individuality. In this way, Smith's story, with its ardent declarations of singularity, embodies the positive potential for independence and integrity that jazz offers women in these narratives.

At the same time, all three novels present jazz as imposing constraints on women's identities—leading to the kind of alienation and self-denial that "Crazy" also depicts. Morrison, Jones, and Allan all signal that jazz is part of a discourse associated with male hegemony, masculine aesthetics, and limited roles for women. They are all aware that, as a form of social resistance predicated on race, it can at times limit the way its subjects imagine their identity by reducing it down to a narrow position of diametric otherness. In *Jazz* and *Corregidora* the most important aspect of jazz-as-identity-marker is its capacity for multiplicity. Both novels are structured around multiple voices and emphasize the polyphonic potential of jazz as a social narrative: it allows characters to express not only individuality, but dissonant individualisms within a group dynamic. The evocation of jazz structurally in both novels is therefore intrinsically tied to the idea of jazz as a model of communal idiosyncrasy. While *Valaida* does mirror the use of time in these novels, it also resists their polyphony: the only voice that Allen cultivates is that of her protagonist. Unlike the characters of Morrison or Jones, moreover, Allen's Valaida finds herself on the outside of jazz discourse, unable to achieve an antiphonal exchange or integrate her own individuality with others'. This is why she resists the public expressions of loneliness that characterize bebop (at least as it is constructed in the novel) and remains structurally suspended in a liminal position by the novel's framing chapters.

OUT THERE

Jazz and the Out-Narrative

Whether in literature or in real life, loneliness is essentially an intense experience of individuality. Given the negative connotations associated with lonely states, such experiences are sometimes narrowly defined as a kind of solipsism—as if they were the product of defective individuals unable to look beyond themselves. But as writers like Morrison and Jones show, loneliness can be reformulated in the positive as solitude—an affirmative, heightened sense of self. Outside of jazz fiction, there are many writers who have depicted it as an empowering form of individualism, and even when it is distressing, such writers often suggest that it can provide a strange comfort. In his 1976 novel *Coming Through Slaughter,* Michael Ondaatje imagines his subject and sometime narrator, the eccentric jazz innovator Buddy Bolden, as experiencing this latter kind of loneliness. Retreating to a cabin in the woods, Bolden admits that he "was annoyed till I admitted to myself I had been lonely and this comforted me."[1] Here Bolden does not simply accept his loneliness—he adopts an active process of appropriation, turning a negative label into an affirming, comforting experience. And jazz fiction, more than any other form, is particularly well placed to model this kind of reclamation.

Unsurprisingly, much of the recent psychological research into broader, national patterns of loneliness strongly indicate that experiences of isolation are more common in cultures that value individualism. Ami Rokach and Felix Neto, for instance, argue that "North American culture emphasizes individual achievement, competitiveness, and impersonal social relations," to the extent that loneliness is "quite pronounced in the face of such socially alienating values."[2] What interests me is how Rokach and Neto invert the kind of relationship we might expect. Although from one perspective loneliness is individualistic, from the standpoint of Rokach and Neto it can also be seen a reaction *against* individualism—emerging from individuals' inability to align with social narratives that privilege the values of collective isolation. In other words, loneliness is not a mainstream attribute (the result of conforming to individualistic expectations), but a marginal one, associated with those on the periphery of society who cannot identify with the values of late-stage capitalism.

Even as it increases one's sense of singleness, therefore, loneliness remains intrinsically tied to the social, and our relationship to larger group identities or narratives; fundamentally, "loneliness is expressive of the individual's relationship to the community."[3] But what happens if you are part of a subcommunity—a group marginalized by a dominant culture? Contrasting the experiences of loneliness in Portuguese and North American adolescents, Rokach and Neto note that "the difference amongst cultures and the ways in which people's social relations are organized within them will result in cross-cultural variations in the way people perceive, experience and cope with loneliness." But to this date, little psychological research has been conducted into the cross-cultural variation between groups *within* the same society. Surely, if individuals feel a heightened sense of isolation in the face of "alienating values," smaller, marginalized groups might *collectively* experience this kind of cultural loneliness, experiencing a different kind of isolation from the dominant groups of that society?

Cacioppo and his colleagues, however, have drawn some broader conclusions about the way that loneliness clusters (and even spreads) around the peripheries in Western cultures. Those who are marginalized, they argue, tend to "have fewer friends," and so are already vulnerable to feeling isolated.[4] Cacioppo even argues that, while feelings of loneliness can drive lonely people on the periphery "to cut the few ties that they have left," they "tend to transmit the same feeling of loneliness to their remaining friends" before cutting these ties. Such a model of loneliness suggests that, because of the "reinforcing effects" of loneliness, "our social fabric can fray at the edges."[5] In contrast to this model of increased atomization, however, narratives of jazz—whether in popular discourse, musicology, or fiction—regularly call upon the image of those on the edges being drawn back together. So surely there must be more than one way we can understand the relationship between loneliness and marginalized groups.

One alternative way of imagining such alienated communities comes from scholars of critical race theory, who term them "outgroups." This concept suggests both their marginalization by the dominant culture, and their role in imaginatively defining mainstream values— they are the "other" against whom normativity is measured. Indeed, Richard Delgado describes outgroups in terms that intertwine their marginalization with their cultural significance: they are "groups whose marginality defines the boundaries of the mainstream, whose voice and perspective—whose consciousness—has been suppressed, devalued, and abnormalized."[6] Equally, however, the idea of outgroups can be used positively—just as such groups, themselves, often develop a politics of affirmative difference. Their opposition to mainstream narratives and structures can lead to innovative aesthetics and alternative perspectives that at once critique the status quo and assert the validity of other voices and consciousnesses. Identifying as an outgroup is both a challenge to conventional values and a defense against isolation.

As a form of expression that developed out of precisely such politics of affirmative difference, jazz provides a striking example of these *out* qualities. The comparison is particularly obvious from the 1940s onwards when, as Burton Peretti notes, "young jazz musicians in big cities imitated the bebop rebels and created a *subculture* of learned behaviours and beliefs."[7] This subculture defined itself, moreover, directly against the values of ingroups; as Elworth explains, bebop "allowed black musicians to seize their discourse from the white-dominated culture industry and to create something less likely to be appropriated. The various social codes stressed by bop are a part of this creation of a counterdiscourse."[8] In a telling turn of phrase, musicologist David Such has even argued that the terms "avant-garde jazz" and "free jazz" should be replaced with the term *"out jazz"*—derived, he suggests, "from metaphors like 'out of this world' and 'far out,'"—in order to emphasize its status as an oppositional discourse to Western musicology, and reflecting the way that, "for musicians, the term *out* often describes startling moments when the musicians strive to extend the normal boundaries that characterize most forms of Western music."[9]

From both a cultural and a musicological perspective, jazz has defined itself through its alterneity, at least since the advent of bebop. Through musicians like John Coltrane, Charles Mingus, and Ornette Coleman it continued to emphasize its own *out* status. But the eminent jazz scholar Ted Gioia has gone even further, to argue that, from its inception, jazz has acted as a counter-discourse because of its emphasis on *process* over *product*. In direct contrast to the dominant Western aesthetic impulse—toward the ideal of perfection and completion, codified in terms like artistic integrity—Gioia argues that jazz aspires toward an "aesthetics of imperfection," challenging the very value system against which art is judged. By its very improvisational nature, such theorists argue, jazz is intrinsically *out*.[10]

This oppositional energy—challenging both the aesthetics and the larger cultural structures of dominant social groups—helps account for the popularity of jazz within marginalized communities both domestically and internationally. As a musical mode, and as a cultural sign, jazz offers a way of positively articulating difference. One fascinating, in-depth study of this cultural value was conducted by Steven Feld, whose 2012 book *Jazz Cosmopolitanism in Accra* explores the significance and adaptation of jazz in Ghana through interviews, performances, and historical research.

Through the case study of Ghana, Feld moves toward a broader explanation of the appeal of jazz, suggesting that we imagine "jazz cosmopolitanism as the agency of desire for enlarged spatial participation"—an agency "that plays out in performances and imaginaries of connectedness."[11] In Feld's view, jazz is attractive outside of the United States because of its ability to create social bonds and allow both fans and performers to expand their network and cultural identity beyond their own limited context. This suggests one of the paradoxes of considering jazz as a countercultural form: while within the United States it was seen as opposing the dominant cultural values (white, middle class, heteronormative), outside of America it was elided with American national values. From this point of view, it is clear that critics need to be aware of the contradictions in many literary evocations of jazz: even as it is used to signal marginality and resistance to power, it can also be appropriated by dominant groups to advance their own agendas. As Feld pithily puts it, particularly during the Cold War, "jazz was America and America was jazz."[12]

This elision goes back to the earliest expatriate performances of jazz, particularly in continental Europe following World War I; the process culminated in the 1950s, when "American policymakers" felt "for the first time in history that the country should be represented by jazz."[13] Indeed, Penny von Eschen has explored in great detail how jazz musicians were co-opted into America's narratives of self-representation during the Cold War because of the music's association with outgroups, pointing out that "the prominence of African American jazz artists was critical to the music's potential as a Cold War weapon." Jazz could be used to signal an American openness to other cultures, helping assuage concerns in Asia and Africa regarding the intransigent racism in United States society. This exploitation neatly underlines the extent to which jazz enjoyed a different cultural status inside the United States and in the wider world; members of the State Department would, quite consciously, "insist on the universal, race-transcending quality of jazz while depending on the blackness of musicians to legitimize America's global agendas."[14] Jazz has continued to be defined as a form of cultural capital based on this hypocrisy: an officially sanctioned marker of outsiderness—particularly important when American culture is invoked by countercultural groups in an act of protest against their own society. But this paradox does not detract from its force as an aesthetic influence toward inversion and counter-narrative.

Jazz provides a unique kind of cultural capital to writers wanting to express their isolation as part of an outgroup. A form that, historically, developed among communities themselves marginalized from mainstream America, jazz is characterized at once by countercultural aesthetics within its music and a broader community that has traditionally identified as outsiders and rebels. In musicology and cultural criticism alike, jazz is routinely imagined as a counter-discourse. It therefore offers individuals a model of constructing an alternative identity, but also (on a more abstract level) a set of symbols that signify opposition.

I want to suggest the term "out-narratives" to describe these jazz-inflected counter-narratives, in order to capture this second-order cultural association—where characters adopt not just jazz structures but a self-conscious cultural signification. I also want to capture the mixture of independence—even isolation—and collectivity that these narratives evoke, particularly given their tendency to focus on experiences of loneliness, the moment of the jazz solo, and on the single artist, while nonetheless moving toward a larger group identity. When advocating for a narrative approach to the issue of race in the law, Delgado noted that "stories create their own bonds, represent cohesion, shared understandings, and meanings. The cohesiveness that stories bring is part of the strength of the outgroup. An outgroup creates its own stories, which circulate within the group as a kind of counter-reality."[15] Within a literary context, the use of jazz by writers from outgroups can likewise be both unifying and destabilizing; where the "narratives told by the ingroup remind it of its identity in relation to outgroups, and provide it with a form of shared reality in which its own superior position is seen as natural," the narratives of outgroups "aim to subvert that reality."[16] Reading the way marginalized authors use jazz through the framework of out-narratives, then, not only clarifies the kind of isolation to which they are responding, but focuses critical attention toward the kind of alternative—counter-reality—that their use of jazz suggests.

MORE THAN A SINGLE STORY: BUDDY BOLDEN AND AESTHETIC MULTIPLICITY

Today, *Coming Through Slaughter*—Ondaatje's fractured, poetic meditation on pioneering jazz trumpeter Buddy Bolden—is regarded as a central pillar in the (sometimes awkwardly defined) canon of jazz fiction. If we are to believe the blurb proudly displayed on the back of my 2004 Bloomsbury edition (taken from a review in the now defunct magazine *The Musician*), it is, in fact, "the best jazz novel ever written." Broken into scattered reflections, fragments of conversations, and unfinished images, the novel shifts fluidly through the accumulated layers of New Orleans, from the contemporary moment back to the late-nineteenth, then early twentieth century. Its sometimes narrator, an investigator named Webb, feels a painful urgency to understand Bolden's story, yet the book itself constantly resists narrative closure, or even coherence. It is hardly surprising that, on publication, the novel was met with a certain critical resistance—a *New York Times* reviewer condemned it as "self-conscious and arty," clearly frustrated that, despite offering "shards of various techniques," the author "leaves it to us to infer the final form"—but this discomfort quickly faded, so that *Coming Through Slaughter* rapidly came to be seen as the stylistic successor to *Invisible Man*.[17]

This shift in status was neatly illustrated in a short 2012 piece for the *Guardian* by Nigerian American author, photographer, and critic Teju Cole, in which he described Ondaatje as his "hero." Having earlier included *Invisible Man* amongst his "Top 10 Novels of Solitude" in an article for the same newspaper, Cole went on to praise Ondaatje for a similar attention to isolation: his novels "taught me how to be at home in fragments, and how to think about a big story in carefully curated vignettes. All his books were odd, all of them 'unfinished.'"[18] Cole's sympathy toward these two writers' works is telling: like *Invisible Man*, *Coming Through Slaughter* draws on jazz as both a unifying image—helping to explain the protagonist's profound solitude—and as a counter-narrative structure that helps circumvent the expectations of conventional, linear narrative fiction.

Indeed, critics have already listened closely to the music of the novel—by which I mean, they have sounded out parallels between Ondaatje's shifting narrative structure and the musical modalities of jazz. Natalie Diebschlag has paid particular to the "the self-reflexive visceral experimentalism in Ondaatje's work," which, she argues forcefully, should be read not within a literary framework, but rather a musical one, unpacking the text as a specifically *"non-verbal* articulation of the historical conditions in turn-of-the-century New Orleans."[19] She is interested equally in "the depiction of jazz and its emulation on the textual level," to the extent that, without intending to, she comes close to thinking about the text as an out-narrative. By suggesting that readers should approach "Ondaatje's text in terms of Derrida's understanding of literature as a perpetual tension between generality and singularity," Diebschlag implies that the text's individualism resists the generalizing tendencies of the literary mainstream.[20]

Brent Edwards makes a similar observation, noting that "*Coming Through Slaughter's* own form is elliptical, piecemeal, an awkward mélange of different sorts of texts (not only fictional narrative but also something more like historical writing, as well as set lists, song lyrics, names of band members, and passages from interviews, oral histories, and institutional records)."[21] For Edwards, this is an attempt by an author to replicate in literary terms the kind of structures the author finds in the jazz subject; as he maintains, Ondaatje's novel "mirrors or parallels the approach to aesthetic form it 'hears' in Bolden, or in the received figure of Bolden." Diebschlag goes further, however, to set the novel in terms of convention and exception. She argues, convincingly, that the *individualizing* tendencies of jazz are called upon in direct opposition to conventional Western musical aesthetics, in a form of "antagonistic co-habitation" that is "expressed through two musical models": the dominant "complexity of European classical music" as marked "by the establishment of modern notation," and "the music of the West African diaspora, similar to oral storytelling," which Diebschlag argues "cannot be dissociated from the social fabric in which it takes place."[22] On the conceptual level, then, critics have already begun to understand Ondaatje's text as a kind of counter-narrative, structurally opposed to the expectations of genre and form through the appropriation of jazz-like individuality.

In spite of this willingness to consider Ondaatje's text as a form of social critique, critics have shied away from the larger countercultural implications of Bolden's destabilizing jazz in its own right. Instead, critics like Titlestad have tended to focus on the way Ondaatje uses the counter-narrative structures of jazz to critique the specific treatment of jazz musicians. Certainly, Titlestad convincingly argues that "certain literary texts," particularly *Coming Through Slaughter*, "can be read as representing alternative forms of embodied-subject formation (in the course of jazz performance) which challenge hegemonic, and significantly detrimental, myths about the music and its practitioners."[23] Edwards places the novel within a similar framework, which he terms "transmedial consonance."[24] Rather than thinking solely about the novel as a challenge to narrative myth, Edwards's model instead follows the "proposition that the resonance of the Bolden legend—its traveling power, one might say, as an origin story, even if the claim of locating origin is always ultimately a ruse— has everything to do with the multiple media it puts into concert." For Edwards, then, it is Ondaatje's use of the conjunction of "sound and print" that short-circuits these hegemonic narratives about jazz musicians.

But while Ondaatje's deployment of jazz as a "code-breaking performance" does certainly help to undermine the value system of European music—and its attendant artistic culture—I think this reading too narrowly construes the impact of such structural opposition.[25] From the very start of the novel, the marginalization of Bolden, his circle of collaborators, and jazz musicians more generally is aligned directly with the response to the wider black community of Storyville, New Orleans; the narrator parallels "the black whores and musicians shipped in from the suburbs," before asserting that "by the end of the Nineteenth Century, 200 prostitutes were working regularly. There were at least 70 professional gamblers. 30 piano players took in several thousands each week" (3). In spite of their financial success (the narrator seems to relish the fact that "prostitution and its offshoots received a quarter of a million dollars of the public's money a week"), the musicians and prostitutes alike are still marked as outgroups by profession, race, and geography. Even Bolden is aware of this social isolation, imagining the denizens of Storyville as a "dead crowd around him" (35)—yet, because of their shared status as social outliers, he is also able to enjoy an unspoken affinity with them: when "listening to others' problems," he finds his "mind became the street" (37). As Ondaatje conceives of it, jazz is intrinsically opposed to Western musical structures, and so offers a framework for the wider marginalized culture of New Orleans to reimagine their identity in positive, oppositional terms—reframing social isolation as positive difference.

It is worth moving beyond the abstract, however, and considering how Ondaatje represents jazz itself within the novel. While it may provide conceptual architecture for the depiction of black lives in New Orleans, signifying opposition to dominant aesthetic and cultural values, jazz is also a vivid, richly imagined subject of the book, with its own contradictions and idiosyncrasies. In fact, rather than either elevating it to high art or valorizing it as purely demotic, Ondaatje treats jazz as a cultural hybrid, so that Bolden can play "the blues and the hymns sadder than the blues and then the blues sadder than the hymns"; one fellow musician, Dude Botley, even describes it as "the first time I ever heard hymns and blues cooked up together" (78). Jazz thus collapses the distinction between body and spirit, in the process confusing the boundary between music and noise, becoming a "muted howl" (30). Such a fluid soundscape naturally evokes shifting images for its audience—Botley is mesmerized as "the picture kept changing with the music" (78)—which, Maria Marinkova argues, is reflected even in the shifting visual appearance of the text, "destabiliz[ing] the initial drive for optical uniformity."[26]

It would be easy to view this as Ondaatje simply marking jazz as polyphonic—an individualistic mode of expression that breaks traditional generic boundaries through its multiple voices. But these contradictory descriptions are loaded with particularly affective language; the sadness Botley feels indicates Bolden's own emotions when performing. The narrator imagines Bolden aiming "for the gentlest music he knew" by using "every sweet stylized gesture that he knew no one could see"; his haunting evocation of Bolden playing "till his body was frozen and all that was alive and warm were the few inches from where his stomach forced the air up through his chest and head into the instrument" (28) emphasizes that there is something intrinsically isolating about this music: it is tied to a personal vision that the musician is unable to communicate entirely to his audience. Throughout the novel, jazz is repeatedly associated with a failure of recognition. At the climactic moment of performance, when Buddy walked "jauntily out of the crowd into the path of a parade," playing "so hard and so beautifully" (10), both Webb and the narrator understand that Bolden's brilliance is lost on his audience. Webb doe not even "wait for the reactions of the people" before leaving—keenly aware of the audience's inability to understand the profundity of the performance, he instead imagines a "roar ... crowding round to suck that joy. Its power" (31). So as much as jazz links the community of *Coming Through Slaughter,* it also marks internal divisions, demarcating the loneliness that inhibits total recognition. From this perspective, is it any wonder that Webb fails to solve the "mystery" of Bolden?

This is not to disparage Webb as an investigator; Bolden is uniquely difficult to understand because he himself looks at world from an alternative perspective, upsetting the balance and rules of society in direct parallel with his musical expression. Early on, the narrator acknowledges the conventional narrative around Bolden—explaining that "many interpreted his later crack-up as a morality tale of a talent that debauched itself"—before quickly overturning any such assumptions, instead proposing an alternative way of seeing him: "his life ... had a fine and precise balance to it, with a careful allotment of hours" (7). Validating Bolden's alternative viewpoint, the narrator at once emphasizes its fundamental incompatibility with the world around him—"his own mind was helpless against every moment's headline" (9)—and affirms this dissident perspective as the source of Bolden's talent. The novel enshrines him as "the best and loudest and most loved jazzman of his time," while nonetheless confirming him to be "never professional in the brain" (8)—and this unorthodox brilliance, based on an *unprofessional* way of seeing the world, is reflected in Bolden's interest in storytelling and journalism. Publishing a bizarre local newspaper, *The Cricket,* Bolden not only sees the world through an out perspective, but gathers, cultivates, and curates other out-narratives: *The Cricket* "respected stray facts, manic theories, and well-told lies," drawing stories from "customers in the chair and from spiders among the whores and police that Bolden and his friends knew" (18). Bolden conceptualizes these stories as a "sub-history," running beneath and counter to the dominant historical narrative, and in the same way, his musical expression has an insurgent quality, undercutting the aesthetic values and commercial structures of mainstream music. Ondaatje makes much of the fact that none of Bolden's music was ever recorded; within the novel, peers note that "he stayed away while others moved into wax history" (32), suggesting at once his resistance to the official structures of society, and the improvisational power of his individuality, which resists such static confinement.

In spite of its potential to unify marginalized individuals, ultimately it is this individuality that is central to Ondaatje's use of jazz. As much as it can draw together the outgroups of Storyville—the black musicians and prostitutes who affirmatively identify with jazz—or endow narrative unity on the disparate voices of the different jazz musicians that Webb interviews in search of Bolden (whose perspectives are presented as first-person notes), jazz is still insistently represented as individualistic and fragmentary. This is best shown by Bolden's own irrepressibly singular vision: describing him as "obsessed with the magic of air, those smells that turned neuter as they revolved in his lung and then spat out in the chosen key," Ondaatje defines Bolden's musical expression through personal sensory experiences. From this perspective, Marinkova is right to explain the novel in terms of its "contestation of political universalism"—so long as the political is understood as mediated by the aesthetic and affective.[27]

In fact, for the narrator of *Coming Through Slaughter*, the political is always expressed through aesthetic multiplicity; what Sally Bachner describes as "Bolden's exclusion from emerging histories of jazz" is, for Ondaatje, a deliberate act of resistance, part of an aesthetic embrace of "sub-history" evinced in the alternative narratives of *The Cricket* and the multiple voices of his music.[28] Individuality, however, does not imply limitation; Bolden's music is beautiful because it contains multiple voices, so that when he describes something through his trumpet, "he would be describing something in 27 ways. There was pain and gentleness everything jammed into each number" (33). In *Coming Through Slaughter*, it is through this ability to embody multiple visions and emotions that jazz really deconstructs what Marinkova calls the "hegemonic" understanding of "the self as unitary and contained, negatively defined against an other and teleologically driven toward absolute knowledge and control of their environs," and instead affirms an alternative ontology—one that is personal, subjective, changeable, and not reliant upon contradistinction with others.[29]

LIVING GHOSTS: JAZZ AND CULTURAL MULTIPLICITY

Feld's encounters with the jazz community in Ghana give just one instance of the number of cultures outside of the United States that have turned to jazz to contest these narratives of limitation. Ondaatje himself is a Sri Lankan Burgher who has lived in Canada since 1962—a double outsider. This ongoing and widespread currency of jazz as a marker for social isolation is particularly obvious in Maori poet and short-story writer Phil Kawana's 1996 collection *Dead Jazz Guys,* whose tongue-in-cheek title suggests the sometimes diffuse, but nonetheless central, value of jazz as a marker of identity for its Maori protagonists. Nowhere is this more obvious than in the opening, titular story, where Mike Arapeta, a young Maori man leading an undercover life as a bone carver in an unidentified New Zealand city, begins a relationship with the lithe, scarred, blonde Pakeha, Lee.[30] Jazz allows Mike to bypass the cultural narratives that would restrict him to playing a part, and to find a way of being that is more idiosyncratic.

Mike is introduced to us in the public library, "sitting cross-legged on the floor reading through a biography of Miles Davis" (7) and, in contrast to Lee's reading habits (they meet when she drops a book by George Bernard Shaw on his head), his interest in jazz immediately signifies his outsider status. Kawana reinforces Mike's position *outside* in a number of ways: he wears a "tatty flannel shirt," (8), eats "fish and rice, mostly" (a fact so unusual that another Pakeha, Janice, asks if this means he is a "tofu muncher" [11]), and is particularly conscious of the way he wears his hair—in an unusual topknot. As soon as Lee has left, he "wondered what she had thought of his hair," describing it as "very short on top, shaved to the scalp and the back and sides, leaving a topknot that was ordered into twelve thin dreadlocks, reading down to below his shoulder blades" (8). So although he casually shows off his familiarity with Shaw (8), Mike clearly identifies more with the "dead jazz guy," Davis. But Kawana does more than simply contrast colonial and New World cultural identities.

Indeed, Kawana reveals that Mike's self-consciousness about his own idiosyncrasies is a product of his conflicting relationship with dominant European–New Zealand values. Despite their initial attraction to one another, it is clear that Mike displays such self-consciousness of his nonconformity because of his interaction with Lee. Aware that he has "never been out with a *real* pakeha before" (11), the attention he receives from her crystalizes an underlying sense of alienation that even his vanity cannot assuage: although he "tried to assure himself" that he did "look good," Kawana notes in a typical understatement that Mike "wasn't feeling quite that confident" (8). His response is an act of overcompensation. Although "he didn't really know what to expect" from their planned date, Mike does recognize that Lee seems to like "a bit of an edge," and so plays the role of an outsider by "dress[ing] like a hood" (13). The gesture almost misfires: Lee wonders if he is "a drug dealer" (16), and Mike in turn wonders if she does not look "a little disappointed" (17) when he says no. Kawana highlight the extent to which both Lee and Mike try to match themselves—and each other—to meta-narratives about ethnic identity; Mike's anxiety about dating a *"real* pakeha" indicates his own concerns about his authenticity as a Maori, and the extent to which Lee has exoticized him.

Despite the danger that both characters run of falling into stereotypes, the story still concludes with the two making love accompanied by jazz. The significance of the music shifts here—from a symbol of marginalization, it becomes an image of productive exchange as, just like the lovers' bodies, "John Coltrane's saxophone and Don Cherry's trumpet writhed and danced around each other. Supple, sinewy and alive" (19). But the music nonetheless retains a transgressive charge, drawing them together in a moment of shared isolation from the world. Kawana describes them as wrapped "in shadows" (18), "in the darkness," at the "edges of a fantasy" (19), suggesting through this free indirect discourse that both characters are flirting with a forbidden alternative to convention. For both, the relationship at once marks a rebellion against social expectations, and moment of consolation that provides reprieve from their everyday loneliness.

In this way, Kawana draws on jazz as more than just a ready-made symbol for standing outside or against the dominant social group. Instead, he weaves it into a larger, complex network of motifs that aligns different outgroups into a coherent pattern by affirming alternative ways of looking and being. While he clearly prefers the "exploration, experimentation," and "exultation" (19) of jazz, for instance, Mike also identifies with Rastafarianism, and other stories in the collection match references to Coltrane and Davis with images of dreadlocks and Bob Marley, not to mention Ice-T, Cheech and Chong, sombreros—even Kraftwerk. The characters in this collection all look for parallels to their own isolation, but Kawana also allows them an awareness of the limits to any claims of authenticity. Mike recognizes that he is not a "proper Rasta," but "likes dreads . . . that's all" (11); while in the story "Moko Carved in Rimu," the protagonist's grandfather protests: "you all run around like you were living in Harlem or something. I hate to shatter your illusions, Andrew, but you're a Maori, not a Negro" (23). Urging his grandson to find alternative parallels—ones that still remind him of his specificity—the grandfather cuts into his walking stick, explaining, "see that cut. That's history. That's a place. That's me. Keep it, give it to your own mokopuna when they're old enough to begin to understand" (24). This is why jazz has such a pronounced effect on Mike: it seems temporally, locatively specific, despite its different cultural origin—"the perfect accompaniment for the moment" (18). Although Coltrane and Cherry might be culturally removed from small-town New Zealand, their music seems to have been "resurrected . . . just for him and Lee."

While Andrew's grandfather might be upset at younger Maori looking for role models from Harlem, Kawana himself is obviously aware of the generative possibilities that can come from conversations between other experiences of marginalization. The most interesting comes from another parallel that Mike draws, adding a layer of complexity to his identification with jazz: he imagines himself as looking "more like a Native American than a Maori. High cheekbones and dark eyes—legacy of his part-Samoan mother—over a straight nose, all painted a smooth and flawless coffee brown" (8). When Lee's friend, Janice, comments that he looks "almost Indian . . . like that guy in *Last of the Mohicans*," Mike is flattered, clearly feeling his self-image reinforced. Lee, however, is puzzled at this, asking "Daniel Day Lewis' brother?"—before Janice replies, "No . . . Magua, the evil one" (12). On the one hand, Kawana is clearly signaling a shared history of marginalization. Mike's positive identification with another indigenous culture is easily inverted into an alienating view of all difference (here in the form of brown faces) as "evil."

This comparison suggests a different way of understanding the experience of being an outsider—one that gains strength from multiplicity. From this perspective, Kawana's book could be thought of in Chadwick Allen's terms as a fundamentally trans-indigenous text. As a way of figuring productive conversations between different indigenous cultures, Allen suggests that, "similar to terms like *trans*lation, *trans*national, and *trans*form, *trans*-Indigenous may be able to bear the complex, contingent asymmetry and the potential risk of unequal encounters borne by the preposition *across*."[31] Individuals like Mike can bring multiple traditions to bear on their own lives, in the process giving new meaning to previously dormant signs. Allen argues that "indigenous signs travel across generations, in other words, not to become enigmatic and dead, but rather to be (re)interpreted by readers who are multiply situated and multiply informed"; within *Dead Jazz Guys,* Maori, Native American, and jazz traditions are all "resurrected," taking on a new affirmative force.[32]

At the same time as providing positive affirmation, however, these cross-cultural connections also implicate Mike (and the other outgroup characters of Kawana's collection) in a process of destructive opposition. In advancing the concept of the trans-indigenous, Allen notes that such modes of identity threaten the hierarchies of official discourses, from larger national narratives to the "discipline of American Studies," whose white, normative perspective "necessarily implies both a binary opposition and a vertical hierarchy of the Indigenous (always) tethered to (and positioned below) the settler-invader."[33] Jazz does more than identify opposition, then—it actively contributes to a larger, epistemological alternative to the pakeha mainstream in Kawana's New Zealand. Crucially, this alternative is not predicated upon an inverted hierarchy. The opening might tap into certain narrative codes, suggesting that the story will offer Miles Davis as an alternative to George Bernard Shaw, flipping a pakeha Eurocentrism. But instead we see a relationship that allows movement laterally, not just vertically; Mike can talk Shaw, and Lee listens to Davis, Coltrane, and Cherry. As the story progresses, moreover, Kawana reveals that the pair are further connected by their position outside the capitalist system of work and consumption (despite differing levels of privilege). For an astute, farsighted writer like Kawana, jazz is more than just a literal symbol or trope for (a) rebellious alterneity, or (b) easy cross-racial harmony. Instead, it is aligned with a larger mode of being that involves standing outside of the dominant culture and its values, and finds parallels in difference. The story might leave lingering questions about the permanence of this solution; in another moment where Mike's voice seems to take over the narrative, he recognizes that "at some time they would have to awake, return to the deadness of the everyday, enshrouded by elevator music" (19)—but *Dead Jazz Guys* nonetheless suspends their togetherness, contrasting the possibility of loss with the vibrancy of jazz, "supple, sinewy, and alive."

Although jazz may not be quite so obviously in the spotlight in Anishinaabe author Gerald Vizenor's formally experimental 2003 novel *Hiroshima Bugi*, it is still imagined as a vital countercultural force—one that the protagonist, a half-Japanese, half-Anishinaabe storyteller named Ronin, synthesizes with other forms of counter-narrative. The novel alternates between chapters or stories told in Ronin's distinctively jarring "kabuki" style and commentaries provided by an Anishinaabe veteran (a friend of Ronin's father, with whom he served in World War II); indeed, it is structured around the idea of isolation through its sequence of counter-narratives.[34] Unlike the characters in Kawana's collection, moreover, Ronin integrates jazz into his identity as part of an active strategy of resistance to cultural marginalization—one that he terms "survivance." In one of the commentaries that follow Ronin's stories, the Anishinaabe commentator notes that this term is "not merely a variation of 'survival,' the act, reaction, or custom of a survivalist," but a state of being, a new kind of identity, at once "a vision and a vital condition to endure, to outwit evil and dominance, and to deny victimry" (36). The concept of resisting dominance is crucial, for as both Ronin and the commentator know, domination is based on binaries; outgroups are othered because of a process that insists on pure categories. Ronin's survivance, however, is synthetic, resisting ideas of purity and instead valuing hybridity and multiplicity: he "creates words, names, and turns combinations of words, some native words, to intimate desire and the critical thrust of new ideas." Throughout the novel, moreover, he inhabits multiple different personae, and in this respect, Vizenor's novel is not just oppositional in the sense of offering a contrast to the mainstream, but because it actively upsets the logic of domination—and jazz is an integral component of this.

But why is this survivance necessary? From the opening images of the novel, Vizenor foregrounds Ronin as painfully alone, an outsider in the country of his birth, Japan. Ronin tells the reader that his "stories are separations of time and family" (4), and as attested to by his half-caste status and anachronistic name (referring to a masterless samurai, or "man of the waves"), he is both physically and temporally out of sync, cut off from those around him. He is stigmatized because his father was an American soldier, part of the occupying forces at the end of World War II, and recognizes that his mother "could not protect or nurture an *ainoko*, a *hafu*, or halfbreed child, born of the erotic sensibilities of the occupation" (17). Keenly aware of this rejection, Ronin develops an attitude of resistance to the country that has isolated him, centering this on protests against peace and the memorialization of the bombing of Hiroshima. This manifests in his "nuclear kabuki theatre in the ruins" around Hiroshima, where he aims to "forever haunt the obedient peacemongers" (23). For both Ronin and the Japanese, these two qualities—his racial otherness and his social iconoclasm—are inextricably linked; he imagines himself as "dead Amerika Indian, hafu, peace boy, out to sea" (16), while newspapers report his actions as those of an "ainoko peace buster" (51). Ronin's isolation and his resistance, moreover, are implicitly tied to jazz. Part of his social isolation comes from his mother's profession: Okichi was "a boogie, or bugi, dancer," someone who embraced not only a foreign man, but a foreign form of music. In turn, Ronin's protests adopt something of the jazz sensibility of boogie—Vizenor even suggests this in the title: Ronin is dancing around the meaning of Hiroshima, riffing off its imagery.

While Ronin eventually travels to America in search of his father, and manages to integrate into the Anishinaabe community of the White Earth Reservation, his relationship with his father's land turns out to be similarly compromised. In part, this comes from his separation from his father; he admits that "my parents are shadows" (15) and lists a genealogy that suggests his feelings of rejection from America: "My life ended before the bomb. My life started with the occupation.

My father sent me away. My father was an army sergeant. My mother was a cripple. My mother was a bugi dancer. My only friends are lepers. My only friends are orphans." Once he is in America, however, he finds himself further alienated. He is at once a reminder of the war with Japan—and thus an uncomfortable reminder of America's use of the atomic bomb—and, as a Native American, a member of a marginalized community and signifier of a continental genocide. Vizenor draws the reader's attention to this paralleled experience of isolation, noting that "thousands of ainoko, or hafu children, were the untouchables of war and peace in two countries"; while "Japan would never embrace the progeny of the occupation," America also "enacted very restrictive immigration laws" (22). Ronin is only able to enter America because he was "adopted by the tribal government at the White Earth Reservation"—emphasizing that he is outside of mainstream society, and instead a member of a marginalized outgroup. Despite these coercive social forces pushing Ronin outside, however, he resists adopting the stance of victim. His storytelling and "atomic kabuki theatre" generate new narratives—ones that deny victimhood and affirm creative agency.

The Anishinaabe narrator of the commentaries that alternate with Ronin's first-person stories particularly admires this element of the *hafu*'s writing, maintaining that "his native stories evade closure and victimry" (64). Intriguingly, the commentator here identifies Ronin's narratives as *native*—suggesting at once Native American and native to the country of his birth, Japan. In other words, Ronin adapts different kinds of counter-narratives that are at once "heartfelt, and inclusive" (64), strengthened by their shared alterneity. Certainly, the community of the White Earth Reservation—and the Hotel Manidoo, in particular—identify Ronin as an Anishinaabe storyteller, bestowing upon him their title of "storier" (9), and comparing him to their figure of the raven ("ravens create stories of survivance in our perfect memories" [7]). At the same time, the commentator freely acknowledges that Ronin has drawn on the tradition of kabuki theater, having "create[d] dialogue in a kabuki theatre style, short, direct, positional words and sentences" (12). The counter-narrative force of kabuki does not simply come from its opposition to Western aesthetics, however, but from its insurrectionary force within Japan. Following the war, "military censors had reduced the great kabuki tradition to a tincture of feudalism" because it was "a dangerous art" (20), later characterized as a "living theatre" (640) that resists singular identities and instead embraces multiplicity, "creat[ing] many new identities" (21). Ronin likewise lays claim to multiple performative identities. Crucially, these are unified in their opposition to the dominant values of their respective societies.

From this point of view, Vizenor is clearly drawing parallels between the kind of countercultural identity associated with jazz, and the insurrectionary force of kabuki theater and Anishinaabe storytelling. These forms of resistance are linked by a shared emphasis on agency and exaggeration—the narrator repeatedly draws attention to Ronin's "empty theatrical smile" (7)—which suggests that their importance lies in the way they can be appropriated. These are performative models of resistance; they allow individuals to self-consciously craft alternative identities. In a moment that is reminiscent of Mike in *Dead Jazz Guys,* Ronin embraces different identities in explicit parallel to a kind of jazz performativity. At a climactic moment of protest he shouts, "my skin is hafu, but my heart is mine, not an orphan heart," before explaining that he is echoing the dancer and performer Josephine Baker, who once called out to a racist audience "You have white skins but black hearts. . . . I have a black skin but I have a white heart" (31). Here Ronin draws together the underlying parallel that Vizenor has built between jazz, storying, and kabuki. In other words, he is acknowledging the disjunction between his "natural" state and the choices he makes in how he crafts his own identity. Other models of being—like jazz and kabuki—are attractive to him precisely because they offer a way of bringing integrity to his position as an outsider. In a telling phrase, he imagines Baker as "a hafu of another world" (31); she offers a model for his own experience, mapping a way for him to imaginatively inhabit other minds and perspectives.

Ronin's identification with Baker is but one of many affinities he finds with other outsiders; in many ways, the narrative consists of a series of staged encounters with members of different outgroups, including orphans, lepers, and the homeless. Nor does Ronin shy away from addressing their status outside the mainstream, lamenting that "my friends died too, outcasts, suicide by desolation" (5). Vizenor is interested in more than just moments of identification, however, and instead depicts Ronin as actively blending their identities with his own, so that at one moment he can claim "the police snatched my body and confined me on an island for sixty years" (4), incorporating the history and experiences of a leper into his own personal narrative, reconfiguring his sense of self. Rather than capitulating to the logic of alienation in the face of difference, Ronin actively embraces the experiences of other outgroups, joining them in acts of paralleled resistance. For instance, in relation to the Ainu—the indigenous culture of northern Japan—Ronin observes that "the Ainu and the *anishinaabe* told similar stories about natural reason, their creation, animal totems, and survivance" (51), drawing attention to the importance of narrative within both cultures even as he uses it to create new modes of survivance for himself.

On one level, then, jazz could be seen as just one small part of a complex, multifaceted response to isolation—one of several strategies that Ronin employs in constructing an alternative identity. Although Vizenor introduces jazz through the title of the book, the figure of Baker, and the early remembrances of Ronin's mother, it is not until the late story/chapter "Ronin of Matsue" that jazz enters the narrative in significant detail. Here, Ronin encounters "jazz musicians gathered at dusk under the streetlights in the park" (183), finding a special connection to their music. He imagines them as a counterpart to Lafcadio Hearn (a Greek-Irish writer who settled in Japan, taking on the penname Koizumi Yakumo), who he describes as "a hafu in a weird, courteous, and obscure culture . . . my hafu muse" (179). Together, Hearn and the jazz musicians provide Ronin with a framework for analyzing the world with an alternative critical perspective, and just as he observes that jazz "might have reversed [Hearn's] literary concentration on a cricket or a smile" (183), so the reader might wonder whether jazz in turn helps inflect Ronin's own slanted aesthetic lens. But here jazz is not simply another way of looking at the world. Vizenor uses it as an alternative aesthetic structure that is profoundly anti-linear. Listening to the performance in the park, where "the blues, a fusion of wiles, bruises and cares, bounced on the canal and roused the somber kami spirits of the samurai in the castle," Ronin focuses in on the way that jazz creates new, anti-linear relationships between past and present; he even describes it as the "beat of a new cultural memory" (183). On a larger scale, the narrative structure of *Hiroshima Bugi* embodies this idea of a new cultural memory, presenting Ronin's stories as fragments that twist past and present, self and other.

The commentaries on each story accentuate this structure, making the process of retelling that creates cultural memory into something material and tangible; the reader follows the narrative as it is retold, interpreted, rearranged, and reimagined. This transformative quality is precisely what Ronin admires in jazz, venerating Naoko Terai's ability to "transform... two audiences with a marvellous rush, beat, and tease of tones" (183). Structurally, *Hiroshima Bugi* truly *is* a boogie, in the sense that it similarly teases and transforms. Another way of looking at the patterned stories and commentaries of the book is in terms of an antiphonal exchange. Certainly, Ronin's stories are performed in a way that implies a connection to the call-and-response of jazz; the commentaries reveal that at the Hotel Manidoo, among the Native veterans, "*Hiroshima Bugi* was read out loud at dinner by the storier named for the day," with the commentator imagining that "Ronin would be pleased to hear the creative counts that became part of his tricky stories, and, of course, my commentaries" (9). These last asides suggest that the commentator recognizes the same concept of call-and-response *within* Ronin's stories themselves—that they also respond, in a jazz-like conversation, to the stories that Ronin has gathered from others.

As far as possible, I try to avoid trite inter-artistic equations—I don't want to simply impose a loose analogy between the novel and certain tropes about jazz. Instead, I want to explore a correspondence that Vizenor himself draws between jazz as a conversational form of music and the processes of conversation in which the characters engage. Indeed, this parallel is integral to the novel's ambitions as a counter-narrative: Ronin tells the reader early on that "survivance is a creative, concerted consciousness that does not arise from separation, dominance, or concession nightmares" (9); instead, it relies on finding shared experiences of alienation, common ground on which to improvise. This is why Vizenor's characters constantly search for such parallels: their strategy of resistance is to find affinity with the stories of others and, together, create new hybrid narratives—ones that, as in jazz, bring together distinctive individual voices—without enacting their own process of marginalization, which might happen in a process that simply inverted binaries (or imposed new ones).

Instead, as the commentaries reveal, this process relies on active, open-hearted interpretation. The Hotel Manidoo occupies the figurative heart of the novel as a place where a whole band of individuals, rejected by the nation-state, can affirm a new identity through responding to Ronin's stories. By the end, they have "deciphered his scenes, teases, and descriptions into an elaborate catchword guide and chronicle," but only because they have proceeded "with great respect and humor" (118). It is this combination of active interpretation and optimism that most differentiates Vizenor's trans-indigenous vision from Kawana's. Where the characters in *Dead Jazz Guys* only enjoy a temporary connection, often fumbling toward moments of transcendence and limited in their ability to critique their affinities with others, the characters of *Hiroshima Bugi* embrace other stories, seeking them out and drawing them into their own.

At the same time, both writers frequently mobilize images of ghosts and resurrection. The "dead jazz guys" of Kawana's stories have a relatively innocuous and certainly benign afterlife, especially when compared to Vizenor's ghosts. But both writers seek to make connections between traditional ways of being and responses to contemporary life and conditions—the "beat of a new cultural memory" that Allen identifies. The ghostly presence of jazz, transfigured from living, vital music to something spectral does not diminish the music's power—resigning it to the past, without importance for the present—but shows its continued animation. For both writers, jazz helps characters to bridge the gap between the past and their current condition, reimagining their identities as outsiders in the affirmative light of resistance and cultural autonomy.

HOW NOT TO THINK LIKE EVERYONE ELSE: MURAKAMI, JAZZ, AND THE DANGER OF CONNECTING

For Japanese novelist and translator Haruki Murakami, jazz and literature are so intertwined as to be almost indistinguishable. Unlike writers such as Ondaatje or Vizenor, who draw on its imagery or motifs for a particular work, or even figures of the Harlem Renaissance like Langston Hughes, who used the aesthetics of the music as both image and structure for periods of their careers, Murakami has developed an entire writing practice out of his love of jazz. An "acknowledged expert" on the subject, the writer's intimate connection to the music blossomed after seeing Art Blakey live in Kobe in 1964 when Murakami was fifteen.[35] Before he had graduated university, he had already opened a jazz café in Tokyo—the evocatively named "Peter Cat." Admitting that "practically everything I know about writing ... I learned from music," Murakami has described his initial steps toward writing as an attempt to translate musical aesthetics into prose—to "write like playing an instrument."[36] Complementing this formal ambition, almost all of his fourteen novels (and the majority of his dozens of short stories) contain references to jazz, typically in conjunction with the experience of personal isolation. While it may be closely associated with moments of individual loneliness throughout his extensive oeuvre, however, jazz also provides a framework for Murakami's solitary characters to find connection—what the writer himself sometimes refers to in the appropriately musical terms of harmony and improvisation.

Unlike Bolden in *Coming Through Slaughter* or Ronin in *Hiroshima Bugi*, Murakami's protagonists seldom belong to an identifiable outgroup. This is not to say that there is nothing countercultural about Murakami's evocation of jazz; as recently as 2016, Nathen Clerici has suggested that the concept of "subculture" might constitute "a missing link in the ever burgeoning field of English-language scholarship" on Murakami's work.[37] But whether you are considering a specific work, or looking longitudinally across Murakami's fictional output, it quickly becomes apparent that his "jazz characters"—the ones who listen to Bill Evans, hang posters of Miles Davis on their dormitory walls, and quote aphorisms from Thelonious Monk—are not part of any particular subculture; instead, they are liminally placed between the mainstream and identifiable countercultural groups. In other words, they suffer a double layer of social isolation. Perhaps nowhere is this more obvious than in Murakami's bestselling *Norwegian Wood*, where the narrator, Toru, finds himself alone on a university campus, isolated from both the normal students and the radical protestors, such as "a helmeted girl student" who was "painting huge characters on a sign with something about American imperialism invading Asia."[38] Here he experiences a total cultural isolation, "a kind of loneliness new to me, as if I were the only one here who was not truly part of the scene" (103), where his intense experience of loneliness comes from the recognition that he is part of no group—not even one that is socially oppressed.

Critics have tended to read such moments of isolation as part of a wider cultural critique; Clerici notes that many of Murakami's earlier novels develop "a criticism of Japan's mainstream consumerist culture and the former dissidents who so easily joined it."[39] Equally, it could be seen as a nod to Murakami's position outside the two streams of Japanese fiction: although from the start of his career it was clear Murakami "was not part of the *jun bungaku* [pure literature] crowd," critics like Matthew Strecher also point out that, his writing was nothing like the "pop" fiction that made up the other end of that continuum, "*taishū bungaku* ('mass literature'), whose chief quality seemed to be its endless repetition of predetermined formulas and, as a result, its easy predictability."[40] But such larger interpretations easily mask what is surely one of the most appealing aspects of Murakami's writing: his focus on coming to terms with loneliness and loss purely on the level of the isolated individual.

From this perspective, Murakami's jazz embodies a paradox: it is at once painful—a reminder of how separate each individual is from others—and beautiful, for the way this recognition heightens our senses and experiences of the world. Following on from his campus revelation, Toru travels to a rural sanatorium to visit his childhood friend, Naoko. On this trip, his isolation is reinforced in a moment of intense existential awareness: left alone in the small house shared by Naoko and an older patient, Reiko, he finds a "Bill Evans album" and realizes it was "the record I had played in Naoko's room on the night of her birthday"; as he listens to the music, he is transported back to "the night she cried and I took her in my arms. That had been only six months ago, but it felt like something from a much remoter past" (141). Here jazz at once increases Toru's pain, "distort[ing] my sense of time", and emphasizes his distances from that moment of physical and emotional connection. At the same time, it heightens his attention to beauty: the moon is "so bright" he turns "the lights off and stretched out on the sofa to listen to Bill Evans' piano," allowing him to enjoy a lyrical moment of intense beauty as "the moonlight cast long shadows and splashed the walls with a touch of diluted Indian ink"—indeed, Toru is so consumed by the piano that "the moonlight seemed to be swaying with the music." This moment of heightened reality allows Toru to articulate his own erstwhile distance from the world, which he describes as a sense of disconnection in ordinary interactions, to the point where he feels that "this isn't the real world. The people, the scene: they just don't seem real to me" (223).

In spite of Toru's almost overwhelming isolation, jazz is not simply an individualistic experience; throughout *Norwegian Wood*, it also provides him a connection to others who find themselves caught outside any social group. It is significant that Toru and Naoko only sleep together on one occasion: while Bill Evans is playing. And as the novel progresses, Toru forms a close bond with the former piano prodigy Reiko who, despite her classical training, is particularly interested in "certain jazz piano styles ... Bud Powell ... Thelonious Monk" (200). The two talk about listening to "Thelonious Monk playing 'Honeysuckle Rose'" (225), and eventually sleep together—a necessary step, Murakami suggests, toward their integration back into society at large.

In this sense, jazz parallels the role played by American fiction in the novel, by acting as a marker of individualism that simultaneously affords connections with others who exist outside conventional social groups. For Toru, American jazz and literature both offer a way to be comfortable with his solitude: in one moment of existential crisis, he buys "a copy of Faulkner's *Light in August*" and goes "to the nosiest jazz café" he can think of to read "my new book while listening to Ornette Coleman and Bud Powell," precisely so that he can feel "quiet, peaceful and lonely" (262) Moreover, Toru signals his own isolation from fellow students through his reading habits: while his "favourites" are "Truman Capote, John Updike, F. Scott Fitzgerald, Raymond Chandler," he is aware that he "didn't see anyone else in my lectures or the dorm reading writers like that. They liked Kazumi Takahashi, Kenzaburo Oe, Yukio Mishima" (37). It is only the aloof, hedonistic Nagasawa who shares his reading tastes; the two form a close friendship over their shared love of Fitzgerald's *Great Gatsby* (significantly, a novel closely associated with jazz), and the two explicitly identify their relationship in terms of shared isolation. Nagasawa sees this in a more solipsistic light than Toru, however, arguing that they are "a lot alike"—neither "is interested, essentially, in anything but ourselves . . . we can think about things in a way that's totally divorced from everyone else" (274). Ultimately, it is Toru's rejection of this outright solipsism that ends their friendship (perhaps indicating a difference between a literary and a musical way of seeing the world), but Nagasawa's defense of his peculiar reading habits does seem to reinforce the importance of jazz as a sign of independent thinking for Murakami: in one of the novel's most quoted phrases, Nagasawa contends that, "if you only read the books that everyone else is reading, you can only think what everyone else is thinking" (39).

Certainly, people are constantly telling Toru that he sees the world—and talks about it—in an entirely unique way. But, in turning away from Nagasawa's vision of self-contained isolation, Toru comes to recognize his need for making connection with others. This leads to a final divergence in his relationship with Naoko, who, by contrast, is unable to bring herself to truly connect to others. Murakami indicates this bifurcation through music: where Toru listens to jazz, Naoko prefers the Beatles—especially the titular "Norwegian Wood." Although their shared taste for western music aligns them as outsiders, their individual preferences also signal a fundamental difference. Naoko tries to describe their difference in terms of self-sufficiency, explaining to Toru that "I can't do what you do: I can't slip inside my shell and wait for things to pass" (111)—but it seems that Naoko's problem is precisely that she is too much inside her own shell. When she listens to "Norwegian Wood," for instance, she feels completely isolated, imaging herself "wandering in a deep wood. I'm all alone and it's cold and dark, and nobody comes to save me" (143). Slowly, this crippling interiorization overcomes her: where earlier in the novel she is able to reply to Toru's letters (although she does admit she only reads his letters "at night when I'm lonely and in pain" [307]), eventually she is unable to break out of herself at all. It is simply too difficult to externalize her feelings and reply, so she instead communicated with Toru through Reiko. Eventually, she acts out her previously imagined separation from the world by hanging herself in the woods. In contrast, Toru chooses to find connections with others. He admits that he has "a need for human warmth," precisely because he gets "so lonely [he] can't stand it" (273); where Naoko refuses to connect, Toru commits, telling his friend Midori that "all I want in this world is you" (386).

Of course, Toru's call to Midori is only meaningful if it falls on receptive ears. For Murakami, a successful jazz character—or on a larger scale, a successful jazz narrative like *Norwegian Wood*—is one that can build a connection with others. This is a relationship that Murakami imagines in terms of the musical conversation between performer and audience. Indeed, the parallel between Toru as character and Murakami as writer is apt: Toru's plea maps out, on a micro scale, the larger call articulated by the book: to acknowledge individuality, and find connections through this mutual recognition. Murakami certainly conceptualizes his role as a writer in terms of a jazz performance, describing the "high you experience upon completing a work—upon ending your 'performance,'" as "the most important thing" in writing—provided that you "get to share that sense of elevation with your readers (your audience)." Such a "marvelous culmination that can be achieved in no other way" seems to be precisely what *Norwegian Wood* aspires toward: the final image of Toru, alone, reaching out to Midori (and by extension, to the reader 'listening' to his story) provides the narrative with a structured moment of connection between writer and audience—the kind of call for response that Morrison will later use at the end of *Jazz*. In this sense, Murakami draws on jazz to coordinate his writing on three interrelated levels: it works simultaneously as a model for Murakami's composition, as a metaphor in characterization, and as a structure for the novel as a whole.

As a strategy for creating empathy with outsiders, this aspiration toward connection also works to support alternative ways of being, much as the novel finally endorses Toru's lifestyle (insofar as he doesn't have to give up his peculiar way of seeing the world). Instead, Murakami shifts the burden onto his audience to listen and respond. As Jay Rubin, Murakami's frequent translator has noted, the motif of listening plays an important role in most of his fiction; he cites an interview between Murakami and a psychologist in which the author explained that "listening to a lot of other people's stories is very healing for me." There is a sense, then, that in inviting his audience to invest themselves in his characters, Murakami is also asking them to undergo a kind of healing—by validating their own idiosyncrasies, coming to terms with their own stories.

Murakami's explanation of his writing process shows a keen awareness of the risk attendant in reaching out: the feeling of elation that he craves depends on a response from readers, and Murakami recognizes that this is impossible to guarantee. His fiction similarly addresses the danger of exaggerated individualism—evident in a character like Nagasawa, whose casual solipsism devastates those around him (including a long-term girlfriend who eventually commits suicide)—suggesting that intense individualism can be alienating as much as affirming. Another attendant danger is articulated in a later short story, "Tony Takitani," namely the consequences of losing this connection with an audience, of being trapped indefinitely alone.

The story, collected in English in the anthology *Blind Willow, Sleeping Woman*, follows the life of the eponymous son of a "fairly well-known jazz trombonist" who, typically of Murakami's protagonists, is caught in a liminal space as an outsider not clearly part of any group.[41] In fact, at first glance, he appears to be an ainoko, or mixed-race child like Ronin in *Hiroshima Bugi*; even though his mother and father "were both 100 per cent genuine Japanese," he was "often assumed to be a mixed-blood child" because of "his name and his curly hair and his rather deeply sculpted features" (225). Tony is "teased" for being a "half-breed," and this ostracizing leads to intense isolation; as the narrator observes, "such experiences served only to close the boy off from the world. He never made any real friends" (230). Surprisingly, however, the tragedy of "Tony Takitani" is not the protagonist's loneliness per se. As a child, he is untroubled by his isolation, finding it "natural to be by himself; it was a kind of premise for living" (231). Instead, the turning point comes when Takitani falls in love, and "suddenly his solitude became a crushing weight, a source of agony, a prison" (235). Acknowledging that "very fact of having ceased to be lonely caused him to fear the possibility of becoming lonely again," Tony recognizes the danger of falling in love—or, in Murakami's musical terms, finding a connection with an audience—is that, if the love is lost, he will never be satisfied with being alone again.

At first, Murakami seems to contrasts Tony's isolation and difficulty in forming connections with his gregarious, trombone-playing father. Shozaburo Takitani displays unusual charisma and originally leaves Japan in the 1930s because of difficulties in some of his amorous adventures, crossing "over to China with no baggage but his trombone" (225). The narrator describes him as "deeply self centred," and he seems to revel in casual affairs. Yet the superficial connections he can make mask an underlying sense of isolation that mirrors his son's. Although he was "young, handsome and good on his horn," he still "stood out like a crow on a snowy day wherever he went" (226), and indeed his distaste for intimacy derives from an almost nihilistic acceptance of this solitude: Shozaburo "felt that, eventually, life had to turn out more or less like this. Everyone ended up alone sooner or later" (228). Prefiguring the fate of his son, Shozaburo falls in love, and the sudden death of his wife (Tony's mother) causes a change in his behavior, which manifests in his music—it becomes stultifying, frozen in place in spite of the musical innovation going on around him. Tellingly, Murakami envisages this new, heightened loneliness as a kind of musical blockage—a "flat, disc-like thing" that "had lodged itself in his chest" (229). It is only when he has found love himself, however, that Tony can recognize this blockage in his father. Attending one of his performances after his marriage, Tony is paralyzed by the loneliness he hears in his father's music as "something in the music began to make him feel like a narrow pipe filling slowly, but inexorably, with sludge. He found it increasingly difficult to breathe" (237). In this grim foreshowing of his own eventual paralysis, Tony's horror at his father's music reflects his own increased anxiety about the dangers attendant in forming connections.

And in turn, Tony does succumb to the same ossifying isolation as his father: after his wife is hit by a car, Tony is unable to move forward with his life, trapped in stasis. Here, Murakami offers the counter-image of Toru in *Norwegian Wood,* who *is* able to escape his own interiorization through a meaningful connection. Without his one positive relationship, Tony reverts inwards, his claustrophobic isolation realized in his wife's room-sized closet. An avid shopper, his wife had amassed enormous quantities of luxury dresses and shoes; following her death, Tony hires a young woman to wear his wife's clothing, but this substitute only exacerbates his awareness of his isolation. Selling her collection off, Tony leaves "the room empty for a long, long time," turning the room into a kind of shrine to solitude: "he would go to the room and stay there for an hour or two, doing nothing in particular, just letting his mind go blank" (246). The depth of his loss is reflected in his inability "to recall the things that used to be in the room," so that "the only thing that remained tangible to him was the sense of absence." As ever in Murakami's fiction, jazz is never far from loneliness: when his father dies not long after, he leaves behind "his instrument, and a gigantic collection of old jazz records" (247), which Tony adds to the room, so that his loneliness is intertwined with his father's music. Jazz, Murakami is suggesting, can be dangerous. Here, it is connected to a kind of blockage that leads to paralyzing isolation. Translator Jay Rubin has noted the importance of ears and listening to Murakami—his "characters take extraordinarily good care of their ears"[42]—so it is significant that, following his loss, Tony can no longer listen to this music—he has, metaphorically, shut out the outside world.

For each of Murakami, Vizenor, Kawana, and Ondaatje, jazz signifies a positive response to social isolation. All are interested in how loneliness is connected to marginalization—which is perhaps why, although all four do employ jazz as a kind of coordinating metaphor, here the music is less important as a practice or lifestyle and more significant as a marker of individual identity. Characters across their novels and stories all mobilize jazz as an affirmative sign of difference: they might be excluded from mainstream society—in Murakami's case, may even be excluded from countercultural movements, too—but by identifying with a music that valorizes the very status of being outside, they can reclaim their marginal position as valuable and fulfilling.

In the same way, jazz also validates their experience of loneliness, allowing them to recast their solitude as something that comes close to a political statement or philosophical manifesto. But if Ingrid Monson is right, and "saying something" is the underlying aim of jazz musicians, then for these jazz identities to really work, the characters need someone else to listen. Why else would all four writers thematize the act of conversation, elevating it above mere dialogue to structural principle—whether in the form of letter and written response in *Norwegian Wood,* interview notes in *Coming Through Slaughter,* or written commentaries in *Hiroshima Bugi*? These writers recognize the danger of not being heard, where solitude takes over everything, leaving only what Tony Takitani experiences as "the sense of isolation."

THE REAL STORY

Jazz Autobiographies, Authority, and Agency

It is not just literary authors who are interested in possible translations between musical concepts and linguistic expression; some of the most interesting and insightful writing about jazz has come from musicians trying to invert this relationship. Many share Ornette Coleman's ambition to "express a concept according to which you can translate one thing into another"—in other words, to try and find a way to communicate abstract musical ideas through concrete linguistic ones.[1] Coleman's comments arose during a conversation with Jacques Derrida in 1997, during a wide-ranging interview in which the two covered topics as diverse as improvisation and the event, neuroscience and identity, Coleman's mother, and their shared experiences of racism.

What stands out most about this conversation is Coleman's insistence on paralleling music and writing, where he uses literary images to explain the theories underpinning his unique model of composition. Frustrated at difficulties in collaborating with the New York Philharmonic, for instance, he explained that their difficulty with his music "had nothing to do with music or sound, just with symbols"; Coleman felt that "the music that I've been writing for thirty years and that I call harmolodic is like we're manufacturing [*fabriquions*] our own words, with a precise idea of what we want these words to mean to people," and he was consequently perturbed at the ensemble's inability to shift modes of language.[2] For Coleman, a harmolodic model of jazz composition was so exciting precisely because it *ought* to be translated; although he never finished the long-promised manuscript that would codify its rules, he did stress to Derrida that "whoever tries to express himself in words, in poetry, in whatever form, can take my book of harmolodics and compose according to it, do it with the same passion and the same elements." On the one hand, Coleman here offers a stinging rebuke to those theorists who argue that musical structures cannot be translated across to literary texts; for Coleman, the two are analogous. But on the other, he seems to be inviting critics and listeners alike to approach his *musical* work from the perspective of literary analysis—the very fact of his interview with Derrida suggests his openness to such a reading.

I have been focusing on various frameworks for reading the relationship between loneliness and jazz in fiction. Whether the context is literary form, group identity, or gender politics, these frameworks reveal the way artists working in one medium—the written word—have turned to sound, specifically jazz, to try to make sense of one of the basic experiences that shape our humanity: loneliness. For some writers, jazz offers a thematic reference point; for others, a model of human interaction. But in every case we see jazz brought in *in parallel* to more traditional, literary modes of narrating and creating identity. What happens, though, when this relationship is flipped? When it is musicians turning to literature to explore loneliness? Like Brent Edwards, I think that "the figure of the musician-writer" demands we go "beyond the positing of a parallel among media, or even of a cross-media influence, in which the practice of one medium can be inspired, provoked, or extended by an attention to the specificities of another."[3] Instead, I want to offer an expanded reading where, just as Edwards argues that "the music can provide the model for criticism because the music already is criticism," so the jazz autobiography as a form imbeds within itself a form of critique.[4]

Although I focus principally on two autobiographies, this is of course not the only written avenue that musicians have pursued.

Some, like Sun Ra, were accomplished poets. Others, like Sonny Rollins, were manic diarists. Many have been actively involved in jazz criticism, writing reviews and articles for magazines. (Duke Ellington was particularly prominent as a spokesman for jazz.) Some have even moved into theory; alongside Coleman and his concept of harmolodics, other major performer-theorists include Ingrid Monson, and Gunther Schuller, who performed on the horn with Miles Davis in the late 1940s before a distinguished academic career. Perhaps the most prolific source of jazz writing, though, comes in the form of liner notes, which often focus as much on giving the album a narrative context as they do on the theoretical scope of the work.

Autobiographies are most relevant here, however, for a number of reasons. To start off with, despite the wide variety of forms that they can take, autobiographies by nature—as a form of "life writing"—take on narrative rhetorical structures. Given how "well versed" professional jazz musicians are "in improvisatory artistic practices," moreover, these narratives have a strong tendency toward invention, exaggeration, and fictionalization; they at once conform to and comment on the "straight" genre of autobiography, and as Ajay Heble rightly points out, thus "offer new ways to think about identity production."[5] Unlike other forms of jazz writing, then, autobiographies are primarily personal, rather than philosophical, political, or polemical (although they can certainly stray into this territory). In some cases, musicians even prefer a linguistic conversation about their music. Coleman certainly found this was the case, explaining that "it interests me more to have a human relationship with you than a musical relationship. I want to see if I can express myself in words, in sounds that have to do with a human relationship . . . because it allows you to gain the freedom that you desire, for yourself and for the other."[6] As such, it is in life writing that jazz artists most clearly articulate their individuality—and in so doing, approach the question of loneliness and isolation.

If writers are drawn to jazz as a motif for conceptualising loneliness, what kind of terms might the musicians themselves use when turning to a literary form? What relationship do they imagine might exist between solitude and a jazz solo? Is their music fueled by loneliness, or does it help provide relief? And how does loneliness fit into their broader imagination of their music? Underlying these questions, of course, is a larger contest over the meaning of jazz; by reading autobiographies of practitioners against the work of fiction writers and cultural critics, I hope to contrast two discourses on jazz that at times overlap—and at others, diverge. Indeed, as Eric Porter has argued, this is in itself a strong incentive to approach jazz writing through literary analysis; what other texts are better placed to complicate "our understanding of the changing meanings of jazz in American culture"?[7] Not all scholars or critics have been so willing to treat artists' writing in so generous terms, with many keen to maintain a romanticized image of the musician as constantly immanent, in the process of becoming and thus outside the process of historicization; to a degree, even novels like *Coming Through Slaughter* are culpable for the same valorization of jazz as process. But as Scott DeVeaux and Garry Giddins point out, particularly from the early 1950s, jazz musicians took an active role in shaping the discourse of their music and recuperating its history, "setting up their own schools and exploring jazz history in books, magazines, and public discussions. Jazz had begun to look at itself as a historical phenomenon with distinct roots and a proud lineage."[8] Although they were not published until the 1970s, Duke Ellington's *Music Is My Mistress* and Charles Mingus's *Beneath the Underdog* both work actively to shape the broader discourse of their music.

RIFFING: JAZZ AUTOBIOGRAPHY, IMPROVISATION, AND FORMAL CRITIQUE

Before turning specifically to loneliness, it seems worth thinking a little more broadly about the form of the jazz autobiography. As some of Coleman's comments suggest, in many cases, jazz writers take to language out of frustration with misconceptions about their music. Even today, autobiographies continue to be written in direct response to the popular or critical discourse around jazz; reading them in literary terms is a way to acknowledge the value of their written contributions to the way jazz is heard, discussed, and imagined—to recognize that their music is not their only language. An early example of such writing back comes in Sidney Bechet's *Treat It Gentle*, published in

1960, just after the pioneering soloist's death. Bechet begins the autobiography by challenging popular misunderstandings of jazz, and in doing so, redefines the parameters suggested by the label "autobiography"; the book is less about the individual, and more about his medium. Explaining that "there's people, they got the wrong idea of Jazz. They think it's all that red-light business," Bechet engages directly with the wider discourse around jazz, where even the name is "a name the white people have given to the music."[9] From the opening pages, it is clear that a narrative impulse drives Bechet's work. The only way for him to reply to the misunderstanding of his music is through a literary response—by telling "the real story I've got to tell, it's right here."[10] On a basic level, then, literature offers the musician a way of validating his own understanding of his music.

That "serious" jazz musicians should turn to concrete expression is all the more unusual given the importance of abstraction to jazz musicians. As Monson has eloquently explained, jazz sought legitimacy through a traditional romantic conceptualization of art as irreducible to language, particularly during the 1940s when bebop artists like Thelonious Monk "demanded that their music be taken seriously" by "adopting and cultivating this quintessentially romantic concept."[11] From this point of view, Monk's famous "reluctance to verbalize—to interviewers, musicians seeking instruction, and even friends and family members," was not taken as a sign of illiteracy or deficit in artistic ability, but instead signified further "evidence that music was his true language." This is not to say that by turning to literary forms Bechet, Ellington, and Mingus were relinquishing their authority as serious musicians. Instead, it is to highlight what Porter identifies as "the contradictory social positions of African American jazz musicians as intellectuals working both within and outside culture-producing institutions."[12] While their romantic aura may have endowed their work with a countercultural cachet, it also compromised their legitimacy within certain culture-producing institutions. A literary mode of expression, by contrast, offered not only an alternative channel, but a different set of conventions and structures.

But as Bechet's autobiography suggests, these conventions often proved to be anathema to jazz—especially when they were tied to larger, official structures, which sought to delimit either the music or its (black) practitioners. So while Bechet certainly explains the origins of jazz through a kind of historicization, he is also wary of placing too much emphasis on dwelling on the past—indeed, part of his aim in the book is to contest a prevailing official nostalgia for earlier eras of jazz, which he believes limits or suppresses alternative accounts of the music and its meaning. When critics and audiences get too hung up on nostalgic definitions of jazz, and "get to think in a memory kind of way all about this Jazz," they miss the new developments and innovations that, for Bechet, are part of the dynamic energy of the genre; to him, it is "more than a memory thing. . . . it's happening right there where they're listening to it."[13] His emphasis on a more expansive understanding of jazz—so that, for instance, when his "family beat time with their hands on drums . . . that's Jazz too. . . . you can just beat on the table and it can be jazz"—is thus part of a larger aim to free its discourse from the narrow confines of a formal definition.

In the process, Bechet also tries to move the discussion of jazz away from individual talents. He is quite happy to affirm that "no music is my music. It's everybody's who can feel it," thereby affirming a more inclusive—but also more subjective—understanding of jazz. While on the surface this might seem to undermine his ability to tell the "real story," detracting from the personal authority on which the autobiography genre depends, it complements the approach Bechet takes in *Treat It Gentle*. By writing his own life—and framing it in narrative terms, as a *story* rather than history—Bechet at once frees himself, as a musician, from the control of others, as he frees jazz from the confines of a single, historical meaning. This second-order reflectivity, moreover, builds into the very text a critique of the official, codifying rules on which autobiography is predicated. As a piece of writing that lays claim to a factual, official status, the autobiography conforms to the kind of hegemonic, authoritative power structures that (in Bechet's view) are responsible for limiting the scope of what jazz can mean. In turning to often suspect stories and overtly fictional narrative techniques, therefore, Bechet ironically undermines the form to which he apparently conforms.

From this point of view, the typical question posed of autobiographies—Did it really happen?—becomes more than just a question of the author's trustworthiness. As Heble convincingly argues, this kind of retelling of the self is drawn from a musical model of improvisation, and in practice serves to trouble the binary distinctions of mainstream culture. So, Billie Holiday's well-known *Lady Sings the Blues* may have "mixed large doses of fiction with a smattering of facts," but her willingness to move into a fictional mode of representation is precisely what lifts the text above an (accurate) collection of gossip: it provides the perfect counterpart to a novel like *Invisible Man*, showcasing how jazz artists translate the performative strategies of improvisation into literary techniques and forms, in contrast to literary authors adapting jazz imagery and structure. I agree with Heble's conclusion that this textual "improvisational dynamic works both to broaden the horizon of what gets represented and imagined in autobiography and to trouble the role that the very distinction between factual and invented worlds has played in terms of our understanding of the genre."[14]

One way in which such jazz-autobiographies resist, even subvert, literary conventions is by insisting on the specificity of jazz music as a form produced by individuals in particular places and in particular ways. Their frequent recourse to picaresque anecdotes (especially when exaggerated) is a way to emphasize the specific conditions out of which their music arose. In an insightful essay on the authority of jazz musicians, composer and pianist Vijay Iyer uses the autobiography of Horace Tapscott as an example of this tendency toward the particularities of place, noting the way he "speaks and acts from the vantage point of a socioculturally situated musician."[15] By focusing on the "rooted functionality" of his musical expression—tied to his own peculiar experiences, even developing in direct response to them— Tapscott's autobiography "'answers back' to the forces of globalization by insisting on the primacy of the local and the particular, the importance of being home." In this sense, such life writing might seem to align closely with literary representations of jazz—which consistently draw on the music as a marker of individuality, often taken to the point of solipsism or solitude. In contrast, however, many jazz autobiographies use such sociocultural positioning as a way of emphasizing the opposite: their place within a community. Tapscott thus treats "every achievement as a collaborative effort that was deeply situated in, contingent upon, and inextricable from its community setting," so that his personal, intellectual authority becomes a sign of his community's value as a whole.[16] Just as I have argued that Bechet uses autobiography to escape the external control of his narrative, so Iyer argues that the form offers artists a way to break out of the commodification of jazz—as opposed to "definitive" histories like the *Oxford Companion to Jazz,* which "treats jazz predominantly as a series of de-situated musical objects, commodified for consumption."

Indeed, it is precisely this tendency toward understanding jazz as commodity—the natural corollary to its cultural capital—that has meant critics have been reluctant to treat this genre seriously. As Daniel Stein points out, jazz autobiography "has generally been dismissed as the literarily insignificant, often ghost-written self-promotion of jazz celebrities trying to further their careers, or as memoirs of marginal figures seeking to cash in on the financial rewards offered by the market value of jazz."[17] By foregrounding the literary qualities of their own stories, however, jazz musicians have not only crafted a way to assert the legitimacy of their own, individual voice, but a way of critiquing the commodification of their music on a broad level.

There is, however, an obvious danger in too narrowly construing the value of literature for musicians. Instead, I want to open up an expansive inquiry into why musicians might turn to literary arts. After all, writers themselves turn to jazz in search of cultural capital, imaginary potential, structural models, even paradigms for composition. So surely literature represents a similar array of possibilities for jazz performers. In this sense, I draw inspiration from the expansive way that artists like Bechet, Holliday, Ellington, and Mingus have not only adopted but actively adapted the genre of life writing. Kathy Ogren notes that, in jazz musicians' autobiographies, "the participatory performance dynamics of jazz music" is "translated into the musicians' persona," suggesting at once a central element of much jazz writing—the desire to emulate the antiphonal dynamics of jazz—and a common motivation: to craft "self-fashioned personas" that sit alongside the musicians' identities as performers.[18]

While Ogren concedes that these "highly subjective accounts" tend to be "suspect as definitive versions of historical events," she argues that this does not detract from their value as "textual performance in which musicians, sometimes in concert with their amanuensis, create personas equally as fascinating as those developed musically."[19] Conceptualizing autobiographies as a different kind of performance helps draw attention to the way that these written texts draw on stock jazz gestures like quotation, which provide "the jazz artist with modes of expression that are otherwise blocked by forces based in race, class, and popular taste."[20] So literature is not only a chance to seize control of one's narrative as it is for Bechet—a chance to take charge of how one's own identity is mediated to others—but an opportunity to bridge the perceived gap between literary and musical expression. Where for authors, jazz is often attractive because of its opposition to writing, as an abstracted form of expression, for musicians, literature is attractive precisely because of its analogies with jazz.

Given this tendency toward an inter-artistic imagination of jazz, I want to give particular attention to the way that jazz musicians see themselves as molding narrative to jazz patterns. I am wary of simply reading loose analogies between literary structures and musical ones; instead, I want to focus on a distinct phenomenon: the claims that musicians themselves make toward blending jazz and fiction. In line with both Ogren and Stein, I see this as part of a larger performance of identity, where "the narrative strategies the musicians mobilize to fashion autobiographical selves ... echo the complexities and dynamics of jazz practices."[21] Indeed, as Stein argues convincingly, it is in their construction of an "autobiographical self" that is deliberately "unstable and shifting, improvised and performed," that musicians frame their texts as "musical improvisation ... translated into autobiographical narration through the invention of a self that cannot be pinned down and that is conjured as an element of an overall self-mythology." This broader comparison provides an important alternative to the way literary artists have tried to approximate jazz aesthetics in prose; musicians are less interested in comparing literary techniques to musical ones (although these musicians are often very well versed in these) than in a larger analogy between improvisation, identity, character, and performance.

UNDERDOGS BARKING UP MY MISTRESS'S SKIRTS: MINGUS, ELLINGTON, AND THE CHALLENGE TO EMPATHY

If jazz autobiographies are the site of contesting narratives about the meaning of jazz, then it should not be surprising that *Music Is My Mistress*—the autobiography of acclaimed jazz pianist, bandleader, and composer Duke Ellington—has itself been the focus of critical dissent. First published late in Ellington's career, in 1974, the book has been characterized as at once almost shamelessly personal—Ted Gioia describes it as an "elegant kiss-and-tell-little memoir"—and at the same time as lacking in any insight into Ellington's inner self, as a "book that mostly reflected his public diplomatic persona rather than any inner dialogue or insight."[22] It has come to be regarded as one of the definitive histories of the growth of jazz, playing a central role in not only the various biographies of Ellington, but many critical studies of the music, Gioia's monolithic *History of Jazz* included. But despite this near-ubiquity, it is often dismissed as crassly commercial, with critics including Gioia drawing attention to both its high commission and unhappy gestation, reflecting what Harvey Cohen calls Ellington's "distaste for books about himself."[23] Whatever financial incentives might have been involved, however, it is worth bearing in mind Ellington's own literary bent. A natural storyteller, Ellington was also a fierce public champion of jazz—and frequently turned to literary analogies to help explain and defend his music. While there is "no doubt Ellington viewed his own life in storybook terms," surprisingly little attention has been paid to the way Ellington also viewed *jazz* in literary terms—yet in inverting the usual recourse of writers to the abstract qualities of music, *Music Is My Mistress* disarmingly subverts conventional narratives about the meanings of jazz.[24]

That many readers should underappreciate the complexity of Ellington's work is not strange, given the composer's reputation as a charming producer of a popular form of music that was often seen as transcending the category of jazz altogether—particularly as the genre became more associated with technical complexity and intellectual difficulty. By contrast, Ellington's apparently "easy" works gave him a broad appeal that was recognized posthumously in a special Pulitzer Prize for music, with one British critic describing him as producing "the most distinguished popular music since Johann Strauss."²⁵ Indeed, in his introduction to the *Cambridge Companion to Duke Ellington* (the existence of the volume in itself a sign of Ellington's cultural capital), Edward Green makes the case that Ellington "was the most influential composer of the twentieth century—for jazz, with its various stylistic offspring, has had more impact worldwide than any other form of modern music. And Ellington is acknowledged almost universally as the greatest of all jazz composers."²⁶ Whatever we might think of Green's syllogistic case, it is clear that the stakes in Ellington's autobiography are high—not only for the meaning of Ellington himself, but for the broader meaning of jazz. This status is only exacerbated by his prominence as a "cultural ambassador" during the 1960s, where his global tours were co-opted by the U.S. State Department as an act of cultural propaganda that included a well-publicized tour of the U.S.S.R.²⁷ However secure Ellington's cultural significance may seem, however, the musician himself was well aware of both the specific critiques of his work and the more problematic status of jazz, first as a subversive, low-brow popular form, then as overly complex, highbrow art music.

Ellington's commitment to defending jazz is attested to by the wide range of articles and interviews he engaged in throughout his career—from his early prominence in 1930 right up until his death in 1974. More importantly, perhaps, Ellington conceptualized his own work as taking place across multiple media. Edwards points out that "black musicians," in which group he places Ellington, "so often insist on working in multiple media, not as autonomous areas of activity but in conjunction, insistently crossing circuits, rethinking and expanding the potential of each medium in the way it is like and unlike the other," suggesting that, in turn, critics need to "shift the fringe of contact between music and language."²⁸ I would not be the first to note the literary streak that runs through Ellington's music and writing alike; Laurie McManus is one of many to see "Ellington's eloquence and love for word play" (189), while Edwards points out that "Ellington based a number of his compositions on literary sources" (327).²⁹

Edwards, however, goes further, to argue that Ellington's criticism invokes literature as a model for jazz. Focusing on Ellington's 1931 essay "The Duke Steps Out," Edwards notes that, although Ellington initially seems to be "in keeping with an assumption that black music articulates a sense of the world that could not be expressed otherwise—that it 'speaks' what cannot be said openly," he shows that, as the essay progresses, "what we so often suppose to be the dynamics of influence between black music and literature is inverted—in Duke's view the achievements of the literary renaissance are a model for his own aspirations in music."[30] And Ellington's music bears out this comparison. Inverting the logic of his close contemporary Langston Hughes, who turned to jazz as a source of inspiration for both poetry and prose, Ellington's own compositions often attempted to tell "stories in ways that combined words and music," and indeed "almost all of the extended works were conceived with this kind of literary component, even though Ellington's attempts at mixing narrative with music were for the most part dismissed by critics."[31] This desire to bring a narrative quality to jazz derived in part from Ellington's awareness of the importance of jazz history—what Ryan Raul Bañagle calls "Ellington's compositional concern with historical narratives" (5).[32] But, as *Music Is My Mistress* shows, it is also intrinsically tied to Ellington's conceptualization of jazz itself—more, I feel, than either Bañagle or Edwards allow.

Admittedly, on the surface, Ellington's defenses of jazz do appear to focus on the music's popular appeal. Regularly invoking jazz as the musical spirit of the era, he echoed Fitzgerald in declaring that, as the defining feature of contemporary life in the 1930s, "jazz will have to be used to describe this, the jazz age."[33] As many commentators have observed, however, as much as Ellington valorized jazz, he also tried to move away from narrow definitions of his work, explaining that "I am not playing jazz. I am trying to play the natural feelings of a people."[34] Fundamentally, such claims simply reiterated his definition of jazz as "the kind of music that catches the rhythm of the way people feel and live today."[35] Such broad affective claims have a tendency to mask the more complex critical ambitions of his music. Explaining that the aim of his orchestra was "not so much to reproduce 'hot' or 'jazz' music as to describe emotions, moods and activities which have a wide range, leading from the very gay to the somber," Ellington at once linked his work to a literary mode of engagement—description—and complicated the romantic tendency to imagine jazz as a spontaneous outpouring of uncritical emotion.[36] Not only did Ellington recognize the way that music could arouse, even manipulate an audience (observing cannily that "music is the most vital thing in swaying the emotions of a multitude"), but he conceptualized jazz as a form of intellectual and emotional exchange that could be summarized as 'harmony.'[37]

For Ellington, harmony had a dual function. In the making of jazz, it could fuel creative production, and Ellington's frequent disavowals of talent—such as his explanation that "what little fame I have achieved is the result of my special orchestrations, and especially of the cooperation of the boys in the band"—were less a profession of modesty than an acknowledgment of the close connectedness that drove his creative process.[38] But harmony was also the ideal *effect* of jazz, and as such could act as a catalyst for social change. Ellington elliptically bridged the two meanings when he claimed that he naturally "had a kind of harmony within me, which is part of my race, but I needed the kind of harmony which has no race at all but is universal," signaling both his innate faculty for jazz, and the kind of music he aspired to make.[39]

One elaboration of this trope came in an unpublished article from late 1957, titled "The Race for Space," where he played with the various ways that harmony could be used as a metaphor for racial unity, by contrasting American racial inequality with Russian accomplishments in the space race. Although he is critical of Soviet "regimentation of thought," he admires the fact that it "doesn't permit race prejudice as we know it," so that the Russians could experience, "as in music, harmony—harmony of thought," which "must have prevailed in order for the scientists to make a moon that would work [*referring, here, to Sputnik 1*]. To attain harmony, the notes are blended in such a fashion that there is no room for discord."[40] Set against this ideal of musical fraternity, Ellington declares (surprisingly baldly) that "in America we simply don't have this all essential harmony."[41] From this perspective, his rather general observations about jazz as a cultural marker take on a more critical edge. For Ellington, jazz was not simply a popular form that can sway emotions, but a complex art form that requires intense interpersonal exchanges, and can in turn bring about larger social transformations.

/ / /

Of course, many readers will recognize the possible dangers inherent in Ellington's emphasis on "harmony." By skewing the racial divide in America toward a positive image of mutual conversation, it could be argued that Ellington was ignoring the basic disparity between white hegemony and centuries of black oppression. And indeed Heble notes that unlike other jazz autobiographies—say, that of Mingus or Holiday—Ellington actively "downplays or sidesteps issues of race throughout the text," going so far as to "frame his achievements precisely in the context of the dominant white social order."[42] In this sense, Ellington was by no means the first or last commentator to draw such optimistic, if not naive, parallels between social and musical harmony. But, as his focus on jazz as "description" suggests, what sets Ellington's theorization apart is the extent to which he draws on literary language to explain the social potential of jazz.

In contrast to the historical romanticization of jazz, reducing the music to pure emotion, Ellington saw jazz as "an expression of sentiment and ideas—modern ideas" and sought to shift the popular discourse around jazz toward ideas of communication and meaning, rather than sensation and feeling.[43] In part, he did so through familiar tropes, for instance framing musical improvisation as a discourse where musicians "argue back and forth with our instruments."[44] But in more distinctive terms, he tried to argue that "music for me is a language. It expresses more than just sound." It was not, as he sometimes suggested, simply an expression of people's emotions, but rather a form of language that relied on narrative structures—so his then-current project, "Boola," "tells the story of the Negro in America" (249). From this perspective, his interest in reincorporating the historical traces of jazz take on a distinctly literary light. He maintains that "the tragedy is that so few records have been kept of the Negro music of the past. It has to be pieced together so slowly. But it pleases me to have a chance to work at it." What he is describing sounds less like a form of musical composition than one of narrative history.[45] Long before he turned to a full-scale literary composition, then, Ellington was already fluently adapting narrative and linguistic ideas into his conceptualization—and promotion—of jazz.

From this point of view, it makes sense that Ellington spends so much of his book discussing other musicians. He is not simply paying lip service to friends, colleagues, and peers (as some more cynical commentators have suggested), but instead is emphasizing the extent to which an individual can be intimately connected to others—even, at times, constituted of them. The long sequences of character sketches thus form a series of orchestrated portraits that at once reflect his compositional practices as a musician and support his broader social aspirations: Ellington is drawing disparate individuals into a unified whole, implying that a coherent self is one that can recognize that multiple voices compose it, much as he admonished America to recognize the strength of its own multiracial makeup.

Drawing on his literary resources, Ellington reinforces this concept of identity through recurring images of communal life, governed by a semimystical sense of a shared life force, describing New York as "a dream of a song, a feeling of aliveness, a rush and flow of vitality that pulses like the giant heartbeat of all humanity" (65). In another sketch, he imagines "the city of jazz" where everyone "assume[s] that they know one another. For instance, when they meet for the first time they embrace warmly like old college chums" (129). This spirit of mutual support helps explain his desire to move beyond ideas of jazz as isolating and depressing. Discussing one of his sidemen, Juan Tizol, he notes that, whenever he "had some problems with myself, I'd go visit, and [Tizol and his wife] would feed me some of their good cooking and words of encouragement"; the mutual support intrinsic to jazz is incompatible with isolation, so Ellington "always left feeling better than when I went" (56). Returning to the autobiography's coda—"When I got to the next corner, there would be someone else standing there to tell me where to go. And this is how my whole life has been all along" (56)—Ellington reveals his peripatetic structure as the narrative counterpart to harmoniously orchestrated jazz.

Ellington's autobiography stands out not simply as an extended written text—by far the longest of Ellington's career—but for the way he self-consciously plays with literary tropes. The prologue is framed as a traditional fairy tale—"once upon a time a beautiful lady and a very handsome young man fell in love and go married" (x)—and throughout the book Ellington frequently returns to the flourishes of what Trevor Weston and Olly Wilson call an at once "insightful and fanciful narrative." In many ways, the text is formally experimental; the narrative prose is broken into eight "Acts" and is punctuated with rich—sometimes exaggerated—imagery, such as Ellington's evocation of night life: "Night Life is cut out of a very luxurious, royal-blue bolt of velvet. It sparkles with jewels, and it sparkles with tingling tones" (63). Although it begins with Ellington's conception, the book quickly subverts the standard chronological structure of a "life story," breaking into sections of extended character studies and brief portraits, switching to diary mode, and even transitioning into an extended interview with his own reflection. In part, these must be a product of Ellington's own fragmentary mode of composition. But the deft handling of different genres, and the stretches of engaging, even elegant, prose reveal not only Ellington's eloquence but his fluency with a wide range of literary works.

Music Is My Mistress certainly emphasizes the early importance of literature to Ellington; one of the most prominent routines of his early youth was the exchange of pulp western novels with his cousin, and Ellington lingers on the time spent in "isolation with the good and bad guys of those mighty Westerns" (16). There is also a distinct note of pride in his announcement that, "by the time I was eleven or twelve years old, I had read Sherlock Holmes, Cleek of Scotland Yard, and Arsène Lupin, and I knew all the literary burglar's theories as well as the murder devices" (16); despite veering into verse, and his obvious comfort with other genres, his early predilection for traditional narratives of growth and adventure helps explain his interest in episodes and personalities. Ellington reimagines his life as a kind of a picaresque-cum-bildungsroman, offering in his foreword what becomes a narrative refrain: "every time I reached a point where I needed direction, I ran into a friendly advisor who told me what and which way to go to get what or where I wanted to get or go or do" (x).

Even as Ellington is interested in personal growth, then, he also insistently frames it through his relationships with others, reflecting his obsession with harmony as a social principle. As he continues, "every intersection in the road of life is an opportunity to make a decision, and at some I had only to listen" (x). Both this focus on listening to others and acting in concert, and the very composite style of the book, structured around "vignettes and portraits," seem to affirm Ellington's distinctive model of jazz orchestration. Ellington was well known for hiring impressive sidemen with "distinct musical personality," and his compositions developed out of his understanding of their individual talent, creating "the precise musical framework to enhance and expand that personality by challenging the artist to explore new musical forms and contexts."[46] As Weston and Wilson note, although he "worked within the received framework of communal collaboration," Ellington "was a composer because his overall conception shaped the final result." On the surface, then, Ellington's polyphonic text could be read as the literary product of his sophisticated musical composition strategies drawing multiple distinctive voices together into a coherent overall piece. Of course, there is a question here to which readers repeatedly return—where, in all of this, is the "real" Ellington? Why, in a text ostensibly about the great composer, does he spend so much time hiding behind stories of others, or behind fictionalized versions of himself? Crucially, Ellington himself draws attention to the fissures between the stories—the points where they fail to adhere, describing it at one point as made up of "fragments" (345). As much as the disparate elements of the narrative appear to work together—as if Ellington were orchestrating many voices—it is my contention that Ellington's text also overtly points to its own lack of cohesion. Like Bechet or Holiday, Ellington deliberately undermines the conventions of the genre he is working within.

Not content to trouble the reader's identification of the subject in quite so subtle ways, Charles Mingus opens the first sentence of his autobiography, *Beneath the Underdog*, by declaring that, "in other words, I am three."[47] In this bold statement, he at once signals his debt to, and divergence from, his sometime-collaborator Ellington. As John Goodman observes, Mingus was certainly motivated to turn to writing after he learned that Ellington was working on an autobiography: "the fact that Duke, whom Mingus worshipped, had done his 'life in music' also must have influenced him."[48] Along with their professional experience working together, the two also shared a similar charisma and reputation for eloquence; Gene Santoro draws attention to Mingus's "charm, intelligence, humor, vulnerability, verbal dexterity, flashes of insight."[49] But where, at least on the surface, Duke imagined jazz as a process of defining the self through connections with others, Mingus saw it as a way of defining the self in *contrast* to others—or, as he baldly declares, "I'm talking about opposites" (294). On the one hand, this association is political and affirmative: jazz offers Mingus a way to take ownership of his identity by affirming his right to perform his life on his own explicitly narrative terms. But on the other hand, as Mingus is all too aware, seeing the world in opposites means foregrounding one's loneliness and isolation.

The link between narrative and loneliness in both Ellington's and Mingus's often problematic autobiographies can be found by focusing on this very literariness—one of many qualities that connect the two texts. To make this connection, I draw on the concept of "autofiction"—a French term that dates back to the 1970s work of Serge Doubrovsky, but which has enjoyed a new popularity in Anglophone criticism over the last five years in the wake of contemporary novelists' increased, overt application of biographical details to their erstwhile fiction. As Marjorie Worthington explains, while Gerard Genette defined the term, autofiction refers to "to a text in which the protagonist shares a name with the author, but the work itself is fictional"; today the term more broadly relates to a work that "masquerades as an autobiography or memoir but is actually a novel."[50] This might seem like an ill match for two texts that—however else they envisage themselves—never reach for the mantle of "novel." But Ajay Heble makes the keen observation that, in *Beneath the Underdog*, Mingus "registers a sophisticated self-consciousness around questions of literary self-invention" (105)—and that, in spite of his apparently straight tone, Ellington's subtle play with different images of the self "raise profound questions about the nature of identity formation."[51] So while the term, as strictly construed, might refer to overtly fictional works, theories of autofiction clearly provide a useful framework for thinking through the larger issues involved in the way fiction and truth are invoked when constructing a literary version of the author.

Here I find an ally in Nicholas Dames's recent account of autofiction for *The Atlantic*. Taking a latitudinal view of contemporary autofiction, he notes that the narrators of these texts "aren't characters embedded in fiction. They are voices that tease a reader into identifying the narrator with the author while casting doubt on that identification."[52] This is a particularly clarifying framework for reading Mingus's and Ellington's self-representation, particularly given that this kind of autofiction, as Dames argues, is characterized by its extreme focus on individualism. On its own, this may not sound like the most compelling case; after all, the short story's similar focus on individuals does not mean that the form is inherently concerned with loneliness. But as Dames shows, the way that writers stage the competing claims to truth and fiction in autofiction creates a block to empathy that spotlights, even exacerbates, loneliness in both the narrator and the reader.

Dames sets his reading of solitude against recent developments in neuroscience, which have affirmed the 1980s pragmatists' belief in the power of fiction to engender empathy. He cannily points to two alternative implications of this equation: If reading fiction helps breed empathy, then what happens in an age when novel reading is on the wane? And more importantly, what happens when writers shut down the reader's avenues for making empathetic connections? While the "most critically acclaimed and influential novels of recent years" may share "a ruminative first-person voice," this individualism tends to solipsism, "given to self-expression more than to distinct characterization." Such narrators have "little interest in becoming specialists in empathy," which Dames describes as an "odd stereopsis that allows us to stay rooted in ourselves while also registering the world through some other perspective." Clearly, with an obsessive focus on the self, these novels immediately shut out alternative perspectives. What makes this kind of writer different from, say, the selfish authors—the kind who point to the dangers or limits of empathy—is that their blending of fiction and autobiography creates a process that "estranges us from any conventional sense of intuitive insight into others."

What is the imaginative consequence of this kind of radical solitude? Dames argues that, by "explicitly . . . rejecting the goal of generating empathy," such texts not only create the opposite effect—an increased isolation—but actively generate a negative experience: a "spectacle of aloneness." While I do not believe Mingus and Ellington were writing solely (or even principally) to reject empathy and cultivate loneliness, I do think the mechanics Dames describes are totally apposite for these quasi-autobiographies. Just like contemporary writers of autofiction, in both *Music Is My Mistress* and *Beneath the Underdog* the authors use strategies to blur the line between fiction and autobiography, break down the possibility for empathy, and exacerbate the text's acts of performance—the staging of what Dames calls "the thrilling and dismaying isolation of the voices." Mingus's and Ellington's autobiographies call for connections—between the lonely individual and the other, whether soloist and band members, or musician and audience—but simultaneously cultivate a distance through blurring of real self and literary creation. Clearly this plays out in different ways across Mingus's and Ellington's work, but the two books are nonetheless connected by a "voice that distrusts, or disbelieves in, the possibility of communication."

The polarized reception of *Music Is My Mistress* suggests that the initial readers of Ellington's book recognized this failure to communicate—or, at least, struggled with the fragmentary structure. In particular, they found it hard to decide whether the book was another representation of Ellington's public persona—the performer, activist, and ambassador—whether it reflected something more intimate and private, or whether it was something in-between. Ironically, for all their ostensible indication of cohesion, Ellington's comments about harmony show that the elision of personal and critical was a deliberate strategy. From a musicological standpoint, critics have had no difficulty in identifying Ellington's interest in "opposites" that are brought "convincingly, beautifully together"; Green points to the confluence of "vibrant energy and deep thoughtfulness, passion, and control" in a typical Ellington composition, which "swings with intensity, yet also with natural ease."[53] Clearly, the same is true of his prose—quite aside from his more serious criticism on jazz, Ellington was "fond of provocative statements often couched in elliptical language, and over the course of his lifetime he offered an array of cryptic and sometimes seemingly contradictory statements on jazz and its meanings."[54] Even its emotional register charts a similar conjunction of extremes, so that even where it charts moments of deep sorrow and loneliness, Ellington almost perversely maintains that "the thing which ultimately matters most, is joy." Reflecting on this contradictory current throughout Ellington's writing, Green observes that "this joy is philosophic; it is present when the thing we yearn most to see, we do see: the profound friendship that is possible between ourselves and the outside world."[55] But as Dames's logic suggests, the dissonance between fictive and "real" selves in Ellington's work does not draw the reader closer, but in fact effects the opposite: it creates a distance between the reader and the text, drawing attention to Ellington's isolation among different images of himself.

Indeed, it is this self-reflective fragmentation that distinguishes *Music Is My Mistress* from Ellington's earlier writing and his focus in conversation and interviews. Here, rather than talking abstractly about the meaning of jazz, or making comments about its external effects, he hones in on the relationship between his music and his sense of self—that is, on what literary writers readily construct as a jazz identity. This is most obvious in the way he introduces himself into the narrative, through a dramatic entrance in the third person: "A grinning fellow enters. He bounces along, almost swaggering, apparently casual but trying to hide the stage fright he expects any minute. When he gets to the microphone, no matter what position it's in, he has to readjust it, or fidget with it, or fondle it" (3). Given this willingness to detach from the first person and present multiple, exteriorized versions of himself, it is no wonder that critics have found the book lacking in personal details; from the first pages of his first "Act," Ellington sets revealing details, like his underlying nervos and insecurities, in contrast to a charming, composed, and dapper exterior. Indeed, if we take up the premise of autofiction and consider jazz autobiographies as a medium for the writer to play with crafting different personae, Ellington is certainly not afraid of showing the artifice of his own stage presence, revealing the discordance between a "true" self and the performance.

The crucial implication of this play between surfaces is the reader's recognition that behind the performance—what might be seen as Ellington's superficial charm—is an isolated individual who suffers from loneliness. The multiplicity of selves—just like the positive image of harmony—is held in tension with a solitary figure cut off from others. At its most existential, this loneliness manifests in stage fright, which recurs, as often in his last tours as it does in his teenage job selling food at baseball games. What makes this loneliness at once more obvious and yet difficult to engage with directly is the layer of performativity that Ellington applies. Even in the face of a crushing disappointment—like the decision by the Pulitzer committee to reject a nomination that he receive a special prize in 1965—Ellington the public persona (here, crucially, also Ellington the literary character) apparently refuses to dwell in blue emotions. Because he was "not too chronically masochistic," he explained, he "found no pleasure in all the suffering that was being endured" (286). Instead, he returns frequently to his own pervasive optimism, aligning with the overwhelming focus in his critical writing on the importance of joy in the performance of jazz.

But this joy is not a spontaneous, *uncritical* overflowing of emotion; Ellington tempers his focus on optimism with an insistence on the need for self-reflection. He even goes so far as to say that "much of the adventure in one-nighters is in the anticipation of approaching confrontation with one's self," because when one is "face to face with one's self, or looking one's self in the eye, there is no cop-out.... So the question is, was, and always will be: have we been true to ourselves?" (298). Such a profoundly critical self-interrogation sits awkwardly against the expectations that literary authors made of the jazzman: typically, he symbolizes an abstract, inexpressible state of being—a pure connection between instinct and artistry that often stands in contrast to overt self-reflection. The way that Ellington constructs a manifold, plural identity within the narrative of *Music Is My Mistress*, then, at once highlights his awareness of his own isolation (even, as we have seen, to the point of loneliness) and an intrinsic multiplicity.

In particular, his epilogue, "The Mirrored Self," self-consciously maps out a series of multiple personae: imagining himself gazing into a pool of water, he catches sight of "the reflection of ourselves, just as we thought we looked" (451) The relief of self-recognition is punctuated by the awareness of permutations—"as we savor the wonderful selves-of-perfection we suddenly realize that just below our mirror, there is another reflection that is not quite so clear, and not quite as we expected"—which Ellington imagines as "our other selves." From one perspective, these levels of identity reflect the polyphonic structure of Ellington's book—and they might also recall his work as a composer bringing unity to multiple personalities, and his interest in recovering traces of African American musical history. But there is a tension between these multiple personae that fails to resolve. McManus rightly suggests that "Ellington's rhetoric of 'reflections' and 'parallels' indicates his own attempts to create a music that seemed to comment on, but not appropriate other musical identities."[56] In his autobiography, Ellington plays with multiple identities in precisely this way, imaging himself through a kind of composite identity, composed of "the thinker-writer, the okayer, the nixer, the player, the listener, the critic, the corrector" (451), where the different voices never fully cohere. It is in his turn toward the traditional realm of the literary, moreover—characterization, even to the extreme of caricature—that his work is paradoxically at its most avant-garde. Like contemporary autofiction, his work destabilizes the reader's ability to pinpoint a fixed identity. In other words, where most novelists and short-story writers value their version of a jazz identity for its connotations of individuality, Ellington valorizes it in precisely the opposite terms, mapping out a self that is plural and multivocal.

This constant flux of identity—a shifting between different voices and hiding behind other characters—is precisely what has frustrated so many critics of Ellington's work. To return to the problems readers have identified, it is clear the charges are all interrelated: Ellington's refusal to reveal candid details about his "true" self is linked to his unrelentingly positive description of others; both of these moves toward multiplicity contribute to the widely sounded claim that Ellington fails to critique the racial politics of the United States; in effect, he is refusing to offer a coherent argument, either about himself or his culture. Although many have read his "failings" in these areas—indeed, his very act of writing an autobiography—as an act of capitulation, giving in to white narratives of identity and culture formation that sideline the radical in both Ellington and jazz at large, it is clear that Ellington coordinates the fragments of this text so as to undermine the generic conventions of the autobiography, just as his refusal to reveal himself is a way of (perhaps subtly, but no less deliberately) contesting claims on his story and identity.

So we don't need to be anachronistic and try to argue that Ellington was consciously attempting autofiction *avant la lettre*; it is clear that he is still working within an autobiographical framework, but applying innovative strategies to critique both the form and its discourse. The framework of autofiction instead helps us bring the *effects* of these strategies into focus. In particular, the way that Ellington at once raises other perspectives and then limits them, in conjunction with his own divided reflections on himself, works to block the reader's channels to empathy, creating a loneliness whose intensity feels paradoxical, given Ellington's emphasis on harmony. It would be short-sighted to ignore the extent to which Ellington tries to parallel the dynamic of jazz and a larger social harmony. Moreover, he clearly turns to narrative techniques repeatedly, in composition and essay as much as autobiography. As he puts it in one of his hipper moments, in the world of jazz, "they communicate, dad. Do you get the message?" (130). For Ellington, jazz performance is intimately tied to the telling of stories, and to their active reception; the episodes he recounts in *Music Is My Mistress* seem to stage these reparative interactions in miniature, modeling the harmonizing effect of good jazz. But Ellington holds this communicative function in tension with an awareness of limitations—reflected in the fragmentary nature of the text. I don't think it is enough to say that this is simply a product of Ellington's piecemeal composition of the book—he spends too much time actively drawing attention to failures in cohesion.

Heble has suggested one other useful way to think about Ellington's strategies of deliberately discomforting the reader. He points to Ellington's frequent use of the term "dissonance" to describe the place of African Americans in U.S. culture—both part of, and at odds with the mainstream. In interviews and essays, Heble points out, this motif of dissonance works at once as "a representation of a deplorable condition and as a strikingly innovative and enduring response to that condition."[57] In the context of *Music Is My Mistress,* Ellington uses dissonance to disrupt the reader's expectations of a coherent self—critiquing both the process of homogenization and the very narrative form he is using. As a form of active resistance, such disruptions turn, to borrow Heble's phrase, "that space of dissonance into something profoundly empowering." This is why the presence of loneliness and its structural emphasis are so important in a text that otherwise seems so relentlessly positive: they further this critical destabilization by acting as another form of dissonance. This helps to explain why Ellington turns to a narrative mode of expression. The form of the autobiography—expanded with fictional riffs—affords him a space to map out not just a cohesive conversation between multiple voices, but also to show gaps and places where these identities fail to cohere. Affectively, he can place loneliness against harmony, without the two needing to be resolved; if anything, the insistent presence of loneliness is precisely the point.

Turning to *Beneath the Underdog*, the ripples of disquiet that we see in *Music Is My Mistress* are magnified to waves. Like Duke, Mingus relishes the opportunity to play with multiple versions of his self—but unlike Ellington, whose vision of jazz returns to the collaborative, Mingus's focus in *his* work is on his own incomparable talent. Even the scope of his original draft—famously more than three times its final, edited length of three hundred pages—speaks to the forcefulness and singularity of the bass player and bandleader's vision of himself. The dazzling introduction is framed as a set-piece dialogue between Mingus and a Jewish psychiatrist, which shows a more complex, deliberate construction of a multivalent identity than Ellington's image of a rippled reflection:

> One man stands forever in the middle, unconcerned, unmoved, watching, waiting to be allowed to express what he sees in the other two. The second man is like a frightened animal that attacks for fear of being attacked. Then there's an over-loving gentle person who lets people into the uttermost sacred temple of his being and he'll take insults and be trusting and sign contracts without reading them and get talked down to working cheap or for nothing, and when he realizes what's been done to him he feels like killing and destroying everything around him including himself for being so stupid. But he can't—he goes back inside himself. (1)

If Ellington dramatizes a multiplicity of self, then Mingus goes one better, to disorient the reader from the start. Perhaps even more distancing is his confident declaration on his three selves, when probed by his psychiatrist, that "they're *all* real." This contrasts strikingly with Ellington's own uncertainty as to whether any of his rippled images are substantial, and where Ellington's self-image is projected outward (just as his narrative focuses on his connections outside himself to an external community) from the start, Mingus's gaze is directed inward. His ability to step outside himself and deconstruct his identity into three different characters suggests not only his facility for fiction, but also his wider motivation for turning to literature. Rather than following Ellington's ongoing contrast between social coherence and individual dissonance, Mingus uses the autobiography as a place to explore his solitude—not just what it is that makes him unique, but what it is that cuts him off from others.

This initial set-piece dialogue (to which Mingus returns repeatedly) thus signals the general movement of the book, which turns from apparent extroversion to a surprisingly sensitive interiority. Indeed, at first glance it seems strange to see the notoriously fiery Mingus so willing to show weakness and internal conflict; on only the second page the psychiatrist remarks, "you're crying again" (2). But this readiness to show emotion is a deliberate strategy on the author's part—a way for Mingus to signal that he is not interested in defining himself for others, but for himself. To borrow Dames's terms, it is not to solicit empathy that Mingus reflects an image of himself in tears, but in fact to block it. After all, as he asks his psychiatrist in one of many moments he appears to be addressing the reader, "what do I care what the world sees, I'm only trying to find out how I should feel about myself." Such disregard for the opinion of others is grounded in a sense of confrontation—for Mingus believes "they're all against me"—which helps explain his determined self-exploration: he is using narrative as a way to construct an alternative image of himself that can stand in opposition to attempts by others to shape or co-opt his image. A direct response to the commodification of his persona by the jazz industry, *Beneath the Underdog* seeks insistently to craft a counter-narrative through which Mingus can assert control over his own story.

What stands out most about this process of self-realization is how deliberately, sometimes disarmingly, literary it is. In his introduction to a 1995 edition of *Beneath the Underdog*, music writer Richard Williams describes it as closer to Ondaatje's *Coming Through Slaughter* than to traditional autobiographies, pointing to the "literary method" that underpins his "riveting work of highly subjective reminiscence and tortured self-analysis."[58] Certainly, like Bolden in Ondaatje's novel, Mingus displays a clear predilection for fantasy and invention, fictionalizing and exaggerating many of the episodes in his life. Gene Santoro, in his astute biography, begins by addressing this propensity for self-fashioned mythology, noting that "the stories I knew, the tales widely retold around the jazz world about this Gargantuan character were often myths. Sometimes they distorted facts; sometimes they were just made up. Even the true tales, I saw, offered only glimpses of the man's apparently hydra-headed personality."[59] Krin Gabbard's *Better Git It in Your Soul* painstakingly unravels the fabrication from the facts of Mingus's life, but I am less interested here in how truthful Mingus's writing is, and more in the mere fact of fictionalization. It is not just a sign of Mingus's literary bent—or what is sometimes dismissively seen as his own sense of self-importance. Instead, it is a central strategy for at once asserting agency over his image and destabilizing his reader, blocking a clear connection between audience and subject. Fiction is a way for him to regain authority over his own story, contesting the very "factual" basis on which others seeking to limit him, and contesting the conventions of the genre of autobiography. Even the psychiatrist's question as to which self is "real" shows Mingus's keen awareness of the ways in which others try to limit his identity to a single story.

From this perspective, Williams's one major misstep in his foreword is his attempt—like several readers of Mingus's autobiography—to try to read a universalizing theme onto a self-consciously singular narrative. Although he draws attention to Mingus's fierce individualism, declaring that "never was there music in which violence and tenderness were so thoroughly entwined as that of Charles Mingus," he also contends that it is this complexity that makes the book's message universal, in that it can "speak" or "reflect" the "complexities and contradiction of mankind."[60] Even when he does privilege the individuality that Mingus carefully crafts, he wants to expand that out to the general, arguing that *Beneath the Underdog* is "the startlingly bold expression of an identity crisis that extends far beyond the individual."[61] Williams's claims seem to match up much more closely to Ellington's image of the self-as-network in his autobiography, where a multiple or divided self is at times connected to social connections and integration into a community. For Mingus, representing the self in multiple is much more overtly a strategy for resisting any such universalization—for spotlighting his own intrinsic individuality.

Part of the way that Mingus aligns jazz expression with literary form, then, is through the emphasis on exaggeration and fantasy that so many readers have noted. From the start Mingus foregrounds this aspect of his autobiography, remarking (in the voice of the psychiatrist) that "there's a lot of fabrication and fantasy in what you say," before conceding that "I did exaggerate some things" (2). As Stein points out, this "selfconsciously violates conventions of autobiography" by calling into question the truth of the narrative—but by drawing attention to this violation, Mingus signals his liberation from commodification by others.[62] Fiction offers a path to resisting the limitation inherent in historical fact, corresponding to the jazz musician's freedom to improvise and invent. Indeed, Goodman sees Mingus's narrative and musical patterns as direct parallels, observing "how Mingus's mind worked" through a process where "one subject flowed into another without much prompting or direct questioning from me, how one association led to another. 'Spontaneous composition' is what he called it in music."[63] As Daniel Stein points out, Mingus draws attention to this parallel himself, telling the reader that, "for the jazz musician/composer, the imagination is an integral part of the autobiographical performance. Questions of narrative composition and literary voice thus lurk behind Mingus's autobiography, as they do over (jazz) autobiography in general."[64] Stein's observation is echoed by Santoro, who also argues that Mingus "had learned the hard-earned value of biography from jazz"; both point to his affirmation of individualism across both musical and literary performances, so that his creative reworking of the autobiographical genre corresponds to the way "the best jazz musicians dedicate themselves to finding their individual musical voices—who they are on their instruments—and to pushing the envelope of technique and conception, rewriting the rules."[65]

While these moments of invention and exaggeration might point to how Mingus elides musical and literary techniques, at the same time they also indicate what it is about a literary mode that drew Mingus to write *Beneath the Underdog*. In fact, invention and exaggeration are just two of a number of deliberate strategies that Mingus deploys to encourage his reader to view the text on literary rather than musical terms; in the same way, music is not transcribed through lyrics or snatches of scores as in Ellington's work, but is instead "represented by ellipses," forcing the reader "to pay attention to the *literary* vision dramatized by the autobiography."[66] Even his opening image of a trifurcated self signals a shift away from the polyphonic coordination that characterized Mingus's bandleading. Novelist Geoffrey Woolf argues that the book "is directed by three narrative conceits: by the conventional first-person voice of autobiography; by the third-person voice of a disengaged Charles Mingus judging the hazardous progress of his alter ego; by a patient's confessions to his analyst"; by splitting the self into such distinctive personae, he already breaks away from the coherent model of jazz he describes within the book.[67] It is in this sense that "the book is meant to be read as a calculated composition and as an ongoing act of therapeutic self-investigation" rather than an affirmation of jazz as a model for identity.

For a book that so brilliantly stages the performance of individuality, therefore, *Beneath the Underdog* actually raises serious questions about the kind of fixed, stable identity that underpins the genre of autobiography. In the same way, Mingus writes about jazz in order to critique some of its guiding aesthetic principles. Writing a letter to a friend, jazz critic Nat Hentoff, Mingus describes a moment of profound disquiet with his genre and his larger mode of being, prompted by hearing a Bartok quartet perform on the radio. In his letter, he points out that "their names were not announced," and instead the musicians were "just 'the Juilliard Quartet,'" before affirming that "that's the way it should be" (280). This comes as a surprise, given his emphasis on individuality and interiorization throughout the autobiography, but for Mingus, it is precisely because they are so good—in fact, "close to perfection"—that their individuality should be ignored. "Their names are unimportant," he contends, because they are devoted to producing transformative music, and describes with envy the effect of such egoless music: "they have the ability to transform in a second a listener's soul and make it throb with love and beauty." Mingus ascribes this transcendence to the quartet's suppression of self, whereby they only focus on "following the scratches of a pen on a scroll." By contrast, jazz is too solipsistic to achieve this kind of perfection, as it has "too many strangling qualities for a composer." As it turns out, then, Mingus is drawn to writing as a way of escaping what he sees as a constraining egotism in jazz discourse. Even as he draws parallels between writing the self and performing jazz in order to validate individualism, Mingus also inverts this logic, calling jazz into question as a way of interrogating the larger idea of independence and authority.

Although he admits that he is "a good composer with great possibilities," listening to the anonymous quartet he becomes painfully aware of his own limitations and starts to feel that the acclaim he has experienced "wasn't really success." I don't want to suggest that Mingus's book wholeheartedly rejects jazz; in fact, in its moments of joy, the book clearly affirms jazz as an individualistic model of music. Mingus's fierce exploration of his own singularity can be seen as an immanent coming-into-being that mirrors the logic of jazz performance and is clearly tied to his understanding of a jazz identity. But ultimately, *Beneath the Underdog* critiques this kind of constricted self-obsession, chafing at the limitations of a solipsistic mode. There is surely something genuine in Mingus's plea "to be the nameless member of a quartet like I heard today!" (281); given how closely he connects jazz to a combination of ego and solitude, it is only natural he should feel that, if he wants to achieve that kind of state, he would "have to leave jazz." This is why I think it is so important to read both Ellington's and Mingus's autobiographies within the framework of loneliness—not only because they focus on singularity (after all, isn't any act of writing to some extent a solitary one?) but because they are structured to highlight loneliness and cultivate a dissonant distance between reader and subject.

As much as he draws parallels between narrative and jazz performance, then, Mingus also deliberately turns to fiction as an *alternative* to jazz. His confession that writing his life has become his driving goal—he described "writ[ing] it down" as "my orders from the Man" (303)—already contrasts with his disavowal of jazz. And by looking for what fiction offers him that music lacks, his tendency toward exaggeration takes on a different function: it is part of a calculated response to the isolation he experiences in the world of jazz. Nowhere is his predilection for fabrication more obvious than in the intermittent chronicles of his sexual exploits; *Beneath the Underdog* has been routinely criticized for its attention to sex, which is often described in such visceral detail as to put some readers off the book. But within the book, Mingus explains quite directly why his prodigious sex life gets such embroidered attention: "the truth is, doctor, I'm insecure and I'm black and I'm scared to death of poverty and especially poverty alone. I'm helpless without a woman" (282).

His inflation of his own affairs and abortive career as a pimp thus serves two purposes. In part, these embellishments help him affirm his individuality, wresting control of his identity away from those who would try to commodify and limit him. But at the same time, they are a response to the loneliness he experiences as an extremely isolated individual; fiction offers him a way to give voice to these negative experiences. In other parts of the work, he imagines the loneliness of the jazz world in particularly claustrophobic terms, such as the account of his treatment in the psychiatric ward of Bellevue Hospital, where he is completely crippled by his sense of being on his own—to the point that he doesn't even feel anger, because "anger is an emotion that has some hope in it" (273). Confined and isolated, Mingus "felt hopeless" (273–74), and echoing his experience of listening to the Juilliard Quartet, he associates this hopeless isolation with jazz, protesting "I *am* mentally disturbed. I'm a musician, I need help" (273). Writers routinely turn to jazz as a way of breaking free from loneliness—the solo validates the musician's individuality; the antiphonic call-and-response of jazz allows individuals to share their loneliness, mapping out the writer's own address. For Mingus, who is motivated to tell his story because of precisely the same kind of loneliness, fiction is a way of expressing something that his musical medium precludes or prohibits. Like Ellington, Mingus foregrounds the very act of performance in his autobiography not to hide his loneliness but to accentuate it.

This use of fiction to interrogate the isolation of jazz is particularly affecting in Mingus's description of the prejudice he experienced traveling "through the South as a member of an otherwise all-white trio"—especially given "in addition to that you've got a white girl travelling with you" (265). In spite of the racism he encounters, he does not respond with violence or anger (as the caricature of Mingus as *The Angry Man of Jazz* would suppose) but instead with obvious, if performative, loneliness and isolation, where even the bouncer "doesn't say anything but you know what he's thinking and he wants you to know." He unashamedly confesses that "it feels very dangerous" and tries to communicate the harrowing, isolating experience of standing out as the only black member of the band: "thank God nobody says anything, they just *look* at you funny." Unlike a story such as Baldwin's "Sonny's Blues," musical performance does not provide any relief here—it only alienates him further.

Even when Mingus seems to be on a high, this is short-lived. At one point he asks the reader directly, "how does it feel when the Redhead's trio is asked to do an important, special television show in *color*?" answering that "it feels great" (266), but then he abruptly discovers he has been replaced with a white bassist. Tellingly, his greatest frustration is not simply that he has been forced out of the trio, but that the others won't communicate with him—after all, "how can you play with guys you can't talk to" (267). It is worth unpacking the effect of this apostrophe. Like much of the book, he stages this chapter as a conversation, using the repeated refrain of "How does it feel?" (with little variations: "How do you do it?" and "What do you say?") to invite the reader to step into his experiences. Writing allows him to convey his feelings in a concrete way that the abstraction of instrumental jazz simply does not allow. In the same way, Mingus uses second-person pronouns to describe himself, encouraging the reader to look at the experiences from his point of view: telling the reader "so now you've got a job again, boy, in a trio, boy," places them directly into his scenario.

Mingus at once builds empathy with the reader by creating a point of identification, inviting the reader to step inside the scenario, into his shoes. But he also cuts off connection with others—at once accentuating the sense of loneliness that readers experience and implicating them within his critique of jazz. As part of the short-circuited conversation, the reader becomes culpable in the loneliness that Mingus suffers. This also contributes to a larger disavowal of the self that depersonalizes the narrative, subverting the individualism intrinsic to autobiography. While the book naturally appears to be about Mingus, it is routinely narrated in second or third person, moving the narrative away from a fixed conversation, into a shifting, dislocating performance that dislocates the reader attempting to get a fix on the "real" Mingus.

While it is easy to trace the network of musical influences between Mingus and Ellington—their shared aesthetics are evident, along with their musical divergences, in their 1962 album *Money Jungle*—it is less straightforward to untangle their relationship as writers. Heble has done important groundwork here, particularly in theorizing their shared turn toward fiction and invention as a form of improvisation. But what strikes me as more important is how both *use* this improvisation. Although there are certainly differences in the underlying "why," both clearly turn to fictionalization, or literary improvisation to adapt Heble's conceit, to achieve the same effect: in order to create multiple images of the self. Mingus's claim to be three matches up exactly to Ellington's fragmentation in front of the mirror. For critics, this has tended to be seen as a flaw in Ellington's work precisely where it has been seen as a strength in Mingus's. To my mind, it is central not only to the way they map out their individual identities across multiple spaces and differing kinds of performance, but also to the reason that both turn to written narrative.

To anyone accustomed to the conventions of autobiography, both musicians' deliberate destabilization of their textual identity seems a clear contravention of the conventions of the genre. For many readers, this was further underscored by Ellington's refusal to reveal personal details, contributing to a broader sense that the elder statesman had failed to deliver what they expected from *Music Is My Mistress*. As current research on autofiction shows, however, this refusal to cultivate an expected singular persona is a strategy *designed* to create distance between the reader and the text. By denying the audience an empathetic connection, the writer underscores their isolation both from the reader and from those around them. As a literary critic, so used to seeing jazz co-opted by writers to help map out pathways that bridge loneliness and build connections, one is fascinated to see the way Ellington and Mingus not only cultivate a distance from their reader, but do so in order to build critiques of jazz itself. They may diverge significantly here—for Ellington, it is the narratives of harmony that he ironically counterpoints with an emphasis on dissonance, while for Mingus it is the culture of ego and failure to converse—but, regardless of their focus, both draw on loneliness as both subject and structural technique to change the way the reader engages with their work and with the larger world of jazz.

EPILOGUE

So What?

While jazz has fueled swathes of writers, providing them with everything from characters, locations, and set pieces to structures, strategies for composition, and cultural capital, literature has also spoken to jazz. It has been the inspiration for innovative compositions, has suggested to musicians new structures for imagining their own performance (particularly the way they interact with one another), and has even offered them an alternative medium for "saying something" in the form of the autobiography. In teasing out this inter-artistic conversation, I have not simply summoned loneliness out of some trite association with the blue moods of jazz, or the hackneyed image of a solitary figure accompanied by muted saxophone. Loneliness is at the heart of the exchange between writers and jazz musicians: each turns to the other's form to help make sense of individuality, isolation, and connection with others. But to channel Miles Davis: So what? How do these exchanges actually change the meaning of loneliness, for writer or reader?

I want to consider how jazz works not simply as a cultural resource, but as a literary technique for writers to at once expand and complicate narratives of loneliness. I have tried to emphasize the extent to which loneliness itself is a narrative condition. Morrison and Smith have explained that "humans are inherently social beings who possess a fundamental need to belong, and when they fail to satisfy this need, loneliness occurs."[1] As they imply, this failure to meet expectations is part of a process of self-narration, so that "in explaining the causes, lonely people are likely to blame themselves and view the social situations as being beyond their control, in a kind of learned helplessness." Cacioppo, Fowler, and Christakis's research has shown the practical consequence of this narrativity: "perceived social isolation," or in other words, an individual's own narrative of loneliness, is "in normal samples... a more important predictor of a variety of adverse health outcomes than is objective social isolation."[2] From this perspective, loneliness can be understood as both the product of narratives, and something that can be *solved* by narratives of connection—as Stein and Tuval-Mashiach rightly point out: because loneliness "is always isolation from something or someone," the very idea of loneliness can "only be understood in a relational context."[3]

When engaging with loneliness, writers have used jazz not just as a subject matter or a theme but as a formal aesthetic. There is a myriad array of styles of jazz to which writers have turned—from the early New Orleans jazz in *Coming Through Slaughter*, to the boogie-woogie in *Hiroshima Bugi*, to the bebop that suffuses *But Beautiful*, to the free jazz listened to by Haruki Murakami's protagonists. But throughout these various modes, jazz is repeatedly employed to structure identity formation and interpersonal relationships. To be more specific, jazz offers characters ways to make connections—whether with other musicians or with their audience. In turn, it models narratives of connection for the reader. But, from the beginnings of jazz fiction, with Langston Hughes's seminal "The Blues I'm Playing," writers have also used jazz to show failures to connect; many of the works considered here use jazz to foreground isolation and exacerbate their protagonist's sense of loneliness. This exacerbated isolation is connected to the broader social status of jazz as a form of counter-narrative. A genre of music that developed amongst outgroups marginalized by mainstream U.S. society, jazz also, structurally, opposed the conventions of western music. By drawing on jazz to emphasize loneliness, writers like Morrison, Ondaatje, and Vizenor critique the social systems that engender loneliness so that jazz becomes an insurrectionary narrative technique.

I want to return to the musician with whom I began—Ornette Coleman—and his theory of jazz improvisation, which he termed "harmolodics." Many musicians and listeners have expressed skepticism about Coleman's theory, and it is easy to see why. Although he often promised a book that would explain this hybrid principal of group performance, it never eventuated; following his death in 2015, critics were left with only some of his gnomic utterances through which to sift. Since I first came across interviews with Coleman in which he described this concept, however, I have been convinced of its usefulness—not necessarily as a complete model for cooperative musical production, but instead as a kind of literary technique. Coleman himself spoke eloquently about language and the relationship between sign and meaning (as witnessed in his detailed conversation with Derrida), and his concept is more clearly grounded in literary structures than in strictly musical ones. So we can use Coleman's system of harmolodics to define the way that writers of fiction and autobiography use jazz to engage with loneliness—more particularly, to show how they coordinate individuality and collectivity, or, in other words, how they deal with loneliness and group belonging.

I am not the first to notice the literary bent of Coleman's harmolodics. While, unlike Charlie Parker, he may not have yet inspired a story like Cortázar's "The Pursuer," his elusive concept looms large over many late-twentieth-century jazz novels. To read alongside, say, Murakami's references to Coleman, Natalie Diebschlag points to the compelling example of *Coming Through Slaughter*, where one character observes that listening to Buddy Bolden was "like talking to Coleman. You were both changing direction with every sentence, sometimes in the middle, using each other as a springboard through the dark" (37). Diebschlag notes that, although the reference to Coleman here could be read as an accurate reference to one of Bolden's contemporaries, it also works as an anachronistic allusion to *Ornette*, "whose musical philosophy of harmolodics has had a considerable impact on what Ondaatje likes to call the architecture of his writings."[4] Diebschlag is exactly right to point to harmolodics as a coordinating structure that helps make sense of the tension built into a novel like Ondaatje's. Describing Coleman's as "the first truly original concept of saxophone playing since Charlie Parker," A. B. Spellman points to harmolodics as "a musical syntax which, though necessarily derived from Charlie Parker, was a copy of no one, and was in fact a kind of syntax that others must eventually copy."[5] A portmanteau word that bridged harmony, movement, and melody, harmolodics constituted a conceptual framework for bringing individual musical voices together in a coordinated whole.

To some listeners, this claim might be confronting; Coleman's music is famously divisive, with Miles Davis once expressing his disdain by claiming Coleman must be "all screwed up inside." Beginning with 1959's *The Shape of Jazz to Come*, Coleman's albums did emphasize individual improvisation to a new degree, with Coleman encouraging his band members toward increasingly unconventional performances that were often labeled discordant. Coleman himself argued that individuality ought to be seen as the mandate of the jazz musician; the genre was the "superior music as far as individual expression is concerned."[6] But where many critics misunderstood his concept of "free jazz" (taken from the title of a 1961 album) to be merely a license for cacophony, the subtitle of his album ("A Collective Improvisation") makes it clear that, as much as Coleman was advocating for individual freedom of expression, he was also deeply concerned with developing a model where individual improvisations could come together in productive, connected ways. At its heart, Coleman's philosophy was grounded in a difference in attitude: where most players were concerned with their own prowess, Coleman wanted them to play in such a way that contributed to a larger aesthetic totality. As he put it:

> what I have always wanted my bands to do is to have every man try to express *anything*, but yet at the same time show the thing that is allowing us to make music together, which has something to do with the person seeing in his mind the difference between making music total together or trying to make someone sound good. I don't like to do something just to make someone sound good because it's giving a false image of you. I like to let the total thing make the music.... As long as they don't do anything to make me sound good but they get with the music, then that's beautiful.[7]

Of course, Coleman's abstract language was not always helpful for band members inured to more technical musical instruction; his difficulty working with the New York Philharmonic attests to the frustration felt by both parties when other musicians failed to grasp his concept of harmolodics. But from a literary perspective, his idea of a totalizing system that recognizes individuality makes sense: it asks musicians to hear and reply to each other's underlying patterns—to respond with an individual voice that shares a common vision, but is defined by boundaries between the individuals. Ajay Heble points to this as the signal difference between Coleman's music and that of his predecessors: his "explicit articulation of conflict as a principle of organization (dissonance, fissure, and a consistently changing rhythm)" contrasted with the dominant expectations of closure and harmony.[8]

Coleman himself frequently invited comparisons between musical harmolodics and literary coherence, declaring his system to be "a concept of sound and feeling that a person can adapt ... the same way that an alphabet can make understandable words, then phrases, then complete sentences." This structure accounts well for the relationship between, say, Sonny and his band in Baldwin's "Sonny's Blues": each band member contributes to a larger, organic narrative, even as that narrative gains its affective power because of the clarity and distinctiveness of individual musical voices. But perhaps more importantly, harmolodics is a structure built around failures to cohere. Heble has gone so far as to argue that the musical development of free jazz improvisation (guided by Coleman's harmolodics) offers a parallel to the literary movement toward semiotics and the suspicion of fixed meaning. Looking at Coleman's album *Free Jazz* (1961), Heble suggests that here "music has shifted from language as perlocutionary utterance to language as a system of signs. The step into atonality is a revolt against stable meanings."[9] Literary harmolodics does not entail a complete rejection of meaning, however, and instead of a "breakdown of all possible communication," we should see harmolodics as a technique for celebrating "multiplicity."

We can think of novels like *Jazz, Coming Through Slaughter, But Beautiful,* and even *Invisible Man* as harmolodic not because they have deliberately drawn on Coleman's theory in writing their novel, but instead because harmolodics models the narrative structures through which these texts hold loneliness in tension with a movement toward conversation and community. In other words, harmolodics accounts for the formal role of jazz in bringing individuality together in a single system without condensing it down to either a totally fragmented loneliness or an oppressive collectivity. Edwards has very sensitively noted that "writings about jazz as cultural phenomena" tend to "open up valuable questions about the complex ways in which identities are constructed and mobilized, and taken up in practices of representation."[10] There are key differences in the different kind of jazz identities that each text models for its characters, often tied to the particular genre of music around which the story revolves. What unifies these texts is the way they insistently valorize loneliness even as they map out new paths for communication.

The very literariness of this structure is, ironically, most evident in the texts that at first glance seem the least likely: the autobiographies of Charles Mingus and Duke Ellington. On the one hand, both writers challenge the generic conventions of life writing by denying their own singularity and instead imagining their own identities as plural and shifting. This reflects not only their resistance to the white narratives that limit the meaning of their music or commodify their image, but also signals their own discomfort with the discourse of jazz itself. In *Beneath the Underdog,* for instance, Mingus moves away from the egotism he sees in jazz through performing an exaggerated, fictionalized version of self and, in the process, breaks down this "self" into multiples. From his declaration that "I am three" onwards, it is actually quite clear that Mingus's jazz is less about singularity than complementary parts. Not only do both musicians represent themselves as composed of multiple selves, they are also keen to stress that these identities are constantly in flux. One only has to think of Ellington's image of the shifting mirror-selves, each different and impermanent, to see how much both autobiographies revolve around the performance of identity, where identity is itself shaped by the act of performing. In this sense, literary writers who turn to jazz as a way of representing loneliness are not simply appropriating the music as a symbol for individuality, but are using jazz to help define a more nuanced model of identity.

What distinguishes their autobiographies as harmolodic, however, is that this multiplicity works together—is, in fact, reliant upon—an intense focus on loneliness. Here I am not simply talking about being an individual, but about the experience of being cut off from others, and feeling this lack of connection as negative affect. As subject matter, this is more obvious in Mingus's work, where he freely, even confrontationally, represents his own painful experiences of alienation. In Ellington's work, this is more subtle, and it is here that it is worth remembering that harmolodics constitutes a formal structure: Ellington sequences his text as fragments, which revolve around surface impressions of others that at once fail to reveal Ellington's deeper feelings and fail to structurally cohere with his own descriptions of himself. The shifting focus of the work, while showcasing multiplicity, also heightens the work's loneliness. This is even more obvious from the perspective of reader response, where both works cue the reader to expect a confessional narrative that opens access for empathy and shows a coherent image of the author-subject. Both Ellington and Mingus subvert this expectation, frustrating the reader's ability to connect with the subject and, in the process, amplifying the alienation they each describe. In Mingus's case, such structural resistance works to negate external control of his identity, turning loneliness into a position of strength. This is what makes loneliness so peculiar within a harmolodic narrative: even as it is shown to be a painful, isolating experience, loneliness is valorized as a mode of being.

A NEW NARRATIVE

But how does such a philosophy help readers? One way to answer this question might be to turn to neuroscience and psychology. While it is a long-standing truism that music soothes the soul, a number of recent studies have more comprehensively investigated the reasons for music's ability to console. Most point to the affective capabilities of music, which help assuage feelings of loneliness by uplifting emotions. As Jenny Groarke and Michael Hogan point out, for most adults, music plays a significant role "in promoting quality of life and managing psychological distress."[11] Several of these studies suggest that jazz has a unique role in relieving negative emotions, offering a source of consolation for the very reason that listeners imagine it to be a "sad" form of music. Annemieke J. M. Van den Tol and Jane Edwards accept that "choosing to listen to self-identified sad music after experiencing negative psychological circumstances seems paradoxical given the commonly-held view that people are motivated to seek a positive affective state when distressed," but they explain that sad music is a major source of mood enhancement because it is associated with "memory triggers" and "high aesthetic value."[12] In other words, even though the music itself provokes emotional responses, its ability to do so is not purely affective, but also rational—our response depends on the wider discourse around particular genres and forms. This suggests not only that literature can change the way we hear jazz and find consolation in it, but that literature itself might provide a form of consolation by changing how we see our emotions.

Certainly, the growing body of research into the neurological phenomenology of reading suggests that literature may affect our emotions in ways similar to powerful music, but what stands out more (in a study of the relationship between literature and jazz) is the way that literature can change the *narrative* around loneliness. Many writers turn to music because they perceive it to be purely abstract—an unarticulated alternative to the concrete, always-articulated specificity of language. But it is because of their awareness of the very narrative conditions of their form of expression that such writers *try* to articulate a musical experience: they are using jazz not just to move people with beauty, but to change how people conceptualize, and thus experience, loneliness. The otherwise disparate images of jazz in fiction are unified by a consistent attempt to engage the reader in a conversation about what it means to be alone; they all draw on jazz as a strategy for re-narrativizing experiences of isolation. In fact, jazz fiction seems to do this more self-consciously than any other genres of writing because it so often breaks out of the usual distinction between reader and fictional world, addressing readers directly and trying to engage them in a conversation.

In turn, jazz is important to so many writers because of its paradoxical ability to turn a negative affective and cognitive state, that of loneliness, into a position of strength and integrity. In particular, the improvisational soloist offers a powerful model for reconfiguring loneliness as an affirmative singularity—and it is telling that so many literary solo-sessions not only spotlight the performer, fading out any supporting instrumentalists, but evoke loneliness in the music itself. From one perspective, jazz autobiographies problematize this neat symbolism; Mingus and Ellington in particular question the universalizing tendencies of writers who seek to use the soloist as a hollowed-out image—and instead try to reinvest jazz narratives with a commitment to specific, personal experiences. Both writers focus in detail on the peculiarity of their own experiences, turning to a picaresque, episode-based structure, and often amplify or exaggerate parts of their lives in order to underline their own idiosyncrasy, reclaiming their lives from blanket observations about the role or meaning of jazz. But as much as their narratives are motivated by a desire to provide a counter-narrative to conventional discourse on jazz and jazz identities, by deploying this kind of literary improvisation, Mingus and Ellington also turn the act of writing *with* jazz into an affirmation of the individual.

I don't want to imply, however, that their texts work counter to the logic of harmolodic fiction. Both texts mirror themes from Cortázar's "The Pursuer": their narratives critique attempts by critics and writers to treat jazz musicians as concepts, not individuals. In doing so, they reinforce the idea that jazz is a field defined by individualism, where idiosyncrasies and quirks can be seen as part of a larger, multifaceted identity. Ben Schnare, Peter MacIntyre, and Jesslyn Doucette have developed the idea of "the individual's concept of his or her musical self"—a psychological model that "summarizes and integrates the various elements of emotional and motivational regulation into a coherent whole."[13] Jazz autobiographies offer a modified version of this "musical self" to readers as a model for imagining their own identities, by placing loneliness as one state in parallel to other ways of being. As part of this kind of multiple identity, loneliness can be a means of insisting on your own peculiarity and resisting attempts to blur away your singularity. Like Dyer's jazz portraits, these amplified, fictive self-narratives suggest that everybody's loneliness is unique, and in doing so actually help define the self as an autonomous individual.

Just as Monson insists that improvisation does not occur on its own, but is a form of "musical conversation," a number of writers draw on jazz to reimagine loneliness as an experience that can be shared with others—that can even provide the basis for relationships and conversations. Even as they valorize the individual, novels from *Invisible Man* to *Hiroshima Bugi* place such individualism within a social context. Returning to Coleman's "Lonely Woman," such texts try to show that, while humans are bound by their loneliness, in recognizing and acknowledging the isolation of others we can find a mutual form of consolation. Often writers turn to the set piece of the performance to underline this idea of shared isolation, staging conversations where musicians respond to each other through solos or move between solo and ensemble.

The climactic moments of "Powerhouse" and "Sonny's Blues" exemplify this dynamic, where Welty and Baldwin focus on the other musicians pulling something unique from the solo artist, creating beauty from shared expressions of isolation. In many cases, this relationship is suggested through allusion rather than representation—the coming together of individuals in *Dead Jazz Guys,* the relationship between Ursa and her foremothers in *Corregidora,* or the juxtaposition of portraits in *But Beautiful.* This conversation can even be staged between the audience and the artist, when a text breaks into apostrophe, speaking directly to the reader as the narrator of *Jazz* does. Such moments do not just signal mutual individuality, but call the reader to action. Drawing on the antiphony of jazz, they encourage the reader to be active in their isolation, and to listen to others. This call is not always responded to—Welty, for instance, leaves Powerhouse's final address unanswered, just as Ellison leaves the question of response to his invisible man hanging. It is possible, the novel implies, that the invisible man may *not* speak for us. But this failure to connect is not a final sucker-punch; it is built into the narrative structures of these texts, which set communication and convergence in tension with loneliness as a place of strength.

NOTES

INTRODUCTION

1. Ornette Coleman, in Mandel, *Miles, Ornette, Cecil*, 186.
2. Sagan, "Narratives of Loneliness."
3. Edwards, *Epistrophies*, 253.
4. Gabbard, "Introduction," 1.
5. Rokach, "Loneliness Updated," 2.
6. Stein and Tuval-Mashiach, "Social Construction of Loneliness," 214.
7. Cacioppo et al., "Alone in the Crowd," 4.
8. Ibid., 3.
9. Rokach, "Loneliness Updated," 2.
10. Cacioppo et al., "Alone in the Crowd," 20.
11. Stein and Tuval-Mashiach, "Social Construction of Loneliness," 217.
12. Morrison and Smith, "Loneliness: An Overview."
13. Stauffer, *Ethical Loneliness*, 5. Hereafter cited parenthetically.
14. Rokach, "Loneliness and Life," 70, 77.
15. Ibid., 78.
16. Ibid., 70.
17. Margalit, *Lonely Children*, 10.
18. Cacioppo et al., "Alone in the Crowd," 4.
19. Moustakas, *Loneliness*, 8. Hereafter cited parenthetically.
20. Bevinn, "Preface," viii.
21. Stein and Solomon, "The Lonely Side of War's Aftermath."
22. Margalit, *Lonely Children*, 1.

23. Riesman et al., *The Lonely Crowd*, 3.
24. Ibid., 5.
25. Ibid., 29.
26. Margalit, *Lonely Children*, 7.
27. Ibid.
28. Ogren, *Jazz Revolution*, 6.
29. Ibid., 7, 6.
30. Ibid., 18.
31. Knight "*Jammin' the Blues*," 14.
32. Gabbard, "Writing the Other History," 1.
33. Ibid., 2.
34. Garber, "Fabulating Jazz," 71.
35. Ibid., 70.
36. Ogren, *Jazz Revolution*, 8.
37. Edwards, *Epistrophies*, 16.
38. Jimoh, *Spiritual, Blues, and Jazz People*, 2.
39. Ibid., 3, 6.
40. Ibid., 5.
41. Ibid., 28.
42. Hobson, *Creating Jazz Counterpoint*, 5.
43. Ogren, *Jazz Revolution*, 147.
44. Ibid., 150.
45. Lott, "Double V," 248.
46. Knight, "*Jammin' the Blues*," 15.
47. Elworth, "Jazz in Crisis," 59.
48. Gendron, "'Moldy Figs' and Modernists," 33.
49. Baldwin, *Going to Meet the Man*, 109. Hereafter cited parenthetically.
50. Lott, "Double V," 249.
51. Monson, *Saying Something*, 1.
52. Harlos, "Jazz Autobiography," 134, 134–35.
53. Edwards, *Epistrophies*, 16.
54. Weiner, "'Zero to the Bone,'" 490.
55. Ellison, *Invisible Man*, 3. Hereafter cited parenthetically.
56. Yaffe, *Fascinating Rhythm*, 86.
57. Porter, *Jazz Country*, 1.
58. Spaulding, "Embracing Chaos," 481.
59. Maier, "The Road to Don Cornelius," 270.
60. Yaffe, *Fascinating Rhythm*, 19.
61. Ellison, *Conversations*, 311, 312.
62. See Borshuk's influential essay "'So Black, So Blue.'"
63. Ellison, "Golden Age, Time Past," 247.

64. Maier, "The Road to Don Cornelius," 268.
65. Gayle, *Way of the New World*, 257.
66. Yaffe, *Fascinating Rhythm*, 74.
67. Steward, "Illusions of Phallic Agency," 527.
68. Gendron, "Moldy Figs," 34.
69. Chambers, "Improvising and Mythmaking," 56.

CHAPTER ONE

1. Jerving, "Early Jazz Literature," 655.
2. Beuka, "Magazines," 283.
3. Caputi, *Kinder, Gentler America*, 65.
4. Elworth, "Jazz in Crisis," 59.
5. Fiedler, "Style and Anti-Style," 155; Howe, "Tone in the Short Story"; Miller, "The Short Story as a 'Young Art'"; Mirrielees, "Short Stories, 1950."
6. Pratt, "Short Story," 175.
7. Ibid., 180.
8. Balder, "Structure of the Modern Short Story," 86.
9. Pratt, "Short Story," 183.
10. Scofield, *American Short Story*, 140.
11. Monson, *Saying Something*, 1.
12. Ibid., 2.
13. Ibid.
14. Lott, "Double V," 249.
15. Ibid., 248.
16. Spaulding, "Embracing Chaos," 482.
17. Monson, *Saying Something*, 2.
18. Sherard, "Sonny's Bebop," 691.
19. Tracy, "Sonny in the Dark," 165.
20. Sherard, "Sonny's Bebop," 681.
21. Tracy, "Sonny in the Dark," 166.
22. Ibid., 167.
23. Feinstein and Rife, *Jazz Fiction*, xi.
24. Chambers, "Improvising and Mythmaking," 55.
25. Ibid., 66.
26. Bearden, "Monkeying Around," 65.
27. Ibid., 67.
28. Ford, "Serious Daring," 25.
29. Bearden, "Monkeying Around," 71-72.
30. Ford, "Serious Daring," 27-28.
31. Bearden, "Monkeying Around," 74.

32. Ford, "Serious Daring," 28.
33. Ibid., 32, 33.
34. Pratt, "Short Story," 186.
35. Cortázar, *Blow-Up*, hereafter cited parenthetically.
36. Robert W. Felkel even argues that the historical relationship between Johnny and Charlie Parker is central to understanding the story, because the protagonist is so closely modeled on Parker that "the line between fact and fiction becomes extremely tenuous, much more tenuous than it may have appeared on previous readings" (21).
37. Garcia, "Time, Language, Desire," 33.
38. Gyurko, "Artist and Critic," 228.
39. Monson, *Saying Something*, 2.
40. Yaffe, *Fascinating Rhythm*, 4.
41. Harlos, "Jazz Autobiography," 134–35.
42. Elworth, "Jazz in Crisis," 59.
43. Titlestad, "Jazz Bodies," 7.
44. Dyer, *But Beautiful*, vii. Hereafter cited parenthetically.
45. Widgery, "Lullaby of Birdland," 44.
46. Bernstein, "Jazz's Dark Forces."
47. Titlestad, "Jazz Bodies," 16.

CHAPTER TWO

1. Smith, Interview with Leyshon.
2. Smith, "Crazy They Call Me."
3. Cacioppo et al., "Alone in the Crowd," 24.
4. Smith, "Crazy They Call Me."
5. Spalding, Interview with Frank.
6. Spalding, Interview with Colapinto.
7. Spalding, Interview with Frank.
8. Ibid.
9. Monson, "Fitting the Part," 280.
10. Ibid.
11. McMullen, "Identity for Sale," 142.
12. Ibid., 143.
13. Titlestad, "Jazz Bodies," 7.
14. Ibid., 10.
15. Stevenson, *Human Rights*, 95.
16. Blumenthal, "Improvisational Soloists," 240; Jewett, "Modality of Morrison's Jazz," 447.
17. Grandt, "Kinds of Blue," 308.
18. Ibid., 305.

19. Small-McCarthy, "Jazz Aesthetic," 293.
20. Grandt, "Kinds of Blue" 308; Scheiber, "*Jazz* and the Future Blues," 471.
21. Rody, "Impossible Voices," 626.
22. Small-McCarthy, "Jazz Aesthetic," 299.
23. Ibid., 294.
24. Morrison, Interview with Schappell.
25. Morrison, *Jazz*, ix. Hereafter cited parenthetically.
26. Morrison, *Conversations*, 93.
27. Brown, "Golden Gray," 629.
28. Hardack, "Music Seeking Its Words," 454.
29. Brown, "Golden Gray," 630.
30. Rody, "Impossible Voices," 626.
31. Nowlin, "Toni Morrison's *Jazz*," 154.
32. Allen, "Role of the Blues," 257.
33. Jones, Interview with Rowell, 44.
34. Jimoh, *Spiritual, Blues, and Jazz People*, 28–29.
35. Yukins, "Bastard Daughters," 227.
36. Jones, *Corregidora*, 3. Hereafter cited parenthetically.
37. Yukins, "Bastard Daughters," 222.
38. Ibid., 231; Li, "Trauma of Resistance," 138.
39. Ansell, "Valaida: A Novel."
40. White, "Second Fiddle?"
41. Fox, "Dance to the Music."
42. Allen, *Valaida*, 3. Hereafter cited parenthetically.
43. Williams, "Trumpet Queen."
44. Dvinge, "Keeping Time," 11.

CHAPTER THREE

1. Ondaatje, *Coming Through Slaughter*, 97. Hereafter cited parenthetically.
2. Rokach and Neto, "Causes," 67.
3. Ibid., 66.
4. Cacioppo et al., "Alone in the Crowd," 23.
5. Ibid., 24.
6. Delgado, *Critical Race Theory*, 60.
7. Peretti, *Creation of Jazz*, 4.
8. Elworth, "Jazz in Crisis," 59.
9. Such, *Performing 'Out There,'* 2.
10. Gioia, "Jazz," 585.
11. Feld, *Jazz Cosmopolitanism*, 49.
12. Ibid., 59.

13. Von Eschen, *Satchmo Blows Up the World*, 3.
14. Ibid., 4.
15. Delgado, *Critical Race Theory*, 60
16. Ibid.
17. Broyard, "Old Jazz."
18. Cole, "My Hero."
19. Diebschlag, "Jazzing the Novel," 161, my emphasis.
20. Ibid., 161, 163.
21. Edwards, *Epistrophies*, 8.
22. Diebschlag, "Jazzing the Novel," 165.
23. Titlestad, "Jazz Bodies," 4.
24. Edwards, *Epistrophies*, 7
25. Titlestad, "Jazz Bodies," 11.
26. Marinkova, *Michael Ondaatje*, 34.
27. Ibid., 2.
28. Bachner, "He Had Pushed His Imagination," 201.
29. Marinkova, *Michael Ondaatje*, 21.
30. Kawana, *Dead Jazz Guys*. Hereafter cited parenthetically. "Pakeha" is the Te Reo Maori term for European New Zealanders, used by many as a positive term of self-identification.
31. Allen, *Trans-Indigenous*, xiv.
32. Allen, "Transnational Native American Studies?" 2
33. Ibid., 3.
34. Vizenor, *Hiroshima Bugi*. Hereafter cited parenthetically.
35. Strecher, *Forbidden Worlds*, 8.
36. Murakami, "Jazz Messenger."
37. Clerici, "Enduring Appeal of Murakami Haruki," 248.
38. Murakami, *Norwegian Wood*, 103. Hereafter cited parenthetically.
39. Clerici, "Enduring Appeal of Murakami Haruki," 256.
40. Strecher, *Forbidden Worlds*, 2.
41. Murakami, *Blind Willow, Sleeping Woman*, 225. Hereafter cited parenthetically.
42. In *Blind Willow, Sleeping Woman*, 3.

CHAPTER FOUR

1. Coleman, "The Other's Language," 319.
2. Ibid., 321.
3. Edwards, *Epistrophies*, 9.
4. Ibid., 10.
5. Heble, *Landing on the Wrong Note*, 92.
6. Coleman, "The Other's Language," 328.

7. Porter, *This Thing Called Jazz*, xii.
8. DeVeaux and Giddins, *Jazz*, 514.
9. Bechet, *Treat It Gentle*, 1, 3.
10. Ibid., 1.
11. Monson, "Monk Meets SNCC," 187.
12. Porter, *This Thing Called Jazz*, xii.
13. Bechet, *Treat It Gentle* 2.
14. Heble, *Landing on the Wrong Note*, 98.
15. Iyer, "Being Home," 465.
16. Ibid., 463.
17. Stein, "Performance of Jazz Autobiography," 173.
18. Ogren, "Jazz Isn't Just Me," 114, 112.
19. Ibid., 112.
20. Gabbard, "The Quoter and His Culture," 93.
21. Stein, "Performance of Jazz Autobiography," 174.
22. Gioia, *History of Jazz*, 194; Cohen, *Ellington's America*, 565.
23. Cohen, *Ellington's America*, 563.
24. Gioia, *History of Jazz*, 116.
25. In Tucker, ed., *Duke Ellington Reader*, 113.
26. Green, "Introduction," 1.
27. McManus, "Ambiguity of Identity," 179.
28. Edwards, *Epistrophies*, 19.
29. McManus, "Ambiguity of Identity," 189; Edwards, "Literary Ellington," 327.
30. Edwards, "Literary Ellington," 327.
31. Ibid., 328.
32. Bañagle, "Rewriting the Narrative," 5.
33. Ellington, "My Hunt for Song Titles," 88.
34. Ellington, Interview with Zunser, 45.
35. Ellington, "Swing Is My Beat," 249.
36. Ellington, "My Hunt for Song Titles," 88.
37. Ellington, "Interview with Zunser," 45.
38. Ellington, "The Duke Steps Out," 48.
39. Ellington, Interview with Mabie, 42.
40. Ellington, "Race for Space," 294.
41. Ibid., 249.
42. Heble, *Landing on the Wrong Note*, 112.
43. Ellington, "Swing Is My Beat," 248–49.
44. Ellington, *Music Is My Mistress*, 249. Further citations appear parenthetically.
45. Ellington, Interview with Mabie, 43.
46. Weston and Wilson, "Edward Kennedy Ellington," 71.
47. Mingus, *Beneath the Underdog*, 1. Further citations appear parenthetically.

48. Goodman, *Mingus Speaks*, xiii.
49. Santoro, *Myself When I Am Real*, viii.
50. Worthington, "Ironic Effects of Autofiction," 472.
51. Heble, *Landing on the Wrong Note*, 105, 111.
52. Dames, "New Fictions of Solitude."
53. Green, "Introduction," 2.
54. McManus, "Ambiguity of Identity," 180.
55. Green, "Introduction," 3.
56. McManus, "Ambiguity of Identity," 183.
57. Heble, *Landing on the Wrong Note*, 20.
58. Williams, "Introduction," iii.
59. Santoro, *Myself When I Am Real*, viii.
60. Williams, "Introduction," vii.
61. Ibid., ix.
62. Stein, "Performance of Jazz Autobiography," 193.
63. Goodman, *Mingus Speaks*, xiii.
64. Stein, "Performance of Jazz Autobiography," 193.
65. Santoro, *Myself When I Am Real*, 79.
66. Stein, "Performance of Jazz Autobiography," 180.
67. Woolf, "Man with a Bass," 110.

EPILOGUE

1. Morrison and Smith, "Loneliness: An Overview."
2. Cacioppo, Fowler, and Christakis, "Alone in the Crowd," 4.
3. Stein and Tuval-Mashiach, "Social Construction of Loneliness," 217.
4. Diebschlag, "Jazzing the Novel," 172.
5. Spellman, *Four Jazz Lives*, 79.
6. Coleman, qtd. in Spellman, *Four Jazz Lives*, 83.
7. Ibid., 143.
8. Heble, *Landing on the Wrong Note*, 55.
9. Ibid., 52.
10. Edwards, *Epistrophies*, 11.
11. Groarke and Hogan, "Enhancing Wellbeing," 769.
12. Van den Tol and Edwards, "Choosing to Listen to Sad Music," 440, 460.
13. Schnare, MacIntyre, and Doucette, "Possible Selves," 95.

BIBLIOGRAPHY

Allen, Candace. *Valaida*. Virago, 2004.
Allen, Chadwick. *Trans-Indigenous: Methodologies for Global Native Literary Studies*. U of Minnesota P, 2012.
———. "Transnational Native American Studies? Why Not Studies That Are Trans-Indigenous?" *Journal of Transnational American Studies* 4.1 (2012): 1–22.
Allen, Donia Elizabeth. "The Role of the Blues in Gayl Jones's *Corregidora*." *Callaloo* 25.1 (2002): 257–73.
Ansell, Gwen. "Valaida: A Novel." *Jazz Times*, 1 Jan. 2006. jazztimes.com/reviews/books/valaida-a-novel-by-candace-allen/.
Bachner, Sally. "'He Had Pushed His Imagination into Buddy's Brain,' or, How to Escape History in *Coming Through Slaughter*." *Rethinking History* 9.2–3 (2005): 197–220.
Balder, A. L. "The Structure of the Modern Short Story." *College English* 7.2 (1945): 86–92.
Baldwin, James. "Sonny's Blues." *Going to Meet the Man*. Dial, 1965. 102–39.
Bañagle, Ryan Raul. "Rewriting the Narrative One Arrangement at a Time: Duke Ellington and Rhapsody in Blue." *Jazz Perspectives* 6.1–2 (2012): 5–27.
Bearden, Kenneth. "Monkeying Around: Welty's 'Powerhouse,' Blues-Jazz, and the Signifying Connection." *Southern Literary Journal* 31.2 (1999): 65–79.
Bechet, Sidney. *Treat It Gentle*. Hill and Wang, 1960.
Bernstein, Richard. "Jazz's Dark Forces and the Artists Who Love Them."

New York Times, 20 Mar. 1996. www.nytimes.com/1996/03/20/books/books-of-the-times-jazz-s-dark-forces-and-the-artists-who-love-them.html.

Beuka, Robert. "Magazines." *F. Scott Fitzgerald in Context*, ed. Bryant Mangum. Cambridge UP, 2013: 283–92.

Bevinn, Sarah J. "Preface." *Psychology of Loneliness*, ed. Bevinn, vii–xi.

———, ed. *Psychology of Loneliness*. Nova Science, 2011.

Blumenthal, Rachel. "Improvisational Soloists in Morrison's *Jazz*." *Explicator* 65.4 (2007): 240–41.

Borshuk, Michael. "'So Black, So Blue': Ralph Ellison, Louis Armstrong and the Bebop Aesthetic." *Genre* 36 (2004): 261–84.

Brown, Caroline. "Golden Gray and the Talking Book: Identity as a Site of Artful Construction in Toni Morrison's *Jazz*." *African American Review* 36.4 (2002): 629–42.

Broyard, Anatole. "Old Jazz." *New York Times*, 24 Apr. 1977. archive.nytimes.com/www.nytimes.com/books/00/05/14/specials/ondaatje-slaughter.html?_r=1.

"But Beautiful: Review." *Kirkus Review*. 1 Jan. 1996. www.kirkusreviews.com/book-reviews/geoff-dyer/but-beautiful/.

Cacioppo, John T., James H. Fowler, and Nicholas Alexander Christakis. "Alone in the Crowd: The Structure and Spread of Loneliness in a Large Social Network." *Journal of Personality and Social Psychology* 97.6 (2009): 977–91.

Caputi, Mary. *A Kinder, Gentler America: Melancholia and the Mythical 1950s*. U of Minnesota P, 2005.

Chambers, Leland H. "Improvising and Mythmaking in Eudora Welty's 'Powerhouse.'" *Jazz Among the Discourses*, ed. Gabbard, 54–69.

Clerici, Nathen. "History, 'Subcultural Imagination,' and the Enduring Appeal of Murakami Haruki." *Journal of Japanese Studies* 42.2 (2016): 247–78.

Cohen, Harvey G. *Duke Ellington's America*. Chicago: University of Chicago P, 2010.

Cole, Teju. "My Hero: Michael Ondaatje." *Guardian*, 17 Feb. 2012. www.theguardian.com/books/2012/feb/17/my-hero-michael-ondaatje-teju-cole.

Coleman, Ornette. "The Other's Language." Interview with Jacques Derrida. Trans. Timothy S. Murphy. *Genre* 37.2 (2004): 319–28.

Cortázar, Julio. *Blow-Up and Other Stories*. Trans. Paul Blackburn. Pantheon, 1967.

Dames, Nicholas. "The New Fictions of Solitude." *The Atlantic*, April 2016. www.theatlantic.com/magazine/archive/2016/04/the-new-fiction-of-solitude/471474/.

Dantzic, Grayson. *Jerry Dantzic: Billie Holiday at Sugar Hill*. Thames and Hudson, 2017.

Deleuze, Giles, and Felix Guattari. *Kafka: Towards a Minor Literature*. Trans. Dana Polan. U of Minnesota P, 1986.

Delgado, Richard. *Critical Race Theory: The Cutting Edge*. Temple UP, 2013.

DeVeaux, Scott, and Gary Giddins. *Jazz*. Norton, 2009.

Diebschlag, Natalie. "Jazzing the Novel: The Derridean Ethics of Michael Ondaatje's *Coming Through Slaughter*." *Mosaic* 49.1 (2016): 161–78.

Dvinge, Anna. "Keeping Time, Performing Place: Jazz Heterotopia in Candace Allen's *Valaida*." *Journal of Transnational American Studies* 4.2 (2012): 1–19.

Dyer, Geoff. *But Beautiful*. Canongate, 2012.

Edwards, Brent Hayes. *Epistrophies: Jazz and the Literary Imagination*. Harvard UP, 2017.

——. "The Literary Ellington." *Uptown Conversations: The New Jazz Studies*, ed. Robert G. O'Meally, Brent Hayes Edwards, and Farah Jasmine Griffin. Columbia UP, 2004. 326–56.

Ellington, Duke. *The Duke Ellington Reader*, ed. Mark Tucker. Oxford UP, 1993.

——. "The Duke Steps Out." *Duke Ellington Reader*, ed. Tucker, 48.

——. Interview with Janet Mabie for *Christian Science Monitor*. *Duke Ellington Reader*, ed. Tucker, 42–43.

——. Interview with Florence Zunser for *New York Evening Graphic*. *Duke Ellington Reader*, ed. Tucker, 44–45.

——. *Music Is My Mistress*. Da Capo P, 1976.

——. "My Hunt for Song Titles." *Duke Ellington Reader*, ed. Tucker, 87–89.

——. "The Race for Space." *Duke Ellington Reader*, ed. Tucker, 294.

——. "Swing Is My Beat." *Duke Ellington Reader*, ed. Tucker, 248–50.

Ellison, Ralph. *Conversations with Ralph Ellison*, ed. Maryemma Graham and Amritjit Singh. UP of Mississippi, 1995.

——. "The Golden Age, Time Past." *The Collected Essays of Ralph Ellison*, ed. John F. Callahan. Random House, 1995. 237–49.

——. *Invisible Man*. Random House, 1952.

Elworth, Steven B. "Jazz in Crisis, 1948–1958: Ideology and Representation." *Jazz Among the Discourses*, ed. Gabbard, 57–75.

Feinstein, Sascha, and David Rife. *The Jazz Fiction Anthology*. Indiana UP, 2009.

Feld, Steven. *Jazz Cosmopolitanism in Accra: Five Musical Years in Ghana*. Duke UP, 2012.

Felkel, Robert. "The Historical Dimension in Julio Cortázar's 'The Pursuer.'" *Latin American Literary Review* 7.14 (1979): 20–27.

Fiedler, Leslie. "Style and Anti-Style in the Short Story." *Kenyon Review* 13.1 (1951): 155–56, 158, 168, 170–72.

Ford, Sarah Gilbreath. "'Serious Daring' in Eudora Welty's 'Powerhouse' and 'Where Is the Voice Coming From?'" *Southern Quarterly* 51.3 (2014): 25–37.

Fox, Sue. "Dance to the Music of Fame." *Independent*, 16 Jan. 2004. www.independent.co.uk/arts-entertainment/books/features/candace-allen-dance-to-the-music-of-fame-73850.html.

Gabbard, Krin. "Introduction: The Jazz Canon and Its Consequences." *Jazz Among the Discourses*, ed. Gabbard, 1–30.

———. "The Quoter and His Culture." *Jazz in Mind: Essays on the History and Meanings of Jazz*, ed. Reginald T. Buckner and Steve Weiland. Wayne State UP, 1991. 92–111.

———. "Writing the Other History." *Representing Jazz*, ed. Gabbard, 1–8.

———, ed. *Jazz Among the Discourses*. Duke UP, 1995.

———, ed. *Representing Jazz*. Duke UP, 1995.

Garber, Frederick. "Fabulating Jazz." *Representing Jazz*, ed. Gabbard, 70–103.

Garcia, Graciela. "Time, Language, Desire: Julio Cortázar's 'The Pursuer.'" *Pacific Coast Philology* 38 (2003): 33–39.

Gayle, Addison. *The Way of the New World: The Black Novel in America*. Anchor P, 1976.

Gendron, Bernard. "'Moldy Figs' and Modernists: Jazz at War (1942–1946)." *Jazz Among the Discourses*, ed. Gabbard, 31–56.

Gioia, Ted. *The History of Jazz*. Oxford UP, 2011.

———. "Jazz: The Aesthetics of Imperfection." *Hudson Review* 39.4 (1987): 585–600.

Goodman, John F. *Mingus Speaks*. U of California P, 2013.

Grandt, Jurgen E. "Kinds of Blue: Toni Morrison, Hans Janowitz, and the Jazz Aesthetic." *African American Review* 38.2 (2004): 303–32.

Green, Edward. "Introduction." *The Cambridge Companion to Duke Ellington*, ed. Green. Cambridge UP, 2014. 1–18.

Groarke, Jenny, and Michael Hogan. "Enhancing Wellbeing: An Emerging Model of the Adaptive Functions of Music Listening." *Psychology of Music* 44.4 (2016): 769–92.

Gyurko, Lanin. "Artist and Critic in Cortázar's 'El Perseguidor': Antagonists or Doubles?" *Ibero-amerikanisches Archiv* 6.3 (1980): 205–38.

Hardack, Richard. "'A Music Seeking Its Words': Double-Timing and Double Consciousness in Toni Morrison's *Jazz*." *Callaloo* 18.2 (1995): 451–71.

Harlos, Christopher. "Jazz Autobiography: Theory, Practice, Politics." *Representing Jazz*, ed. Gabbard, 131–66.

Heble, Ajay. *Landing on the Wrong Note: Jazz, Dissonance, and Critical Practice*. Routledge, 2000.

Hobson, Vic. *Creating Jazz Counterpoint: New Orleans, Barbershop Harmony, and the Blues.* UP of Mississippi, 2014.
Howe, Irving. "Tone in the Short Story." *Sewanee Review* 57.1 (1949): 141–52.
Hughes, Langston. "The Blues I'm Playing." *The Collected Works of Langston Hughes: The Short Stories,* ed. R. Baxter Miller. U of Missouri P, 2002. 72–84.
Hurston, Zora Neale. *How It Feels to Be Colored Me.* Applewood, 2015.
Iyer, Vijay. "Being Home: Jazz Authority and the Politics of Place." *Current Musicology* 71–73 (2001–2): 462–76.
Jerving, Ryan. "Early Jazz Literature (And Why You Didn't Know)." *American Literary History* 16.4 (2004): 648–74.
Jewett, Chad. "The Modality of Toni Morrison's *Jazz.*" *African American Review* 48.4 (2015): 445–56.
Jimoh, A. Yemisi. *Spiritual, Blues, and Jazz People in African American Fiction: Living in Paradox.* U of Tennessee P, 2002.
Jones, Gayl. *Corregidora.* Camden P, 1988.
———. Interview with Charles H. Rowell. *Callaloo* 16 (1982): 32–53.
Kawana, Phil. *Dead Jazz Guys.* Huia, 1996.
Knight, Arthur. "*Jammin' the Blues,* or the Sight of Jazz, 1944." *Representing Jazz,* ed. Gabbard, 11–53.
Li, Stephanie. "Love and the Trauma of Resistance in Gayl Jones's *Corregidora.*" *Callaloo* 29.1 (2006): 131–50.
Lott, Eric. "Double V, Double-Time: Bebop's Politics of Style." *Jazz Among the Discourses,* ed. Gabbard, 243–55.
Maier, Brennan. "The Road to Don Cornelius Is Paved with Good Intentions: The Crisis of Negro Nationalism in Ralph Ellison's Jazz Criticism." *Callaloo* 35.1 (2012): 267–92.
Mandel, Howard. *Miles, Ornette, Cecil: Jazz Beyond Jazz.* Routledge, 2008.
Margalit, Malka. *Lonely Children and Adolescents: Self-Perceptions, Social Exclusion, and Hope.* Springer, 2010.
Marinkova, Milena. *Michael Ondaatje: Haptic Aesthetics and Micropolitical Writing.* Continuum, 2011.
McManus, Laurie. "Ambiguity of Identity in the 'Global Village': Ellington, McLuhan, and the Afro-Eurasian Eclipse." *Jazz Perspectives* 6.1–2 (2012): 179–96.
McMullen, Tracy. "Identity for Sale: Glenn Miller, Wynton Marsalis, and Cultural Replay in Music." *Big Ears,* ed. Rustin and Tucker, 129–56.
Miller, Nolan. "The Short Story as a 'Young Art.'" *Antioch Review* 10.4 (1950): 543–46.
Mingus, Charles. *Beneath the Underdog.* Canongate, 1995.
Mirrielees, Edith R. "Short Stories, 1950." *English Journal* 40.5 (1951): 247–54.
Monson, Ingrid. "Fitting the Part." *Big Ears,* ed. Rustin and Tucker, 267–90.

———. "Monk Meets SNCC." *Black Music Research Journal* 19.2 (1999): 187–200.
———. *Saying Something: Jazz Improvisation and Interaction.* U of Chicago P, 1996.
Morrison, Philip S., and Rebekah Smith. "Loneliness: An Overview." *Narratives of Loneliness,* ed. Sagan and Miller.
Morrison, Toni. *Conversations,* ed. Carolyn Denard. UP of Mississippi, 2008.
———. Interview with Elissa Schappell. *Paris Review* 128 (1993). www.theparisreview.org/interviews/1888/toni-morrison-the-art-of-fiction-no-134-toni-morrison.
———. *Jazz.* Vintage, 2001.
Moustakas, Clark. *Loneliness.* Prentice Hall, 1961.
Murakami, Haruki. *Blind Willow, Sleeping Woman.* Trans. Philip Gabriel and Jay Rubin. Vintage, 2007.
———. "Jazz Messenger." *New York Times,* 8 July 2007.
———. *Norwegian Wood.* Trans. Jay Rubin. Vintage, 2003.
Nowlin, Michael. "Toni Morrison's *Jazz* and the Racial Dreams of the American Writer." *American Literature* 71.1 (1999): 151–74.
Ogren, Kathy J. "'Jazz Isn't Just Me': Jazz Autobiographies as Performance Personas." *Jazz in Mind: Essays on the History and Meaning of Jazz,* ed. Reginald Buckner and Steven Weiland. Wayne State UP, 1991. 112–21.
———. *The Jazz Revolution: Twenties Culture and the Meaning of Jazz.* Oxford UP, 1989.
Ondaatje, Michael. *Coming Through Slaughter.* Bloomsbury, 2004.
Peretti, Burton W. *The Creation of Jazz: Music, Race, and Culture in Urban America.* U of Illinois P, 1992.
Porter, Eric. *What Is This Thing Called Jazz: African American Musicians as Artists, Critics, and Activists.* U of California P, 2002.
Porter, Horace A. *Jazz Country: Ralph Ellison in America.* U of Iowa P, 2001.
Pratt, Mary Louise. "The Short Story: The Long and the Short of It." *Poetics* 10 (1981): 175–94.
Riesman, David, Nathan Glazer, and Reuel Denney. *The Lonely Crowd: A Study of the Changing American Character.* 1950. Yale UP, 1989.
Rody, Caroline. "Impossible Voices: Ethnic Postmodern Narration in Toni Morrison's *Jazz* and Karen Tei Yamashita's *Through the Arc of the Rain Forest.*" *Contemporary Literature* 41.4 (2000): 618–41.
Rokach, Ami. "Loneliness and Life: From Beginning to End." *Psychology of Loneliness,* ed. Bevinn. 69–98.
———. "Loneliness Updated: An Introduction." *Journal of Psychology* 146.1-2 (2012): 1–6.
——— and Félix Neto. "Causes of Loneliness in Adolescence: A Cross-Cultural Study." *International Journal of Adolescence and Youth* 8.1 (2000): 65–80.

Rustin, Nichole T., and Sherrie Tucker, eds. *Big Ears: Listening for Gender in Jazz Studies*. Duke UP, 2008.

Sagan, Olivia. "Narratives of Loneliness and Mental Ill Health in a Time of Neoliberalism." *Narratives of Loneliness*, ed. Sagan and Miller.

———, and Eric Miller, eds. *Narratives of Loneliness: Multidisciplinary Perspectives from the 21st Century*. Routledge, 2018.

Santoro, Gene. *Myself When I Am Real: The Life and Music of Charles Mingus*. Oxford UP, 2000.

Scheiber, Andrew. "*Jazz* and the Future Blues: Toni Morrison's Urban Folk Zone." *MFS* 52.2 (2006): 470–94.

Schnare, Ben, Peter MacIntyre, and Jesslyn Doucette. "Possible Selves as a Source of Motivation for Musicians." *Psychology of Music* 40.1 (2011): 94–111.

Scofield, Martin. *The Cambridge Introduction to the American Short Story*. Cambridge UP, 2006.

Sherard, Tracey. "Sonny's Bebop: Baldwin's 'Blues Text' as Intracultural Critique." *African American Review* 32.4 (1998): 691–704.

Small-McCarthy, Robin. "The Jazz Aesthetic in the Novels of Toni Morrison" *Cultural Studies* 9.2 (1995): 293–300.

Smith, Zadie. "Crazy They Call Me." *New Yorker*, 6 Mar. 2017. www.newyorker.com/magazine/2017/03/06/crazy-they-call-me.

———. Interview with Cressida Leyshon. *New Yorker*, 27 Feb. 2017. www.newyorker.com/books/page-turner/fiction-this-week-zadie-smith-2017-03-06.

Spalding, Esperanza. Interview with John Colapinto. *New Yorker*, 15 Mar. 2010. www.newyorker.com/magazine/2010/03/15/new-note.

———. Interview with Alex Frank. *Pitchfork*, 8 Mar. 2016. pitchfork.com/features/interview/9830-esperanza-spalding-insubordinate-by-nature.

Spaulding, Timothy. "Embracing Chaos in Narrative Form: The Bebop Aesthetic in Ralph Ellison's *Invisible Man*." *Callaloo* 27.2 (2004): 481–501.

Spellman, A. B. *Four Jazz Lives*. U of Michigan P, 2004.

Stauffer, Jill. *Ethical Loneliness: The Injustice of Not Being Heard*. Columbia UP, 2015.

Stein, Daniel. "The Performance of Jazz Autobiography." *Genre* 37.2 (2004): 173–99.

Stein, J. Y., and Zahava Solomon. "The Lonely Side of War's Aftermath: Traumatization and Isolation Among Veterans." *Narratives of Loneliness*, ed. Sagan and Miller.

Stein, J. Y., and Rivka Tuval-Mashiach. "The Social Construction of Loneliness: An Integrative Conceptualization." *Journal of Constructivist Psychology* 28.3 (2015): 210–27.

Stevenson, Nick. *Human Rights and the Reinvention of Freedom*. Routledge, 2016.
Steward, Douglas. "The Illusions of Phallic Agency: Invisible Man, Totem and Taboo, and the Santa Claus Surprise." *Callaloo* 26.2 (2003): 522–35.
Strecher, Matthew. *The Forbidden Worlds of Haruki Murakami*. U of Minnesota P, 2014.
Such, David G. *Avant-Garde Jazz Musicians: Performing 'Out There.'* U of Iowa P, 1993.
Titlestad, Michael. "Jazz Bodies: In Process, on Trial and Instrumental." *Journal of Literary Studies* 16.2 (2000): 1–22.
Tracy, Steve C. "Sonny in the Dark: Jazzing the Blues Spirit and the Gospel Truth in James Baldwin's "Sonny's Blues."" *James Baldwin Review* 1 (2015): 164–78.
Van den Tol, Annemieke J. M., and Jane Edwards. "Exploring a Rationale for Choosing to Listen to Sad Music When Feeling Sad." *Psychology of Music* 41.4 (2011): 440–65.
Vizenor, Gerald. *Hiroshima Bugi: Atomu 57*. U of Nebraska P, 2003.
Von Eschen, Penny M. *Satchmo Blows Up the World: Jazz Ambassadors Play the Cold War*. Harvard UP, 2006.
Weiner, Joshua. "'Zero to the Bone': Thelonious Monk, Emily Dickinson, and the Rhythms of Modernism." *A Companion to Emily Dickinson*, ed. Martha Nell Smith and Mary Loeffelholz. Blackwell, 2008. 68–72.
Welty, Eudora. *A Curtain of Green*. New York: Doubleday, 1941.
Weston, Trevor, and Olly W. Wilson. "Edward Kennedy Ellington as a Cultural Icon." *Cambridge Companion to Duke Ellington*, ed. Edward Green. Cambridge UP, 2014. 67–82.
White, Michael. "Second Fiddle? Not a Chance." *Telegraph*, 14 Jan. 2004. www.telegraph.co.uk/culture/donotmigrate/3610117/Second-fiddle-Not-a-chance.html.
Widgery, David. "Lullaby of Birdland." *New Statesman*, 21 June 1991. 44.
Williams, Richard. "Introduction." *Beneath the Underdog*. By Charles Mingus. Canongate, 1995.
———. "Trumpet Queen." *Guardian*, 14 Feb. 2004. www.theguardian.com/books/2004/feb/14/featuresreviews.guardianreview14.
Woolf, Geoffrey. "Man with a Bass." *Newsweek*, 17 May 1971. 110.
Worthington, Marjorie. "Fiction in the 'Post-Truth' Era: The Ironic Effects of Autofiction." *Critique* 58.5 (2017): 471–83.
Yaffe, David. *Fascinating Rhythm*. Princeton UP, 2006.
Yukins, Elizabeth. "Bastard Daughters and the Possession of History in *Corregidora* and *Paradise*." *Signs: Journal of Women in Culture and Society* 28.1 (2002): 221–47.

INDEX

Allen, Candace, 28, 84; *Valaida*, 90–95
Allen, Red, 58
Antiphony. *See* call-and-response
Armstrong, Louis, vii, 21–23, 38,
   autobiography, jazz, 19, 28, 129–35,
   137–38, 142–56, 158–60, 164
   autofiction, 145–48, 150–51, 160

Baker, Josephine, 115
Baldwin, James, 27, 31, 49, 53; "Sonny's
   Blues," 19, 39–45, 46–47, 49, 85, 159,
   166, 171
bebop, 18–19, 23, 38–39, 43, 53, 56, 74, 90,
   94–95, 98–99, 163
Bechet, Sidney, 131–33, 135–36, 144
Blakey, Art, 119
blues music, 14, 16–17, 33–34, 36, 39,
   43–44, 47–48, 64, 74, 84–89, 105
Bolden, Buddy, 96, 101–7, 119, 154, 164
Borges, Jorge Luis, 66

call-and-response, 36–37, 59, 63,
   74–75, 78, 82, 84–85, 95, 117, 135,
   158, 171
Carney, Harry, 54, 58

Capote, Truman, 121
Chandler, Rayomnd, 121
Cherry, Don, 1, 109–11
Cole, Teju, 102
Coleman, Ornette, 1–2, 28, 99, 121, 128–
   31; "Lonely Woman," vii, 1, 171; theory
   of harmolodics, 164–68
Coltrane, John, 71, 99, 109–11
Cortázar, Julio, 27, 57; "Pursuer, The,"
   49–54, 57, 63, 164, 170

Davis, Miles, 50, 108, 110–11, 119, 130,
   162, 165
Derrida, Jacques, 103, 128–29, 164
Dickinson, Emily, 21
Dyer, Geoff, 27, 65–66, 170; *But Beautiful*,
   54–64, 163, 166, 171

Ellison, Ralph, 21–27, 31, 39, 73, 81, 83,
   134, 166, 171
Ellington, Duke, 21, 28, 130, 132, 135,
   153–54, 156, 160, 170; fictional portray-
   als of, 54, 58–59; *Music is My Mistress*,
   131, 137–52, 157–58, 167–68
Evans, Bill, 119

Faulkner, William, 121
Fitzgerald, F. Scott, 30–31, 121
fragmentation, 16, 33–34, 48, 52, 81, 92–93, 102, 107, 117, 143–44, 147–51, 160, 167–68. *See also* short stories and jazz

gender, 67–73, 79–81, 83–87, 90–91, 93–95
Gillespie, Dizzy, 19

Harlem Renaissance, the, 16, 77, 79, 119
Hawkins, Coleman, 60
Hearn, Lafcadio, 116
Holliday, Billie, 60, 65–69, 72, 82, 144; *Lady Sings the Blues,* 134–35, 141
Hughes, Langston, 27, 43, 46, 48, 53, 56, 71, 119, 139; "Blues I'm Playing, The," 31–32, 33–39, 45, 47, 163
Hurston, Zora Neale, 69–71

immanence, 20–21, 58–59
improvisation, 1, 16–20, 27, 37–39, 42, 44–46, 52, 54–57, 61–62, 74–76, 99, 119, 128, 169–70; autobiographies as, 130, 134, 136, 141, 155, 160, 166
Iyer, Vijay, 134–35

Jones, Gayl, 28, 91, 96; *Corregidora,* 84–87, 92, 95, 171

kabuki, 112–115
Kafka, Franz, 33
Kawana, Phil, 108–12, 118, 126, 171, 178n30

loneliness, as isolation, 1–3, 5, 12, 20–21, 27, 157–60, 85, 96, 103, 162–63, 171; as lack of social connections, 6–7, 8–9, 11–12, 23–24, 28, 97–98; health risks and 7–8, 13, 163; neuroscience and, 168–69. *See also* solitude
Lonely Crowd, the, 11–12, 19, 31

McCullers, Carson, 31
Marsalis, Wynton, 70, 72
Mingus, Charles, 21, 28, 56, 63, 99, 132, 135, 141, 161, 170; *Beneath the Underdog,* 131, 144–47, 152–60, 167–68
Mishima, Yukio, 121
Mitchell, Joni, 68–69
Monk, Thelonious, 21, 61–63, 119, 121, 132
Monson, Ingrid, 19, 37–38, 52, 69–70, 84, 126–27, 130, 132, 170
Morrison, Toni, 28, 92, 96, 163; *Jazz,* 73–83, 91, 95, 123
Murakami, Haruki, 28, 118, 163–64; *Norwegian Wood,* 119–23; "Tony Takitani," 124–26

New Orleans, 17, 18, 102, 104–5,
New York Times, the, 56, 102
New Yorker, the, 66,

Oe, Kenzaburo, 121
Ondaatje, Michael, 28, 108, 126; *Coming Through Slaughter,* 96, 101–7, 119, 131, 153–54, 163–64
outgroups, 98, 100–101, 104, 108–9, 111–12, 114–16, 119, 163

Paris Review, the, 76, 78
Parker, Charlie, 19, 43–44, 49, 53, 57, 71, 77, 83, 164–65, 175n36
performance, 15–16, 20, 27, 34–39, 43, 45–48, 54, 60–63, 68, 72–73, 75, 86, 89, 93–95, 99–100, 105–6, 151, 171; as metaphor for writing, 2, 123, 135–36, 147–49, 155–60, 162, 167. *See also* improvisation

Pepper, Art, 64
Poe, Edgar Allan, 32
polyphony, 15–17, 44, 48 85, 89, 95, 105, 144, 149, 156
Powell, Bud, 62, 71, 121

Ra, Sun, 130
Rollins, Sonny, viii, 130
Russell, Pee Wee, 58

short stories and jazz, relationship between, 30–34, 37, 39, 43–46, 48–50, 52–57
Smith, Zadie, 28, 83; "Crazy they Call Me," 65–69, 72, 82, 90–91
solitude, 10, 13, 21, 23, 29, 46–47, 65–67, 93–96, 102, 121–27, 146
soloists, 15–19, 27, 33, 38, 46–47, 55, 158, 169–71

Spalding, Esperanza, 68–70, 72, 84, storytelling, 20, 27, 44–46, 74, 103, 106, 115, 137, 163. *See also* performance

Takahashi, Kazumi, 121
Tapscott, Horace, 134–35
Tizol, Juan, 142

Updike, John, 121

Vizenor, Gerald, 112–19, 126–27, 163, 171

Waller, Fats, 45
Webster, Ben, 58
Welty, Eudora, 27, 31, 49 53; "Powerhouse," 45–48, 67, 171

Yates, Richard, 31
Young, Lester, 59–63, 66

www.ingramcontent.com/pod-product-compliance
Lightning Source LLC
Chambersburg PA
CBHW022021220426
43663CB00007B/1163